THE PENGUIN CLASSICS

FOUNDER EDITOR (1944–64): E. V. RIEU

Editor: Betty Radice

ARISTOTLE was born at Stageira, in the dominion of the kings of Macedon, in 384 B.C. He studied at Athens under Plato, at whose death he left, and some time later became tutor to the young Alexander the Great. When Alexander succeeded to the throne in 335, Aristotle returned to Athens and established the Lyceum, where his vast erudition attracted a large number of scholars. After Alexander's death he was regarded in some quarters with suspicion, because he had been known as Alexander's friend. He was accused of impiety, and in 322 B.C. fled to Chalcis in Euboea, where he died in the same year. His writings were of extraordinary range, and many of them have survived. Among the most famous are the *Ethics* and the *Politics*.

THOMAS ALAN SINCLAIR was Professor of Greek at the Queen's University of Belfast for twenty-seven years before his death in 1961. He was also Dean of the Faculty of Theology and, for eleven years, Secretary of the Academic Council. Prior to his Belfast appointment, he held posts at Southampton University and Birkbeck College, London, and was a Fellow of St John's College, Cambridge, from which he had graduated. He published a number of books; the most widely known, his *History of Greek Political Thought*, has been translated into several languages.

ARISTOTLE

THE POLITICS

TRANSLATED WITH AN INTRODUCTION BY

T. A. SINCLAIR

PENGUIN BOOKS

Penguin Books Ltd, Harmondsworth, Middlesex, England
Penguin Books Inc., 7110 Ambassador Road, Baltimore, Maryland 21207, U.S.A.
Penguin Books Australia Ltd, Ringwood, Victoria, Australia
Penguin Books Canada Ltd, 41 Steelcase Road West, Markham, Ontario, Canada
Penguin Books (N.Z.) Ltd, 182–190 Wairau Road, Auckland 10, New Zealand

—

First published 1962
Reprinted 1964, 1966, 1967, 1969, 1970, 1972, 1974, 1975, 1976

—

Copyright © the Estate of T. A. Sinclair, 1962

—

Made and printed in Great Britain
by Richard Clay (The Chaucer Press) Ltd,
Bungay, Suffolk
Set in Monotype Baskerville

IN MEMORIAM J.A.K.T.

CONTENTS

INTRODUCTION

ARISTOTLE was born in 384 B.C. at Stageira in Chalcidice which was part of the dominion of the kings of Macedon. He was the son of a physician who attended the family of King Amyntas. Later the throne was occupied by Philip, who spent his life augmenting the power and territory of Macedon and making it dominant among Greek states, whereas prior to his reign it had lain somewhat on the fringe. At the age of about seventeen Aristotle went to Athens and became a student in the famous Academy of Plato. Here he studied mathematics, ethics, and politics, and we do not know what else besides. He remained there, a teacher but still a learner, for twenty years. At this period he must have written those works which Plutarch called Platonic, dialogues on ethical and political subjects, which were much admired in antiquity for their style but which are now lost. After the death of Plato in 346 he left the Academy, possibly disappointed that he had not been chosen to succeed him as head. In any case it was quite time that he left. The Academy offered little scope for his rapidly extending intellectual interests. With a few companions he crossed the Aegean Sea to Asia Minor and settled at Assos in the Troad. Here he continued his scientific studies, especially in marine biology. It is doubtful whether he wrote anything at this period, but the experience had a profound effect on his general outlook on the physical world and his view of man's place in it. Man was an animal, but he was the only animal that could be described as 'political', capable of, and designed by nature for, life in a *polis*. It was at this period of his life also that he married his first wife; she too was a Macedonian. In 343 he returned to his native land whither he had been invited to teach King Philip's young son, the future Alexander the Great. He did this for about two years, but what he taught him and what effect either had upon the other remain obscure. We know very little about the next four or five years but by 336 B.C. he was in Athens with his family.

Politically much had happened at Athens during his ten years' absence. The eloquence of Demosthenes had not been sufficient to stir up effective resistance to the increasing encroachment of Aristotle's own King Philip. After winning the battle of Chaeronea in 338 Philip had grouped most of the Greek states into a kind of federation firmly under the control of Macedon. Preparations were set afoot for an invasion of Asia, but Philip was assassinated in 336 and it was Alexander who led the expedition. At Athens opinion about Philip had long been divided. Macedonian supporters were fairly numerous among the wealthier upper classes and among these Aristotle had friends; he also had the useful backing of the Macedonian Antipater whom Alexander left in charge. So he had no difficulty in realizing his ambition of establishing at Athens a philosophical school of his own. He was a foreigner, not a citizen, and so could not legally own property there; but arrangements were made for a lease, and his school, the Lyceum, with its adjoining Walk (*Peripatos*), was successfully launched. Thus the most important and productive period of Aristotle's life, that of his second sojourn at Athens, coincides with the period when Alexander was conquering the Eastern world – a fact which no one could guess from reading his works. The news of Alexander's death in 323 was a signal for a revival of anti-Macedonian feeling at Athens, and Aristotle judged it prudent to retire to Euboea, where he died in the following year at the age of about sixty-two.

At the Lyceum, Aristotle had a staff of lecturers to assist him. These included the botanist Theophrastus, author of *Characters*, a man whose learning must have been as diversified as that of Aristotle. Perhaps, like the Regents in Scottish Universities in the eighteenth century, the staff were expected to teach a variety of subjects, theoretical and practical, and their surviving writings are a reflection of what they taught. But the distinction between *theoretikè* and *praktikè* was not at all the same as between theory and practice. They were two separate branches of knowledge, not two different ways of dealing with knowledge. The former, regarded as truly philosophical and truly scientific, was based on *theoria*, observation *plus* contemplation. This branch included theology, metaphysics, astronomy, mathematics, biology, botany, meteorology; and on these subjects Aristotle lectured and wrote extensively. To the practical branch belong the works entitled *Ethics*, *Politics*, *Rhetoric*, and *Poetics*. Of course these subjects, no less than the 'scientific' group, must be based on collecting and studying the available data. But the data, arising as they do out of human endeavour, are of a different and less stable kind. Moreover these sciences have a practical aim and the students were expected to become in some measure practitioners. In *Ethics* and *Politics*, for example, it does not suffice to learn what things are; they must find out also what can be done about them.

ARISTOTLE'S *POLITICS* IN THE PAST

There was a story current in antiquity that after Aristotle's death his unpublished works (that is most of the Aristotle that we have) were hidden in a cellar in Scepsis in the Troad and remained there unknown till the first century B.C. The story is probably untrue but there is no doubt that his *Politics* was not much studied during that time. Polybius, who was well read in Plato and would have had good reason to read the *Politics*, shows no real acquaintance with it. Cicero too, who *might* have read the *Politics* if the story is true that the manuscript reached Rome in Sulla's time, seems not to have done so. But Cicero knew Aristotle's earlier and published works, the now lost dialogues, including 'four books about justice'. Besides, teaching at the Lyceum continued to deal with *Politica* after the death of Aristotle, and the works of the Peripatetics Theophrastus and Dicaearchus were well known. Thus in various ways the political philosophy of the Lyceum may have been familiar to the men learned among Romans. Still, there is no denying the fact that both for Greeks and Romans the fame of Plato's *Republic* quite outshone that of Aristotle's *Politics* during classical antiquity. The same is true of Aristotle's work in general; it was little read in the days of the Roman Empire. Some of it (but not the *Politics*) became known in the West through the Latin translations of Boethius in the sixth century A.D. In the East, translations were made into Syriac and thence into Arabic. Some of these Arabic translations eventually found their way to Europe by way of Spain, where they were closely studied by learned Jews, and Latin translations were made from the Arabic before the twelfth century. But again the *Politics* was not included. The influence of the *Ethics* and the *Politics* does not begin to appear in Western Christendom till the thirteenth century; and that beginning was due to three members of the Dominican Order – William of Moerbeke (in Flanders), Albert of Cologne, and, most of all, St Thomas of Aquino.

William of Moerbeke knew Greek sufficiently well to make a literal translation into Latin for the use of Albert and Thomas. His versions of the *Ethics* and the *Politics* are extant, barely intelligible but interesting as exercises in translation. St Thomas made constant use of them, and everything that he wrote touching upon politics, rulers, and states was strongly influenced by the *Politics*. The state itself was for him, as for Aristotle, something in accordance with nature, something good in itself and needed by man in order to fulfil his nature. St Augustine had seen in the state the institutions and laws of the Roman Empire, certainly not good in themselves, but necessary as a curb on man's sinful nature; and this view was not abandoned when the Empire broke up. St Thomas in discarding it does not, of course, accept Aristotle's view of the state in its entirety. He may agree with the philosopher about property and about usury and the need to control education; but to be a good citizen in a good society, to be well-endowed with property, virtue, and ability – this ideal could not be made to fit the contemporary outlook merely by the addition of religion. The good life must needs now be a Christian life and a preparation for Eternity. St Thomas reproduces much of the six-fold classification of constitutions which Aristotle sometimes used and sometimes ignored; but he really had little use for it. He found (as we find) that Aristotle has no clear-cut answer to give to the question 'which is the best form of constitution?' But he found plenty of warrant in the *Politics* for saying that the rule of one outstandingly good man, backed by just laws, is most desirable, if only it can be attained. Besides, here he was on familiar ground. For centuries monarchical rule of one kind or another had occupied the central position in political thought; the contrast between the good king and the bad tyrant had been part of the stock-in-trade since classical antiquity; obedience and disobedience, legal status and legal rights, these were the topics; and above all how to build up what they called a 'Mirror of Princes' for the monarch to copy. We must not forget that the *Policraticus* of John of Salisbury (A.D. 1159) was just as much a precursor of St Thomas's *De regimine principum* as was the *Politics* of Aristotle, which John had not read.

In the domination exercised by Aristotelian philosophy over scholastic thought in the later Middle Ages, the *Politics* had little part to play; its influence and prestige were very great but of a very different kind and in a different field. Dante, for example, in his *De Monarchia* (1311) differed utterly from St Thomas, but his work is just as much permeated by the thought and language (latinized) of the *Politics*. Even farther removed politically from St Thomas is

Marsilius of Padua (*Defensor pacis*, 1324), yet here too the influence of the *Politics* is unmistakable. After the more general revival of classical learning in the fifteenth century, Plato and Cicero were more favoured than Aristotle by the majority of readers, but the *Politics*, which was first printed in 1498 (Aldine press), continued to be part of the essential background of political philosophers such as Machiavelli, Jean Bodin, or Richard Hooker. In the seventeenth century Thomas Hobbes poured scorn on the Aristotle of the Schoolmen, but his own *Leviathan* testifies to his reading of the *Politics*. In the eighteenth century a superficial acquaintance with the *Ethics* and the *Politics* could be taken for granted among educated Europeans. But it was not until the next century, and the publication in 1832 by the Prussian Academy of the great Berlin *Corpus* of his works, that the study of Aristotle *as a Greek author* was really taken seriously. The *Politics* shared in this, and soon began to profit greatly from the industry and application of German scholarship. Political philosophy in its turn derived benefit from the translations and interpretations of nineteenth-century classical scholars and was enabled to see its own ancient antecedents in truer perspective. In the twentieth century this work continued unabated but political philosophy itself began to lose interest for academic philosophers. On the other hand there was a growing interest in the newer disciplines of anthropology and sociology, and the comparative study of political institutions. Where in all this does the *Politics* of Aristotle now stand?

ARISTOTLE'S *POLITICS* TODAY

The *Politics* of Aristotle is still read as a textbook of political science in universities. It may be asked why this is so, why it has not been discarded, since all that is of value in it must surely have been absorbed and taken over by subsequent writers on the subject. Euclid was used as a textbook of geometry till well into the twentieth century, but his discoveries have been embodied in better textbooks for schools. For mathematicians the interest of Euclid is largely antiquarian; he is a part of the history of mathematics. Nor is Aristotle's biology any longer taught. Why is his *Politics* worth studying today for its own sake?

Broadly speaking the reasons are first, that the problems posed by ethical and political philosophy are not of a kind that can be solved once and for all and handed on to posterity as so much accomplished; and second, that the problems are still the same problems at bottom, however much appearances and circumstances may have altered in twenty-three centuries. How can men live together? The world has grown smaller and men are more than ever forced to live together. The problem is larger, more acute, and more complicated than it was when ancient philosophers first looked at it. How in particular can top-dog and under-dog be made to live together? Is it enough to say 'Give the top-dog arms and the under-dog enough to eat'? Or should there be only one class of dog? Then the under-dogs abolish the top-dogs, only to find themselves burdened with a new set. How perennial are the problems of government and how little they have changed are indeed all too clear. Recent events, the expansion of civilization, the spread of technological advances, and the growth of political power in all parts of the world have emphasized this. Western Europe no longer holds its former dominance either culturally or politically; but the *Politics* is not simply part of our Western heritage nor is it tied to the European political concepts which it helped to form. Just as it transcended the city-state era in which and for which it was written, so it has transcended both the imperialism and the nation-states of the nineteenth century. The nascent or half-formed states of Africa and Asia will recognize some of their own problems in Aristotle's *Politics*, just as the seeker after norms of behaviour will learn from his *Ethics*. Neither will find, nor expect to find, ready-made answers to his questions, but it is always illuminating to see another mind, sometimes penetrating, sometimes obtuse, working on problems that are fundamentally similar to one's own, however different in time, setting, and local conditions.

Works written about the science of politics may be said very roughly to fall into two classes, one of which may be called prescriptive, the other descriptive. The one seeks to make a pattern of an ideal state and, in varying degrees according to the taste of the author, to lay plans for the realization of that pattern. The other examines the data of politics, looks at constitutions as they exist now or have existed in the past, and seeks to draw conclusions about the way they are likely to develop. It does not aim at describing an ideal state or at determining what kind of constitution is best. Both types of study have, actually or potentially, a practical use, the prescriptive with a blue-print for the future, the other analysing and comparing. Both may also move in the domain of

pure theory, the one deducing from a set of principles what human
behaviour in society ought to be, the other evolving principles of
human behaviour from the ways in which men do in fact behave.
This does not mean that a descriptive writer suspends value-judge-
ment altogether; he can hardly avoid appraising, by some standard
or other, the work of the constitutions which form the data of his
subject.

The *Politics* of Aristotle belongs to both these classes and moves
in and out of them. It is the only work of an ancient author of
which that could be said. All through antiquity (and in more
modern times too) the utopian method of study predominated.
Long before Plato or Aristotle, the Greeks for good practical
reasons had been asking themselves 'What is the best form of constitution?' And after Plato the fame of the *Republic* and the *Laws*
kept much of political thought fastened to the same topics. In later
antiquity discussions of the ideal state took the form of discussions
about the perfect ruler, the ideal king. The search for the ideal
state and the best constitution are of course the very heart of Aristotle's *Politics*; he had inherited the topic from his predecessors and
is constantly commenting on and drawing from Plato. But he also
had the analytical approach; it was part of his scientific cast of
mind. And it is this that gives the *Politics* part of its special interest
today, when the prescriptive method, from Plato to Marx, is out
of fashion.

It is difficult to be a thoroughly detached observer even of the
data of the physical sciences, virtually impossible when it comes to
the study of man. Among the ancients only Thucydides came near
to it. He observed and analysed human behaviour as manifested
by nations at war, and nothing of that has changed since he wrote;
but he was not a political theorist and nothing could have been
farther from his mind than constructing a form of constitution. Yet
even in the pages of Thucydides it is not difficult to see in broad
outline what kind of polity he would prefer and would regard as
best for Athens. All the more then when we come to Aristotle; his
views about what is best are constantly to the fore and not always
consistent. He draws a distinction between the ideally best, and the
best in the circumstances or the best for a particular people; but his
own ethical standards and political preferences stand out clearly at
all times, even in those parts where the methods of descriptive
analysis and comparison are extensively employed. Hence although we may reasonably say that Aristotle carried over from his

biological studies to his political an analytical mind and a zeal for classifying and understanding all the data of his subject, we cannot claim that his observation is detached and unprejudiced. Nor of course must we fall into the common error of making such a claim for ourselves.

Again, Aristotle had more understanding than most ancient writers of the connexion between politics and economics. Just because the links between these two are nowadays so complex, it may be useful to study observations that are based on a much simpler form of society, however barren they may seem in themselves. The acquisition and use of wealth, the land and its produce, labour, money, commerce, and exchange – such topics as these are perpetually interesting and much of the first book of the *Politics* is devoted to them. Aristotle proceeds from a discussion of household management (*oikonomia*), regarding that as state-management on a smaller scale; goods, money, labour, and exchange play a big part in both. All that he has to say on these matters is strongly coloured by two obsessions, first, his prejudices against trade and against coined money and second, his reluctance to be without a labour-force which was either the absolute property of the employer (slave-labour) or so economically dependent on him as to make their free status positively worthless. In his thinking about these matters Aristotle was saddled with a piece of theory which because of its quasi-scientific appearance had been resting as an incubus on much of Greek thought for a century or more; the notion that whatever is good is according to nature. The *polis* itself was for Aristotle obviously good; it was made by man, but by man acting according to his own nature. But commerce and labour were not so easy. In the matter of trade Aristotle decided that exchange and barter of surplus goods were natural but that the use of coined money as a medium of exchange was contrary to nature, as was also usury. To own property was natural and indeed most meritorious, so long as the property was land. But in accordance with the principle 'Nothing too much' (to which the average Greek paid no more than lip-service) Aristotle lays it down that unnecessary accumulation cannot be allowed. What he has to say about money-making, about the responsibilities of wealth and the possibility of private ownership coexisting with public use of property, has a particular interest today, since the habits, methods, and ethics of money-making have become subjects of interest and importance for a much larger section of the population than formerly.

As regards slavery he was in a dilemma; slaves were both a form of property and a source of labour. He was aware that previous thinkers had shown that the enslavement of human beings, especially of Greek by Greek, was contrary to nature. But he was sure that slaves were indispensable in creating the conditions for the life of culture which was the aim of the *polis*. He could not therefore reject slavery, but he must endeavour to prove that after all it is not contrary to nature and that the slave though a human being is designed by nature to be as a beast of burden. Needless to say the attempt breaks down (see p. 34), as he himself must have been aware. Yet the arguments which he used were still in use among the defenders of slavery in the nineteenth century; the difference between black and white races gave them just that outward manifestation of nature's supposed intention that Aristotle had looked for in vain (Book I, Chapter 5).

Surprise is sometimes expressed that Aristotle continued to write about and to prescribe for the city-state, unaware that its era of independence had come to an end with the Macedonian conquest. But there is really no occasion for surprise; contemporaries cannot be expected to foresee the effects of events. Besides, the city-state was destined to remain the standard form of living for the majority of the Greek-speaking world for centuries yet to come. It is true that the cities had lost their absolute autonomy and notably their military power, so that they could not henceforth oppose the wishes of the Syrian, Macedonian, or other monarchs within whose territory they lay. But even in the time of the Roman Empire city-state life still went on; and if they had no real independence of action, there were still varying degrees of independence and certain privileges to be won.

But there *are* surprising things about Aristotle in his *Politics*. His attitude to slavery, to which reference has just been made, seems strange in one who must have read Euripides; and we do not know whether to ascribe it to callousness or to obtuseness. But he had other blind-spots; we can grant that he could not foresee the effects of the Macedonian domination and of Alexander's conquests. But was it necessary to omit all reference to them as if they were irrelevant to his subject? No one would ever guess from reading the *Politics* that Aristotle himself was a Macedonian or that a Macedonian king was then conquering the world. He has much to say about monarchy, but in spite of one or two casual references to Macedon we cannot see that either the country or its king was of

the slightest interest to him, or that they presented, as they un-
doubtedly did, features worth mentioning. He makes a casual and
unimportant reference to the murder of Philip in 336, but otherwise the latest identifiable event is the loss of Spartan military
supremacy at the battle of Leuctra in 371. So one must conclude
that the silence about modern times was deliberate. All the same it
seems strange in a manual intended for practical use.

Aristotle was a subject of the king of Macedon. His status at
Athens, while he lived there, was that of *metoikos*, resident alien.
As we have seen, he had powerful friends there and his position
was an easy one. But he was not a citizen, and the privileges of
citizenship were to him a matter of supreme importance. Yet never
at any time in his life had he the satisfaction of being a land-owning
citizen of a Greek *polis*. Perhaps that is just the reason for his cease-
less insistence on citizenship (see especially Book III). As he realized
the advantages of being a citizen, so too, one would think, he must
have been fully alive to the disadvantages of not being one. His
own position as a resident alien was tolerable enough, but what, in
theory or in practice, would be the position of all the other non-
citizens, permanent residents trying to earn their living? The number of persons in this category, neither slaves nor citizens but paid
employees, might, in any form of constitution which Aristotle
would tolerate, be fairly numerous, and it is surprising that he has
little to say about them except that they are a possible source of
discontent and a danger to the established order. Modern parallels
in different parts of the world will occur to a discerning reader of
the *Politics*; non-participation in the *politeia*, to use a phrase of
Aristotle's, is a real problem. Aristotle hardly sees it as such, beyond making a plea for moderation (beginning of Book v). Nor did
he see any connexion between these and that other depressed class,
the slaves; their legal status was different, and that was an end of
the matter. In spite of their similar economic positions it was
hardly even suspected that there could be common interests between slaves and free men.

The comparative study of political institutions in different countries is frequently made a part of the normal course of study in
modern political science; and the fact that it began with Aristotle
is an added reason for continuing to read him. He is known to have
written, probably with the aid of collaborators, historical and descriptive accounts of 158 city constitutions. One of these, the
Athenian, has survived largely intact on a series of papyrus-rolls

discovered in Egypt in 1891. Aristotle refers to this collection in the concluding passage of his *Ethics* as being part of the material which he will use in his *Politics* (see p. 24). He needs in particular to have examples to hand of the actual working of constitutions and to note the changes to which the different types are liable (see especially Book v). He also wishes to make comparisons with, and criticisms of, constitutions which only existed on paper, and for this he had in his library not only the *Republic* and the *Laws* of Plato but the work of other predecessors, most of them unknown now except for what he tells us (mostly in Book II.). Thus he uses both actual and imagined states for comparative purposes. Between one source of comparison and another he casts his net pretty wide. Chiefly of course he is concerned with the typically Hellenic product, the city-state, including the non-Hellenic but very interesting Carthage. But not all Greeks lived in city-states, and there are frequent references to the fact that many peoples lived a much less centripetal life in communities of a varying degree of cohesion. (See Aristotle's own note on *ethnos*, Book II, p. 57.) He knows monarchy well and describes many types of it but he shows no particular interest in the Macedonian type. Indeed his interest in monarchy is generally either antiquarian or theoretical.

There is a tendency when reading Aristotle's *Politics* to interpret what he says about the city-state in terms of the modern nation-state. This is natural and in part appropriate, since independent sovereignty was the mark of, and the claim made, by the ancient *polis*, no less than the modern state. But in the history of political thought the notion of a state is not a constant in the way that the notion of triangle is a constant in the history of geometry. Wherever and whenever we read about the theory of the state we are reading about a conception of it current in the author's time or else created by him. About the ancient Greek state two salient points (apart from its size) need to be emphasized which at first sight appear to contradict each other; on the one hand its unity and solidarity, on the other its limited membership. Even in a democracy there would be numerous adult males who would be non-citizens or slaves; they would form no part of the *polis*. The city is made up of its members, its citizens, enrolled as such in accordance with the rules of the constitution. Much of what they do in their daily lives arises directly out of the fact of their membership. Not only the duties of administration, of military service, and of the courts of law, but equally games, religion, festivals, recreation, even eating and drinking, are often closely connected with membership of the state. In short the state embraced a much smaller proportion of the population but a much larger share in the daily lives of each. The extent to which these facts are true of any one state in history varies greatly, but for Aristotle as for Plato they are not only true but right.

Aristotle calls the state the supreme form of human association, not the only one. He recognizes the existence of others, but except for the household or family he has little to say about them separately; he is mainly concerned with organs of government within the different kinds of constitution. But when Aristotle calls man 'a political animal' he has in mind all aspects of life in humane society, all that contributes to 'the good life'. The smaller social units within the larger *koinōnia* of the state have an important part to play here, and one wishes that Aristotle had gone into greater detail. But it is legitimate to take the general principles governing the larger associations as applicable also to the smaller. We need not always be thinking of the modern nation-state as a single whole when we are reading about ancient *politeia*. There is an immense variety of the lesser social units in any modern state. Some of these are closely connected with the constitution, others entirely separate from it; but all contribute in some measure to the life of the citizens and Aristotle would have regarded them as part of the *politeia*. The nineteenth century saw religious organizations becoming separated from the constitution, the twentieth has seen medicine, education, and even sport drawn into it. But all these bodies, great or small, and subordinate bodies under them, are associations of human kind, and much of what Aristotle has to say about the supreme form of association has application also to the lesser.

Like the ancient lawgivers the founders of a club or society, local or national, have to build a framework within which the members will together pursue the objects of their common purpose. A constitution has to be drawn up and rules agreed upon; the constitution will generally be what some ancient writers called a mixed one, the committee being an oligarchic element, the annual general meeting a democratic one. Clearly therefore the manner prescribed for elections to committees is a matter of supreme importance to all members, as Aristotle saw. But how rigid should this framework be? Can it be made to last for ever? Aristotle advises that a constitution should be of such a kind that the majority of its members will wish it to remain in being. But that is certainly no guarantee of permanence. Thus the questions raised in the *Politics* are not always those which concern the state and its rulers; they may be such as affect our daily lives and our social activities.

For Aristotle, as for Plato, the subject of political philosophy, or *politikè*, embraced the whole of human behaviour, the conduct of the individual equally with the behaviour of the group. Ethics was, therefore, a part of politics; we might also say that politics was a part of ethics. It was the aim of political philosophy to establish standards of social behaviour. Aristotle is thinking of both aspects of the matter when he writes near the beginning of his *Ethics*: 'In studying this subject we must be content if we attain as high a degree of certainty as the matter of it admits. The same accuracy or finish is not to be looked for in all discussions any more than in all the productions of the studies and the workshop. The question of the morally fine and just – for this is what political science attempts to answer – admits of so much divergence and variation of opinion that it is widely believed that morality is a convention and not part of the nature of things. We find a similar fluctuation of opinion about the character of the good. The reason for this is that quite often good things have hurtful consequences. There are instances of men who have been ruined by their money or killed by their courage. Such being the nature of our subject and such our way of arguing in our discussions of it, we must be satisfied with a rough outline of the truth, and for the same reason we must be content with broad conclusions. . . . Every man is a good judge of what he understands; in special subjects the specialist, over the whole field of knowledge the man of general culture. This is the reason why political science is not a proper study for the young. The young man is not versed in the practical business of life from which politics draws its premises and its data.' *

Alongside the strong ethical bias in political philosophy went a sense of the need for fixing standards. An ethical code had to be embodied in a code of law, and this code of law in turn described the whole framework of the social and political system and the moral standards under which the citizens were to live, and for which the Greek word was *politeia*, usually translated by 'Constitution'. Inevitably therefore young citizens had to learn these laws; only thus could they learn to live either the life of a citizen or

* *The Ethics of Aristotle* (trans. J. A. K. Thomson, Allen and Unwin, 1953; Penguin Classics, 1957), Book I, Chap. 3.

the life of an individual following accepted standards of right and wrong. Thus when we say that a young Athenian was educated in the *laws* of his country, we do not mean legal education, but moral and social.

There is a short passage at the end of the *Ethics* which some editors omit as being properly part of the *Politics*. At any rate it clearly makes a transition from one to the other and refers to some at any rate of the books of Aristotle's *Politics* as we have them. We will therefore translate this passage* as a preliminary to Book I, remembering, however, that we do not know that Aristotle so intended.

*

The text used is that of O. Immisch (Teubner). It has been translated in its entirety, including those passages which were bracketed by Immisch; but his bracketings and insertions of isolated words have been respected. His use of marks of parenthesis has not always been followed. The printing of some parts of the text as footnotes is due to the translator; it follows a principle now well established in Penguin translations and of proved assistance to the reader. The *Politics* has often before been translated into English, but the only version which has been at all times beside the present translator is that of one of his early teachers, H. Rackham (Loeb Library). It will be evident that the present translation is of an entirely different character. It aims at offering to English readers the *Politics* as a whole. In an attempt to convey something of the complexity of meaning attaching to certain Greek terms different English words have been used to translate them. At the same time the reader's attention is often called to these important terms in the passages (printed in italics) which are at intervals inserted in the text. It is hoped that these will help the reader to follow the drift of Aristotle's discourse, but he should remember, first, that these are no substitute for a commentary on the text, and second that the translator's interpretation of Aristotle's meaning may not always command acceptance. He has attempted to make the *Politics* readable; he could not be expected to make it all easy.

* It is not included in Thomson's translation of the *Ethics*.

THE POLITICS

As our predecessors have not investigated the process of law-making, it would perhaps be a good thing to examine it ourselves. Indeed we ought to go into the whole business of *politeia*, or constitution, in order that we may round off that part of philosophy which deals with Man. Now in the first place, since some good or partly good things have been said about this by our predecessors, we ought to try and evaluate these. Next we should look at my own work *Collected Constitutions* and see from these what kind of procedures do in fact keep states and separate constitutions in going order, and what are those which tend to bring them to a standstill; also what are the reasons why some states are well run and others are not. When these matters have been examined, we should, I think, be better able to get an all-round view of such questions as What is the best kind of constitution? What is the arrangement or structure of each kind of constitution? What are their established codes of law and morals? Let us therefore begin.

I

OUR own observation tells us that every state is an association of persons formed with a view to some good purpose. I say 'good' because in their actions all men do in fact aim at what they think good. Clearly then, as all associations aim at some good, that one which is supreme and embraces all others will have also as its aim the supreme good. That is the association which we call the State, and that type of association we call political. It is an error to suppose that the relationships between statesman and state, between king and subjects, between householder and household, between master and slaves, are all the same. In fact they differ not merely in size but in kind. Size is no criterion; we cannot say that a few people make a master-slave relationship, rather more people a household, more still a monarchical or, it may be, a political community – as if there were no differences between a large household and a small city. And even as between a monarchical and a political or citizen community there is a difference in kind; and it is not right to say that when one person is in control over the rest, that is monarchical, and that it is being political when a citizen takes his turn at ruling and at being ruled according to the principles of the science concerned. This will be quite evident if we examine the matter according to our established principle – the analytical method. We are accustomed to analyse other composite things till they can be subdivided no further; let us in the same way examine the state and its component parts and we shall see better how these differ from each other, and whether we can deduce any working principle about the several parts mentioned.

This first chapter is largely unintelligible until we realize that Aristotle is attacking Plato, who in a work called Politicus *or*

Statesman makes the errors above referred to. *It is typical of Aristotle as a biologist that he now goes on to consider the growth of the state.*

2

We shall, I think, in this as in other subjects, get the best view of the matter if we look at the natural growth of things from the beginning. The first point is that those which are ineffective without each other must be united in a pair. For example the union of male and female is essential for reproduction, since each is powerless without the other; and this is not a matter of choice, but is due to the desire, implanted by nature in both animals and plants, to propagate one's kind. Equally essential is the combination of ruler and ruled, the purpose of their coming together being their common safety. For he that can by his intelligence foresee things needed is by nature ruler and master, while he whose bodily strength enables him to perform them is by nature a slave, one of those who are ruled. Thus there is a common interest uniting master and slave.

It is assumed as self-evident that the male possesses superior intelligence to the female, but slave and female are not on that account to be identified.

Nature has distinguished between female and slave. She recognizes different functions and lavishly provides different tools, not an all-purpose tool like the Delphic knife; every instrument will perform its work best when it is made to serve not many purposes but one. So it is with the different functions of female and slave. Some non-Greek communities fail to understand this and assign to female and slave exactly the same status. This is because they have no section of the community which is by nature fitted to rule or command; their society consists solely of slaves, male and female. So, as the poets say, 'It is proper that Hellenes should rule over barbarians,' meaning that barbarian and slave are by nature identical.

Aristotle thus believes in a natural superiority and inferiority of both races and persons.

It was out of the association formed by men with these two, women and slaves, that the first household was formed; and the poet Hesiod was right when he wrote, 'Get first a house and a wife and an ox to draw the plough.' (The ox is the poor man's slave.) This association of persons, established according to the law of nature and continuing day after day, is the household, the members of which Charondas calls 'bread-fellows', and Epimenides the Cretan 'stable-companions'. The next stage is the village, the first association of a number of houses for the satisfaction of something more than daily needs. It generally comes into being through the processes of nature, as off-shoots of a house are set up by sons and grandsons. The members of such a village are called by some 'homo-galactic'. Composed in this way its government was inevitably monarchical; and the city-states too were at first monarchically ruled as are some nations to this day. For every household is ruled by its senior member, as by a king, and the off-shoot householders because of their blood relationship are ruled in the same way. This patriarchal rule is mentioned in Homer 'Each man has power of law over children and wives.' Homer is referring to scattered families, not to groups in villages, for scattered settlements were common in primitive times. For this reason the gods too are said to be monarchically governed, namely because men were originally ruled by kings and many are so still. Just as men imagine gods in human shape, so they imagine their way of life to be like that of men.

The final association, formed of several villages, is the city or state. For all practical purposes the process is now complete; self-sufficiency has been reached and so, while it started as a means of securing life itself, it is now in a position to secure the good life. Therefore the city-state is a perfectly natural form of association, as the earlier associations from which it sprang were natural. This association is the end of those others and its nature is itself an end; for whatever is the end-product of the perfecting process of any object, that we call its nature, that which man, house, household, or anything else aims at being. Moreover the aim and the end can only be that which is best, perfection; and self-sufficiency is both end and perfection.

Thus for Aristotle the 'nature' of anything is not its first but its final condition. And the process of growth towards it is also described as 'Nature'.

It follows that the state belongs to a class of objects which exist in nature, and that man is by nature a political animal; it is his nature to live in a state. He who by his nature and not simply by ill-luck has no city, no state, is either too bad or too good, either sub-human or super-human – sub-human like the war-mad man condemned in Homer's words 'having no family, no morals, no home'; for such a person is by his nature mad on war, he is a non-cooperator like an isolated piece in a game of draughts. But it is not simply a matter of cooperation, for obviously man is a political animal in a sense in which a bee is not, or any gregarious animal. Nature, as we say, does nothing without some purpose; and for the purpose of making man a political animal she has endowed him alone among the animals with the power of reasoned speech. Speech is something different from voice, which is possessed by other animals also and used by them to express pain or pleasure; for the natural powers of some animals do indeed enable them both to feel pleasure and pain and to communicate these to each other. Speech on the other hand serves to indicate what is useful and what is harmful, and so also what is right and what is wrong. For the real difference between man and other animals is that humans alone have perception of good and evil, right and wrong, just and unjust. And it is the sharing of a common view in these matters that makes a household or a city.

Aristotle has clearly not been giving us factual history but logical reconstruction. This is even more apparent in what follows.

Furthermore the city or state has priority over the household and over any individual among us. For the whole must be prior to the parts. Separate hand or foot from the whole body and they will no longer be hand or foot (except in name, as one might speak of a hand or foot sculptured in stone). It will have been ruined by such treatment, having no longer the power and the function which make it what it is. So, though we may use the same words, we cannot say that we are speaking of the same things. It is clear then that the state is both natural and prior to the individual. For as an individual is not fully self-sufficient after separation, he will stand in the same relationship to the whole as the other parts. Whatever is incapable of participating in the association which we call the state, a dumb animal for example, and equally whatever is perfectly self-sufficient and needs nothing from the state (e.g. a god), these are not parts of the state at all. Among all men, then, there is a natural impulse towards this partnership; and the first man to build a state deserves credit for conferring very great benefits. As man is the best of all animals when he has reached his full development, so he is worst of all when divorced from law and morals. Wickedness armed is hardest to deal with; and though man while keeping his weapons can remain disposed to understanding and virtue, it is all too easy for him to use them for the opposite purposes. Hence man without goodness is the most savage, the most unrighteous, and the worst in regard to sexual licence and gluttony. Justice is something essential in a state; for *right* is the basis of the political association and right is the criterion for deciding what is just.

Aristotle then deals with oikonomia, *which occupies the remainder of Book I. The word literally means 'household management', but, as the sequel shows, Aristotle is not thinking of domestic economy but of economics in a wider context, of state management as well as household.*

3

Now that I have explained what are the component parts of a city, and since these include households, it is essential to begin with the economics of the household. This topic can be subdivided so as to correspond to the parts of which a complete household is made up, namely, the free and the slaves; but our analytical method requires us to examine everything when it has been reduced to its smallest parts, and the smallest division of a household into parts gives three pairs – master and slave, husband and wife, father and children. And so we must ask ourselves what is, and what ought to be, each one of these three relationships. The word 'despotic' is used to describe the first, and we may use 'matrimonial' and 'paternal' respectively to describe the other two, as there is no more exact term for either. We may accept these three; but we find that there is a fourth element, one so important that some people regard it as covering the whole. I refer to what is called 'financial operations'.

Little more (Chapter 12) is said of marital or paternal relations. Aristotle concentrates on the other two in this book; they are essential to his economic theory, whether of household or city. They are also closely connected with each other, since on them both depends the maintenance of a high standard of living for the citizen. In order that some may be really free, others must be slaves. In order that a civilized people may preserve its heritage of culture, other races must be exploited and denied all human rights. Aristotle could see no other way.

First let us discuss master and slave in order to see what essential services are rendered in this way. I think we might be able to find a better way towards understanding this topic than if we started from the suppositions usually made. For example, some people suppose that the work of being a master requires a certain kind of knowledge, and that this is the same knowledge as is required to run a household or to be a statesman or a king – an error which we discussed at the beginning. Others say that it is contrary to nature to rule as master over slave, that the distinction is one of convention only, since in nature there is no difference, and that this form of rule is based on force and therefore wrong.

The slave as property and as tool.

4

Now property is part of a household and the acquisition of property part of the economics of a household; for neither life itself nor the good life is possible without a certain minimum standard of wealth. Again, for any given craft the existence of the proper tools will be essential for the performance of its task. Tools may be animate as well as inanimate; a ship's captain uses a lifeless rudder, but a living man for watch; for the worker in a craft is, from the point of view of the craft, one of its tools. So any piece of property can be regarded as a tool enabling a man to live; and his property is an assemblage of such tools, including his slaves; and a slave, being a living creature like any other servant, is a tool worth many tools. For suppose that every tool we had could perform its function, either at our bidding or itself perceiving the need, like the statues made by Daedalus or the wheeled tripods of Hephaestus, of which the poet says that 'self-moved they enter the assembly of the gods' – and suppose that shuttles in a loom could fly to and fro and a plucker play on a lyre all self-moved, then manufacturers would have no need of workers nor masters of slaves.

Tools in the ordinary sense are productive tools, whereas

property is useful in itself. I mean, for example, a shuttle produces something other than its own use, a bed or a garment does not. Moreover since production and action differ in kind and both require tools, the difference between their tools must be of the same kind, tools proper for production, property for action. Now life is action not production, therefore the slave as property is one of those that minister to action. A piece of property is sometimes spoken of as a part; for a part is not only part of something but wholly belongs to it, as does a piece of property. So a slave is not only his master's slave but wholly his master's property, while the master is his slave's master but does not belong to him. These considerations will have shown what are the nature and functions of the slave: any human being that by nature belongs not to himself but to another is by nature a slave; and a human being belongs to another whenever he is a piece of human property, that is a tool or instrument having a separate existence and useful for the purposes of living.

5

But whether anyone does in fact by nature answer to this description, and whether or not it is a good and a right thing for one to be a slave to another, and whether we should not regard all slavery as contrary to nature – these are questions which must next be considered.

Neither theoretical discussion nor empirical observation presents any difficulty. There can be no objection in principle to the mere fact that one should command and another obey; that is both necessary and expedient. Indeed some things are so divided right from birth, some to rule, some to be ruled. There are many different forms of this ruler-ruled relationship* and they are to be found everywhere.

* The *quality* of the rule depends primarily on the quality of the subjects, rule over man being higher than rule over animals; for that which is produced by or out of better men is a better piece of work; and the ruler-ruled relationship is itself a product created by the men involved in it.

Wherever there is a combination of elements, continuous or discontinuous, and a common unity is the result, in all such cases the ruler-ruled relationship appears. It appears notably in living creatures * as a consequence of their whole nature; the living creature consists in the first place of mind and body, and of these the former by nature is ruler, the latter ruled. Now in dealing with any phenomena dependent on natural growth we must always look to nature's own norm and not base our observations on degenerate forms. We must therefore in this connexion consider the man who is in good condition mentally and physically, one in whom the rule of mind over body is conspicuous. The opposite state, where body rules over mind, being in itself a bad thing and contrary to nature, would be found to exist in bad men or in men in bad condition. However, as I say, it is within living creatures that we first see the exercise of ruling or commanding power, both the absolute rule of a master and the non-absolute or constitutional. The rule of mind over body is absolute, the rule of intelligence over desire is constitutional and royal. In all these it is clear that it is both natural and expedient for the body to be ruled by the mind, and for the emotional part of our natures to be ruled by that part which possesses reason, our intelligence. The reverse, or even parity, would be fatal all round. This is also true as between man and other animals; for tame animals are by nature better than wild, and it is better for them to be ruled by men; for one thing, it secures their safety. Again, as between male and female the former is by nature superior and ruler, the latter inferior and subject. And this must hold good of mankind in general. We may therefore say that wherever there is the same wide discrepancy between two sets of human beings as there is between mind and body or between man and beast, then the inferior of the two sets, those whose condition is such that their function is the use of their bodies and nothing better can be

* It can exist also where there is no life, as dominance in music; but that is hardly relevant here.

expected of them, those, I say, are slaves by nature. It is better for them, just as in the analogous cases mentioned, to be thus ruled and subject.

The 'slave by nature' then is he that can and therefore does belong to another, and he that participates in the reasoning faculty so far as to understand but not so as to possess it. For the other animals serve their owner not by exercise of reason but passively. The use, too, of slaves hardly differs at all from that of domestic animals; from both we derive that which is essential for our bodily needs. It is then part of nature's intention to make the bodies of free men to differ from those of slaves, the latter strong enough for the necessary menial tasks, the former erect and useless for that kind of work, but well suited for the life of a citizen of a state, a life divided between war and peace. But though that may have been nature's intention, the opposite often happens. We see men who have the right kind of bodily physique for a free man but not the mind, others who have the right mind but not the body. This much is clear: suppose that there were men whose bodily physique alone showed the same superiority as is shown by the super-human size of statues of gods, then all would agree that the rest of mankind would deserve to be their slaves. And if this is true in relation to physical superiority, the distinction would be even more legitimately made in respect of superiority of mind. But it is much more difficult to see quality of mind than it is to see quality of body. It is clear then that by nature some are free, others slaves, and that for these it is both right and expedient that they should serve as slaves.

Aristotle must have been well aware that he has not really proved the naturalness of slavery. Apart from the flimsiness of the arguments from analogy he has had to admit that nature, while making obvious and visible the distinction between men and animals, has not done so for free men and slaves. The argument really only amounts

*to saying that in any society there must be hewers of wood and
drawers of water and that such work should be done by those best
fitted by nature for menial tasks – unless of course a Daedalus or a
Hephaestus can provide the right kind of automaton.*

*In the following chapter Aristotle comes astonishingly near to
saying that Might is Right and to dismissing as mere sentimentality
all protests against the enslavement of war-captives.*

6

On the other hand it is not hard to see that those who take
the opposite view are right up to a point. The words
'slavery' and 'slave' have a double connotation. I have
been speaking about 'natural' slavery but there exists also
a legal or conventional slavery. This arises under the convention which provides that all that is captured in war
becomes legally the property of the captors. Against this
right many of those versed in law protest that it is in fact
contrary to law, which should exercise restraint upon
violence. They hold it to be indefensible that a man who
has been overpowered by the violence and superior might
of another should become his property. Others see no harm
in this, and both views are held by expert jurists. The
reason for this difference of opinion, and for fluctuations
between the two, lies in the word 'superior'. Surely it is in
a sense goodness or ability which attains a position of
command and is therefore best able to use force; and that
which is victorious is so in virtue of superiority in some form
of goodness. It seems therefore that force is not without a
goodness of its own and the real dispute is about what is
right, that is to say between those who say that right in
this connexion means human feeling and those who say
that it means 'the stronger shall rule'. No reconciliation is
here possible; arguments based on one view have no
validity or power of conviction for the opposite party, and
reduce us to denying altogether our principle that the
superior in goodness shall rule and be master.

Some claim that enslavement in war has an element of

right in it, simply as being legal; but they do not always say this, since it is quite possible that the undertaking of the war may have been unjust in the first place. Also one cannot use the term slave properly of one who is undeserving of being a slave; otherwise we should find among slaves and descendants of slaves even men of the noblest birth, should any of them be captured and sold. For this reason they will not apply the term slave to such people but use it only for barbarians. But in so doing they are really seeking to define, not the slave by convention, but the slave by nature, which was our starting point, an essential point of which was that there are some who are slaves everywhere, others who are slaves nowhere. And the same is true of noble birth: nobles regard themselves as well-born not only among their own people but everywhere, but to non-Greeks they allow nobility of birth to be valid only in barbarian lands. This involves making two grades of freedom and of noble birth, one absolute, the other conditional.* But in introducing this conditional element they are really basing the distinction between slave and free, well-born and base-born, upon goodness and badness. For they maintain that as man is born of man, and beast of beast, so good is born of good. But though this may be frequently nature's intention, she is unable to realize it. It is clear then that there is justification for the difference of opinion; on the one hand we cannot say that some are slaves and others free by nature, on the other this distinction is in some cases actually made, cases where it is both expedient and just for the one to be slave, the other to be the master, and as ruling and being ruled ought to depend on the natural qualities in each case, so too in being a master. For, if the work of being a master is badly done, that is contrary to the interest of both parties; for the part and the whole, the soul and the body, have identical interests; and the slave is in a sense a part of his master, a living, but as it were a separate, part of his

* In a play by Theodectes, Helen is made to say 'Who would think it proper to call me a slave, who am sprung of divine lineage on both sides?'

body. For this reason also it is advantageous that a feeling of mutual affection should subsist between master and slave, wherever they are by nature fitted for this relationship. But they are not so fitted when the slave-condition arises out of the use of force and out of the convention about captives which we have been discussing.

7

From all this it is clear that there is a difference between the rule of master over slave and political rule. All forms of rule are not the same though some say that they are. Rule over free men is by nature different from rule over slaves; rule in a household is monarchical since every house has one ruler; the government of a state is rule over free and equal persons. A man is not called master in virtue of what he knows but simply in virtue of what he is – a master; similarly with slave and free. That is not to say that there is no such thing as a master's knowledge or a slave's knowledge. The latter kind may be illustrated by a certain man in Syracuse who, for a fee, undertook to train house-boys in their ordinary duties; this kind of instruction might well be extended to include cookery and other forms of domestic service. For the tasks are many and various, some menial, some more dignified; as the proverb has it 'servant before servant, master before master', meaning that there is inequality in both groups. Turning from slaves' knowledge to masters' knowledge, we may say that this consists in knowing how to use slaves; for he is master not in his acquiring slaves but in using them. But the use of slaves is not a form of knowledge that has any great importance or dignity, since it consists in knowing how to direct slaves to do the tasks which they ought to know how to do. Hence those masters whose means are sufficient employ an overseer to take on this function, while they devote themselves to statecraft or philosophy. The knowledge of how to acquire slaves is different from both these; the true and original method was by raiding and hunting.

Getting slaves must be considered along with getting other property. But for Aristotle property, not work, is the basis of livelihood. Yet it is part of household management to see that the household has enough to eat, both now and for the future, so it is often necessary to add to resources – the art of money-making. Aristotle is uncertain whether working for gain is part of management, but he is certain that it is something different. The political importance of this becomes clear when we remember that for Aristotle ownership of a certain amount of property is a necessary condition of citizenship.

8

Let us then, since the slave is part of the property, go on to consider the acquisition of property and money-making in general, still following our usual analytical method. The first question to be asked might be this: Is money-making the same as household management, or a part of it, or subsidiary to it? And if it is subsidiary, is it so in the same way as shuttle-making is subsidiary to weaving, or as bronze-founding is to the making of statues? For these two are not subsidiary in the same way; the one provides instruments, the other the material, that is, the substance out of which a product is made, as wool for the weaver, bronze for the sculptor. It is obvious that household management is not the same as money-making; it is the task of the one to provide, the other to use; for what other activity than running the house is going to make use of what is in the house? But whether money-making is part of management or a different kind of activity altogether – that is a debatable question, if, that is to say, it is a money-maker's task to look around and see from what sources money and property may be derived.

Now property and riches are very comprehensive terms, so that a first question might be whether farming is a part of property-management or something of a different kind, including under farming both the acquisition and the maintenance of stock. But again, there are many different ways of getting food and that means many different ways of life, both of animals and humans; and as there is no life without food, so differences in feeding make different kinds of life. For it is differences in feeding-habits that make some animals live in herds and others scattered about; some are carnivorous, some vegetarian, others will eat anything. So, in order to make it easier for them to get these nutriments, nature has given them different ways of life. Again, since animals do not all like the same food but have different tastes according to their nature, so the ways of living of carnivorous animals differ among their different kinds, as do also those of the vegetarian. Similarly among human beings there are many varieties of life: first there are the nomads; these do least work, for nutriment from domestic animals can be had with a minimum of toil and a maximum of ease, but when the animals have to be moved to fresh pastures, the human beings have to go with them, running, as it were, a mobile farm. Next the hunter, or rather all those who live by what they can catch, some being simply raiders, others fishermen who must live near a lake, a marsh, a river, or a fish-bearing part of the sea; others live off birds and wild animals. The third and largest class lives off the earth and its cultivated crops.

These then are the main ways of getting a living, that is the self-maintaining types, not those which depend on trade or barter. They are the nomadic, the agricultural, the piratical, fishing, and hunting. Many live happily enough by combining some of these, making up for the deficiencies of one by adding another at the point where the former fails to provide; such combinations are nomadism with piracy, agriculture with hunting, and so on. They simply live the life that their needs compel them to. Getting a living in this self-supporting way is clearly given by nature herself to all her creatures, both at the time of their birth and when they are fully grown. For some animals produce at the very beginning of procreation sufficient food to last their offspring until such time as these are able to get it for themselves; for example those which produce their young as grubs or eggs. Those also which produce live

offspring carry in themselves sufficient food for a considerable time – the food which we call milk. Nature also provides for them when they are fully grown; for we must
believe, first that plants exist for the sake of animals, second
that all other animals exist for the sake of man, tame
animals for the use he can make of them as well as for the
food they provide; and as for wild animals, most though
not all of these can be used for food or are useful in other
ways; clothing and instruments can be made out of them.
If then we are right in believing that nature makes nothing
without some end in view, nothing to no purpose, it must
be that nature has made all things specifically for the
sake of man. This means that it is part of nature's plan that
the art of war, of which hunting is a part, should be a way
of acquiring property; and that it must be used both against
wild beasts and against such men as are by nature intended
to be ruled over but refuse; for that is the kind of warfare
which is by nature right.

*Thus Aristotle used the need for a livelihood as an argument in
favour of regarding slave-raiding against inferior peoples as something natural.*

One form then of property-getting, namely getting a livelihood, is, in accordance with nature, a part of the economics
of management; accordingly either the goods must be
there to start with, or this art of acquisition must see that
they are provided; goods, that is, which may be stored up,
as being useful or necessary for providing a livelihood.
This is true whether the organization that we are dealing
with is a household or a state. And I am sure that wealth
in the true sense consists of property such as this. For the
amount of property of this kind which would give financial
independence adequate for a good life is not limitless, as
Solon thought. In one of his poems he wrote 'No bound is
set on riches for men'. But there is a limit; wealth is a tool
and there are limits to its uses as to the tools of any craft;

both in size and in number there are limits of usefulness. Wealth is a collection of tools for use in the administration of a household or a state. It is clear therefore that there is a certain kind of property-getting that is the natural duty of those in charge of a house or a city; and why this is so is also clear.

Wealth should be sought only as a basis for livelihood not for its own sake. Aristotle reverts to using the term money-making (χρηματιστικη), but suggests that it best describes the pursuit of unlimited riches, of which he disapproves; but he does not consistently use it so. It belongs to commercial activity not to the management of a household or a state.

9

But there is another kind of property-getting, to which the term money-making is generally and quite rightly applied; and it is due to it that there is thought to be no limit to wealth or its acquisition. Because it closely resembles that form of acquisition which we have just been discussing, many suppose that the two are one and the same. But they are not the same, though admittedly they are not very different; one is natural, the other is not. This other kind does not come naturally to a man; he has to acquire it by practice. Let us begin our discussion thus: Every article or property has a double use; both uses are uses of the thing itself, but they are not similar uses; for one is the proper use of the article in question, the other is not. For example a shoe may be used either to put on your foot or to offer in exchange. Both are uses of the shoe; for even he that gives a shoe to someone who requires a shoe, and receives in exchange cash or food, is making use of the shoe as shoe, but not the use proper to it, for a shoe is not expressly made for exchange purposes. The same is the case with other articles of property; the process of exchange can be applied to any of them and the practice has its origin in a state of affairs often to be found in nature, namely, too much here and not enough there. It was essential that the exchange should be carried on just so far as to satisfy the needs of the parties. (Clearly the process of buying and selling is different and is not a natural way of getting goods.) The practice of exchange of goods did not exist in the earliest form of association, the household; it only came in with the larger forms. Members of a single household shared all the belongings of that house. But members of different households shared many of the belongings of other houses also. Mutual need of the different goods was the essential basis of these exchanges, and it is on this basis that many of the foreign peoples still practise barter. For barter is the exchange of one class of goods for another, as may be found useful; they take and give wine for corn and so on. But they do not carry the process any farther than this; it remains one of barter.

Interchange of this kind is not contrary to nature and is not a form of money-making; it keeps to its original purpose – to re-establish nature's own equilibrium of self-sufficiency. All the same it was out of it that money-making arose. This is quite understandable; for as soon as the import of necessities and the export of surplus goods began to extend beyond national frontiers, the provision and use of a conventional medium of exchange inevitably followed. Not all the things that we naturally need are easily carried; and so for exchange purposes men entered into an agreement to give to each other and accept from each other some commodity, itself useful for the business of living and also easily handled, such as iron, silver, and the like. The amounts were at first determined by size and weight, but eventually the pieces of metal were stamped. This did away with the necessity of weighing and measuring, since the stamp was put on as an indication of the amount. Once a currency was provided, development was rapid and what started as a necessary exchange of goods became *trade*, the other kind of money-making. At first probably it was quite a simple affair; but then it became more complicated, as men become more experienced and more adept at discovering where and how the greatest profits might be made out of commercial exchanges. That is why money-making is held to be concerned primarily with actual coined money and those who engage in it have to be persons with a good eye for sources where plenty of money is to be made; for that, they say, is the way wealth of any kind is made. Indeed wealth is often regarded as consisting in a pile of money, since the aim of money-making and of trade is to make such a pile.

But some regard coined money as not true wealth at all; the value of a currency is easily debased.

Sometimes on the other hand coinage, along with other usages conventionally established, is regarded as so much artificial trumpery having no root in nature; since, if those who employ a currency system choose to alter it, the coins cease to have their value and can no longer be used to procure the necessities of life. And it will often happen that a man with plenty of money will not have enough to eat; and what a ridiculous kind of wealth is that which even in abundance will not save you from dying with hunger! It is like the story told of Midas: just because of the inordinate greed of his prayer everything that was set before him was turned to gold. Hence we seek to define wealth and money-making in different ways; and we are right in doing so, for they *are* different; on the one hand true wealth, in accordance with nature, belonging to household management, productive; on the other money-making, with no place in nature, belonging to trade and not productive of goods in the full sense. In this kind of money-making, in which coined money is both the end pursued in the transaction and the medium by which the transaction is performed, there is no limit to the amount of riches to be got.

Aristotle sees this as a confusion of means and ends or, as he put it earlier, between the tools and the job.

The art of healing aims at producing unlimited health and every other art aims at its own end without limit, wishing to secure that to the highest possible degree; on the other hand the means towards the end are not unlimited, the end itself sets the limit in each case. But for this kind of money-making the end provides no limit, because wealth and getting money are themselves the end. Household management on the other hand, not being money-making, has a limit, since money-making is not its function, but only a means to an end. So, while it seems that there must be a limit to every form of wealth, in practice we find that the opposite occurs: all those who are amassing wealth in the form of coin go on increasing their pile without limit, not distinguishing this kind from the other because they are so similar. For they are similar in that both are concerned with the acquisition and ownership of property; but in method they are dissimilar; in one case the end is sheer increase, in the other something different. Some people therefore imagine that increase is the function of household management and never cease to believe that their store of money ought to be hoarded or increased without limit. The reason why some people get this notion into their heads may be that they are eager for life but not for the good life; so, desire for life being unlimited, they desire also in unlimited amount what is conducive thereto. Others again, while aiming at the good life, seek what is conducive to the pleasures of the body. So, as this too appears to depend on the possession of property, their whole activity centres on money-making and the second kind of money-making owes its existence to this. For where enjoyment consists in excess, men look for that which produces the enjoyable excess. And if they cannot procure it through money-making, they try to get it by some other means, using all their faculties for this purpose. It is contrary to nature to use all our faculties thus: courage, for example, whose function is to produce confidence, not money, military leadership, or medicine, whose aims are victory and health. But these people turn all qualities into money-making qualities, as though that were the end and everything had to serve that end.

We have now discussed money-making, both the unnecessary, what it is and why we do in fact make use of it, and the necessary, which differs from the other in being concerned with household management and maintenance in a way that accords with nature, and also in being limited and unlimited.

Early in Chapter 8 we learned that money-making was not the same as household management since the user must be distinguished from the producer. Then we learned that it might be regarded as a part, as long as it was concerned with procuring necessities and did not develop into general commercial activity. But now at the beginning of Chapter 10 doubt is cast on the usefulness of money-making even of the right type: if nature does her work, there is no need of property-getting. But this position is not long held and a compromise is reached.

10

The answer also is clear to the question raised at the beginning whether or not it is the business of one engaged in household economy or in political economy to make money and add to property. The answer is that it is not: these should be at hand for his use from the start. Household management ought not to need to make money, any more than political science needs to make men, who are the material which nature provides and which political science takes and uses. Similarly nature can be expected to provide food, whether from land or sea or in some other way. It is only as a result of that that the economist can perform his duty of distributing these supplies. So weaving is not the art of producing wool but of using it, though it is also the art of knowing good yarns from bad and the most suitable types for different purposes. If, on the other hand, we do allow that money-making is a part of management, why, it may well be asked, is not the art of medicine also a part? After all, the members of a household need to be healthy as much as to keep alive and meet their daily needs. The answer is that up to a point it is the business of manager or ruler to see to health, but only up to a point; beyond that it is the doctor's business. So in the matter of money and property, to some extent these are the concern of the manager, beyond that they belong to the subsidiary art. But best it is, as has been just said, that the wealth should be provided at the outset by nature. For it is a function of nature to provide food for whatever is brought to birth, since that from which it is born has a surplus which provides food in every case. We conclude therefore that any form of money-making that depends on crop and animal husbandry is for all men in accordance with nature.

Money-making then, as we have said, is of two kinds; one which is necessary and acceptable, which we may call administrative; the other, the commercial, which depends on exchange, is justly regarded with disapproval, since it arises not from nature but from men's dealings with each other. Very much disliked also is the practice of charging interest; and the dislike is fully justified, for interest is a yield arising out of money itself, not a product of that for which money was provided. Money was intended to be a means of exchange, interest represents an increase in the money itself. We speak of it as a yield, as of a crop or a litter; for each animal produces its like and interest is money produced out of money. Hence of all ways of getting wealth this is the most contrary to nature.

*In practice a man can make a living in a variety of ways; some
fall under the heading of natural, which Aristotle approves, others
do not. He is much less interested in practice than in theory and
refers his more political readers to manuals of instruction. But the
philosopher too may be a practical man and even make money. It is
also now conceded that even commercial money-making may be a
useful adjunct to a country's prosperity and that nature herself
often provides an exportable surplus that can be used for exchange
(cf. Book VI, Chapter 8, beginning).*

11

Now that we have discussed adequately the theory of
money-making, we ought to speak also about its practice.
In matters like this, theoretical speculation is free, but
practical application is tied fast to circumstances and needs.
Some profitable branches of the natural kind of money-
making and the kind of practical knowledge that each
requires will now be mentioned: (1) Stock rearing, experience and knowledge of what kinds are profitable and
where and how, I mean the purchase of horses, cattle,
sheep, and other animals; and further one must know
which of these are most profitable as compared with the
rest, and which kinds in which areas, since some do better
here, others there; (2) a knowledge of tillage, fields to be
sown with crops and fields planted for fruit; (3) of bee-
keeping and of rearing such birds and fishes as can contribute. Those are the three main branches of the most proper
way of making a living. Of the other, the method of
exchange, the main branch is (1) Commerce, subdivided
into (a) shipping, (b) carrying goods, (c) offering them for
sale. In all these there are wide differences according to
whether one looks for high profits or for security. Then
(2) money-lending and (3) working for pay, whether (a) as
a skilled or (b) as an unskilled workman. Somewhere
between these two main categories of natural and unnatural money-getting we might make a third, since it has
elements in it both of nature and of exchange: I refer to

what is got out of the earth itself or grows out of the earth, uncultivated but useful, such occupations as timber-working, and mining of every description. This latter can be subdivided for there are many products that earth yields in this way.

About these ways of getting a living I have spoken only in a very general way, but adequately for the present purpose. For, however useful a detailed account might be for those likely to be engaged in such occupations, it would be out of place to spend much time on them now.* Moreover people have written books on these topics. Chares of Paros and Apollodorus of Lemnos have manuals on agriculture, both crops and fruits, and others on other subjects, so that anyone who is interested may study them in those writers' works. The material is scattered, and it would be advisable to make a collection of all those methods by which men have succeeded in this business of money-making. It would certainly be very useful for those who, like the philosopher Thales, attach much importance to the acquisition of wealth. Thales used a financial device which, though it was ascribed to his skill as a philosopher, is really open to anybody. The story is as follows: people had been saying to Thales that philosophy was useless, as it had left him a poor man. But he, deducing from his knowledge of the stars that there would be a good crop of olives, while it was still winter raised a little capital and used it to pay deposits on all the oil-presses in Miletus and Chios, thus securing an option on their hire. This cost him only a small sum as there were no other bidders. Then the time of the olive-harvest came and as there was a sudden and simultaneous demand for oil-presses, he hired them out at any price he liked to ask. He made a lot of money and so demonstrated that it is easy for philosophers to be rich, if they want to; but that is not their object in life. Such is

* I will just add this: those require most skill which depend least on luck; those are most banausic which cause most deterioration of the bodies of the workers; most slavish where the body has most to do, most ignoble where there is least need of goodness.

the story of Thales, how he gave proof of his cleverness; but, as we have said, the principle can be generally applied; the way to make money in business is to get, if you can, a monopoly for yourself. Hence we find governments also on certain occasions employing this method when they are short of money. They secure a sales-monopoly for themselves. There was a man in Sicily, too, who used a sum of money that had been deposited with him to buy up all the iron from the foundries; then, when the buyers arrived from the various firms, he was the only seller; and without raising the price unduly he turned his fifty talents into a hundred. When the ruler Dionysius heard of this he told the man that he regarded such practices as detrimental to the country's interest and that he must therefore depart from Syracuse at once, though he might take his money with him. The example of Thales and this one are in principle the same; both managed to create a monopoly for themselves. All this knowledge about commodities and supply and demand is useful also for statesmen; for many cities are in greater need of money and of these sources of supply than a household. Hence we sometimes find that those who direct the affairs of a state make this their entire policy.

The short Chapter 12 adds something to what was said at the beginning of Chapter 3 to which it makes reference.

12

There are, as we saw, three parts of household management, corresponding to three types of rule, one as of a master, despotic; this has already been dealt with; next the rule of a father; and a third which arises out of the marriage relationship. This is included because rule is exercised over wife and children, over both as free persons but in other respects differently; over a wife rule is as of a statesman, political, over children as of a king, royal. For the male is more fitted

49

to rule than the female, unless conditions are quite abnormal, and the elder and fully grown more fitted than the younger and undeveloped. It is true that in the majority of those states in which government is truly political there is an interchange of the role of ruler and ruled, which aims at equality and non-differentiation; but so long as one is ruling and the other is being ruled, there is a strong tendency to mark distinctions in outward dignity, in style of address, and in honours paid. (A man becomes entitled to respect when he is made an official, like the statue of a god which Amasis made out of a wash-basin.) As between male and female this relationship of superior and inferior is permanent. Rule over children is royal, for the begetter is ruler by virtue both of affection and of age; and this is the prototype of royal rule. Homer therefore was right in calling Zeus 'father of gods and men', as he was king over them all. For a king ought to have a natural superiority but to be no different in birth; and this is just the condition of elder in relation to younger and father to son.

Thus relationship between the persons concerned is for Aristotle, as a moralist, of greater importance than economics. It is clearly essential that all should possess fitness for the performance of their various functions; and this fitness is described in the very general word 'virtue'. This includes ability, but Aristotle regards moral virtue as equally a part of fitness for a task; and its exercise requires the faculty of reasoning. Since virtue is to be related to function, and since a slave has no function but to serve his master, the virtue of a slave is said to be due to his master. The Greek word is aretē; *goodness, excellence, ability, virtue, are some of the ways in which it may be rendered in English.*

13

It is clear then that in household management the people are of greater importance than the material property, and their quality of more account than that of the goods that make up their wealth, and also that free men are of more account than slaves. About slaves the first question to be asked is whether in addition to their value as tools and servants there is some other quality or virtue, superior to these, that belongs to slaves. Can they possess self-respect, courage, justice, and virtues of that kind, or have they in fact nothing but the serviceable quality of their persons?

The question may be answered in either of two ways, but both present a difficulty. If we say that slaves have these virtues, how then will they differ from free men? If we say that they have not, the position is anomalous, since they are human beings and capable of reason. Roughly the same question can be put in relation to wife and child: Have not these also virtues? Ought not a woman to be self-respecting, brave, and just? Is not a child sometimes naughty, sometimes good?

All these questions might be regarded as parts of the larger question – our inquiry into the relations of ruler and ruled, and in particular whether or not the virtue of the one is the same as the virtue of the other. For suppose we say that they are the same, and that the highest quality of excellence is required of both, why should one completely rule and the other completely obey? (A distinction of more or less will not do here; the difference between ruling and obeying is one of kind; quantitative difference is irrelevant.) If on the other hand one is to have virtues and the other not, we have a surprising state of affairs. For if he that rules is not to be self-controlled and just, how shall he rule well? And if the ruled lacks virtue, how shall he be ruled well? For if he is slack and disobedient, he will not perform his duties. Thus it becomes clear that both ruler and ruled must have a share in virtue but there are differences in virtue in each case, as there are also among those intended by nature to be ruled.

This mention of virtue leads us straight away to a consideration of the soul; for it is here that the natural ruler and the natural subject, whose virtue we regard as different, are to be found. In the soul the difference between ruler and ruled is that between the rational and the non-rational. It is therefore clear that in other connexions also there will be natural differences. And so generally in cases of ruler and ruled; the differences will be natural but they need not be the same. For rule of free over slave, male over female, man over boy, are all natural, but they are also different, because, while parts of the soul are present in each case, the distribution is different. Thus the deliberative faculty in the soul is not present at all in a slave; in a female it is inoperative, in a child undeveloped. We must therefore take it that the same conditions prevail also in regard to the ethical virtues, namely that all must participate in them but not all to the same extent, but only as may be required by each for his proper function. The ruler then must have ethical virtue in its entirety; for his task is simply that of chief maker and reason is chief maker. And the other members must have what amount is appropriate to each. So it is evident that each of the classes spoken of must have ethical virtue. It is also clear that there is some variation in the ethical virtues; self-respect is not the same in a man as in a woman, nor justice, nor courage either, as Socrates thought; the one is courage of a ruler, the other courage of a servant, and likewise with the other virtues.

If we look at the matter in greater detail it will become clearer. For those who talk in generalities and say that virtue is 'a good condition of the soul', or that it is 'right conduct' or the like, delude themselves. Better than those who look for general definitions are those who, like Gorgias, enumerate the different virtues. So the poet Sophocles singles out 'silence' as 'bringing credit to a woman', but that is not so for a man. This method of assessing virtue according to function is one that we should always follow. Take the child: he is not yet fully developed and his function is to grow up, so we cannot speak of his virtue as belonging absolutely to him, but only in relation to the progress of his development and to whoever is in charge of him. So too with slave and master; we laid it down that a slave's function is to perform menial tasks; so the amount of virtue required will not be very great, only enough to ensure that he does not neglect his work through loose living or mere fecklessness.

If this is true of a slave-worker, one will naturally ask whether free workers will not also need virtue to keep them from the disordered living which often interferes with their work. The answer is Yes, but the parallel is not exact; the work may be the same in each case but the manner of life is different; the slave shares his master's life, the workman lives away from his employer and participates in the virtue required for his work in the same measure as he participates in the slavery; for any worker at menial tasks is in a restricted sense in a condition of slavery. There is also this difference that the slave is slave by nature, which cannot be said of a shoemaker or other artisan. It is clear therefore that the master ought to be the cause of such virtue as is proper to a slave. (I refer, of course, to moral virtue and not to the fact that as master he can teach slaves to be good at their task.) Hence they are wrong who would deny all reason to slaves and say that a master has nothing to do but issue orders; suggestion and advice are even more appropriately given to slaves than to children.

The discussion of households in this book has been largely concerned with property and slaves; family relationships have scarcely been touched upon and now once again they are postponed. Something is said of marriage relationships in Book VII, Chapter 16.

So much then for our discussions of these matters. As for man and wife, children and father, and the virtue that appertains to each and their intercourse one with another, what is right in that connexion and what is not, the pursuit of the good therein and the avoidance of the bad – all such matters it will be necessary to discuss in connexion with the forms of the constitution. For these are all matters pertaining to the household and every household is part of a state; and the virtue of the part ought to be examined in relation to the virtue of the whole. This means that children, and women too, must be educated with an eye to the whole constitution of the state – at least if it is true to say that it makes a difference to the goodness of a state that its children should be good and its women good. And it must make a difference; for women make up half the adult free population and from children come those who will become citizens and participate in the political life.

Now that we have finished with these matters, and decided to discuss the rest in another place, we will regard as concluded the subject of households and make a fresh beginning. And let our first topic be those who pronounced an opinion on the best form of constitution.

BOOK II

The final sentence of Book I has forecast the main topic of Book II, a consideration of the Ideal States as imagined by Plato and others. The book contains also an account of some actual states which Aristotle considers to be good. It is the first essay in the comparative study of political institutions.

I

We have undertaken to discuss the form of association or partnership which we call the state, to ask the question what is the best type of such partnership – supposing that we are in a position to choose what we would like. But we must also look at sample constitutions, for example, those that are in use in cities that have the reputation of being well-governed, or any others that have been sketched by writers and appear to be good. Our purpose is partly to see what in them is good and useful and what is not; but we also wish to make it clear that if we keep looking for something different from what we find there, we do not do so out of mere captiousness or a desire to be clever; we have chosen this method simply because in fact none of the existing constitutions, whether written or actual, is entirely satisfactory.

Thus Aristotle apologizes for beginning by attacking all the weakest points in Plato's Republic, *notably its excessive concern with solidarity and unanimity (the reference to his* Ethics *in Chapter 2 is 1132 and 33) and the sharing of wives and property by all the members of the ruling-class, that is, all full citizens.*

As we are discussing a form of partnership, a natural starting point is 'the things shared and the partners who share them'. In a state either all the citizens share all things, or they share none, or they share some but not others. It is clearly impossible that they should have no

55

share in anything; at the very least the members must share in the territory, the territory of a single state, of which single state they are all members. The question then becomes twofold: if a city is to be really well-governed, is it better that all the citizens should share in all things capable of being shared, or only in some of these and not in others? It is certainly quite possible for citizens to go shares with each other in children, in wives, and in property as in the *Republic* of Plato. For in that work Socrates says that children, wives, and property ought to be held in common. We ask therefore, Is it better to do as we now do or should we adopt the practice advised in the *Republic*?

2

The proposal that wives should be held in common presents many difficulties of which these three are the chief: (a) in all that Socrates says there does not clearly emerge any reason why this custom should be made part of the social system; (b) when viewed as a means to the end, for which the state is said in that dialogue to exist, the proposal is unworkable; and (c) it is nowhere laid down how it is to be carried out. I am referring to the dictum of Socrates, 'It is best that the state should be as much of a unity as possible.' But surely this is not true. A state which becomes progressively more and more of a unity will cease to be a state at all. Plurality of numbers is natural in a state; and the farther it moves away from plurality towards unity, the less a state it becomes and the more a household, and the household in turn an individual. I say this because the household is clearly more of a unity than the state and the individual than the household. So, even if it were possible to make such a unification, it ought not to be done; it would destroy the state. For the state consists not merely of men, but of different kinds of men; you cannot make a state out of men who are all alike.

Consider in this connexion the difference between a state and an alliance; the purpose of an alliance is military assistance and its usefulness depends on the amount of that assistance, not on any differentiation in kind; the greater the weight, the greater the pull.* On the other hand for the making of a single state differences in kind among the members is essential. As I have already stated in my *Ethics*, it is the perfect balance between its *different* parts that keeps a city in being. This balance between different parts is essential even among citizens who are free and equal; for they cannot all hold office simultaneously but must do so for a year at a time or for some other appointed period. This does in fact ensure that all rule, just as much as if shoemakers and carpenters were to change places with each other instead of always keeping to the same kind of work. On this analogy it would be better that these in charge of the political partnership should, if it is possible, not change places but always remain the same people. But that is not possible in cases where all are by nature equal; for then it becomes a positive right that all should share in the task of ruling, whether they do so well or ill; this is a true reflection of the twin principles (1) that equals in turn defer to others and (2) that out of office they are all equal. Some rule while others are ruled, and by doing this turn about it is just as if they became different persons every time. There is similar differentiation among those ruling, for they exercise now one function, now another. It is clear from all this need for dissimilarity that the state is not a natural unity in the sense that some people think, and that what has been alleged to be the greatest benefit in societies does in fact make for their dissolution; that which is truly good for a thing makes for its preservation. And here is another indication that excessive unification is a bad thing in a state: the household is more self-sufficient than the individual, the state than the household; and when that moment is reached when the association formed by the people is self-sufficient, then we have a city or state. Since then a greater degree of

* The same difference can be observed between a *polis* and an *ethnos*, even when, as in Arcadia, the people are not scattered in villages but federated.

self-sufficiency is to be preferred to a lesser, the lesser degree of unity is to be preferred to the greater.

3

Again, however much importance we may attach to the principle of unity within the political association, the arguments used in favour of common ownership do not support that principle. Socrates says that if in a city all alike say 'mine' and 'not mine', this is an indication of complete unity in the state. But this is not so; the word 'all' is used in two senses 'all separately' and 'all together'. Used in the former sense this might better bring about what Socrates wants; for each man will always refer to the same boy as his son, the same woman as his wife, and will speak in the same way of his property and whatever else comes within his purview. But that is not at all how people will speak who hold wives and children in common. They may do so all together, but not each separately; and the same with regard to possessions. Thus it is misleading to use the word 'all', which like many other words, such as 'both', 'odd', 'even', owing to double sense lead to highly disputable conclusions in reasoning. So, while it may be an admirable state of affairs where 'all' say the same thing, it is in one sense of the word an impossible state of affairs, in the other it is not conducive to a feeling of solidarity.

There is a further drawback to common ownership: the greater the number of owners, the less the respect for the property. People are much more careful of their own possessions than of those communally owned; they exercise care over public property only in so far as they are personally affected. Other reasons apart, the thought that someone else is looking after it tends to make them careless of it. This is rather like what happens in domestic service: a greater number of servants often does less work than a smaller. Applying this to the proposed communal possession of families, we might say that each citizen has a thousand sons, but these are not one man's sons; any one of them is equally the son of any person. As a result no person will concern himself very much about any of them.

Moreover when a man uses 'my' in this way with reference to a fellow-citizen, he is speaking only as a small fraction of a large number. In saying 'my son' or 'X's son' is 'doing well' or 'not doing well', he is referring to each one of a thousand fathers (or whatever the number of the citizens may be) and even then with some dubiety, since it is uncertain whether any particular citizen is in fact the father of a son, and of one that has survived. Is not our ordinary use of the word 'my' better than this use of it by two thousand or ten thousand people all with reference to the same thing? In the ordinary way one man will call his own son the same person whom another will call his own brother, and whom a third will call cousin, or some other term of relationship by blood or marriage, some direct or indirect connexion. (And yet another will speak of him as a member of his club or his clan.) Anybody would rather have a cousin who really was his cousin than a son shared in the manner described. Again, one could not prevent people from making guesses as to their own brothers, sons, fathers, or mothers. And in view of the likenesses which exist between parents and their offspring, mutual recognition would inevitably be regarded as proof. And this is what actually occurs – according to the reports of those who write about their travels. These tell us that some of the peoples of Upper Libya have community of wives, but they can always tell whose children are whose by their resemblances. And even among non-human females such as horses and cattle there are some which have a remarkable natural power of producing offspring resembling their sires, like the one they called the Honest Mare of Pharsalus.

Aristotle began by criticizing Plato's plan for communally-owned property as not being conducive to solidarity, as Plato had thought. From that he was led on to consider community of wives and children,

*because this too, by watering down the sense of ownership, diminishes
the feeling of solidarity. In the course of this he turns aside for a
moment to mention other objections.*

4

Here are some further evil consequences which could
hardly be avoided by those who would set up such a form of
society – assault, homicide, both intentional and unintentional, feuds and slander. All these are not merely illegal but
unholy, if they are committed against father or mother; the
nearer the relationship, the more unholy the act. Yet such
things are more likely to happen when people are not aware
of any relationship than when they are aware. And when
they do happen, those who know the relationship can at
least make the expiations which religious custom demands;
the others cannot. It is equally objectionable that Plato,
while making sons to be shared by all, wishes to prohibit
sexual intercourse between lovers only but not to prohibit
its most unseemly manifestations, as between brothers or
between father and son, where the passion itself ought to be
prohibited. And why prohibit sexual intercourse that is
otherwise unobjectionable, merely on the grounds of the
powerful pleasure it gives, drawing no distinction between
that and intercourse between brothers, or father and son?
Again, in the *Republic*, community of wives and children is
prescribed for the guardian or ruling class. It would be far
more useful applied to the agricultural class. For where
wives and children are held in common there is less affection, and a lack of strong affection among the ruled is
conducive to obedience and not to revolution.

*Aristotle agrees that affection makes a bond to hold the state together,
but not that kind of affection which strives for absolute unity, such
as that described in Plato's* Symposium.

So, taken all round, the results of putting such laws as
these into practice would inevitably be directly opposed to

the results which good legislation ought to aim at, and which moreover are those which in the *Republic* Socrates thinks can be produced by ordering matters in this way for children and wives. We do believe that the existence of friendly and affectionate feelings in cities is a very great boon to them; it is a safeguard against civil strife. And Socrates is emphatic in his praise of unity in the state, which, as he expressly states, is one of the products of a friendly feeling. In another of Plato's dialogues, one which treats of love, we read that Aristophanes said that lovers because of the warmth of their affection are eager to grow into each other and become one instead of two. In such an event one or other must perish, if not both. But in a state in which wives and children are shared the feelings of affection will inevitably be very lukewarm, father being unable to say 'my son', son unable to say 'my father'. Just as a small amount of sweetening dissolved in a large amount of water does not reveal its presence to the taste, so the feelings of mutual solidarity implied in these terms of affection becomes watered down to nothing; and in a city of this kind there is nothing to make fathers care for their sons or sons for their fathers or brothers for each other. There are two impulses which more than all others cause human beings to love and care for each other: 'this is my own', and 'this I love'. In a state constituted after the manner of Plato's *Republic* no one would be able to say either of these.

One further point – the suggested transfer of children from the classes of farmer or artisan to the class of guardian and also the transfer in the opposite direction – there is the greatest obscurity as to how such transfers shall take place. Those who surrender the children born and those who hand them over must be aware what children they are and to whom they are being handed over. And such transfers would add greatly to the already mentioned risks – assault, manslaughter, illicit passion; for those transferred to one of the two lower classes will no longer use the terms brother, son, father, mother, of members of the guardian class, nor will those raised to the guardian class so speak of the rest of the citizens, which would at least have set them on their guard against such acts on their own kin.

That concludes our discussion of community of wives and children.

Ownership of property and the right to its produce are now discussed, first in very general terms and with a wider reference than Plato's Republic. *Private ownership of the means of production is advocated combined with fair distribution of profits.*

5

Connected with the foregoing is the question of property. What are the best arrangements to make about property, if a state is to be as well constituted as it is possible to make it? Is property to be held in common or not? It will be observed that the answer to this question may well be different from the answer as to children and wives. A possible answer is that while there should be separate households, as is the universal practice, it would be better that property, both in respect of ownership and usufruct, should be held communally. Or ownership and usufruct might be separated; then either the land is held in common and its produce pooled for general use (as is done by some peoples) or the land is communally held and communally worked but its produce is distributed according to individual requirements. This is a form of communal ownership which is said to exist among certain non-Greek peoples. There is also the alternative already mentioned – that both the land and its produce be communally owned. As to its cultivation – any system of communal ownership will run more smoothly if the land is worked by persons other than the citizens; because, if they themselves work the land for their own benefit, there will be greater ill-feeling about the common ownership. For if the work done and the benefit accrued are equal, well and good; but if not, there will inevitably be ill-feeling between those who get a good income without doing much work and those who work harder but get no corresponding extra benefit. Communal life and communal ownership are hard enough to achieve at the best of times and such a state of affairs makes it doubly hard. The same kind of trouble is evident when a number of people club together for the purpose of travel. How often have we not seen such partnerships break down over quarrels arising out of trivial and unimportant matters! In a household also we are most likely to get annoyed with those servants whom we employ to perform the routine tasks.

These then are some of the difficulties inherent in the joint ownership of property. Far better is the present system of private ownership provided that it has a moral basis in sound laws. It will then have the advantages of both systems, both the communal and the private. For, while property should up to a point be held in common, the general principle should be that of private ownership. If the responsibility for looking after property is distributed over many individuals, this will not lead to mutual recriminations; on the contrary, with every man busy with his own, there will be increased production all round. 'All things in common among friends' the saying goes, but it is the personal qualities of individuals that ensure their common use. And politically such an arrangement is by no means impossible; it exists, even if only in outline, in some countries, and in well-governed ones too, either in operation or soon to be. Briefly it would work thus: each man has his own possessions; part of these he makes available for his own immediate circle, part he uses in common with others. For example, in Sparta they use each others' slaves practically as if they were their own, and horses and dogs too; and if they need food on a journey, they get it in the country as they go. Clearly then it is better for property to remain in private hands, but we should make the right to use it communal. It is a particular duty of a lawgiver to see that citizens are disposed to do this. Moreover there is an immense amount of pleasure to be derived from the sense of ownership; every man bears love towards himself and I am sure that nature meant this to be so. Selfishness is condemned and rightly so, but selfishness is not simply love of self but excessive love of self. So excessive greed to acquire property is condemned, though every man, we may be sure, likes to have his bit of property. And there is this further point: there is very great pleasure in giving, helping friends and associates, making things easy for strangers; and this can only be done by someone who has property of his own.

None of these advantages is secured by those who seek through the abolition of private ownership the extremest unification of the state. And, what is more, they are openly throwing away the practice of two virtues – self-restraint in sexual passion (for it is a virtuous thing to refrain from another's wife through self-discipline) and private generosity. The abolition of private property will mean that no man will be seen to be liberal and no man will ever do any act of liberality; for only in the use of money is liberality made effective.

Thus excess of unity means excess of control; if the state controls our expenditure and our sexual relationships, there is no occasion to exercise moral virtue in either of these spheres. In the passage which immediately follows, Aristotle confuses the distinction between public and private ownership with the distinction between individual private ownership and joint ownership. He then reiterates his criticism of excessive unity.

Plato's proposals under this heading might well on first hearing sound attractive and humane; they would seem to promise exceptional warmth of affection among all members of the citizen body and to have a particular attraction for those who blame the prevalent evils of society entirely on the absence of communal ownership. I refer especially to charges and countercharges of broken contracts, of false witness, and of undue influence over wealthy owners. But these things are not due to the absence of communal ownership, they arise out of defects in human character. In fact we find more disputes arising between those who share the use and possession of property than we do among separate owners; but we do find that the number of those who quarrel over common property is small as compared with the great multitude of private owners.

Again, it would be only fair to count not merely the evils of which property-sharing would rid us but also the advantages of which it would deprive us. Such a count would show that to live in the way suggested would be really impossible. The cause of Socrates's error lies in his false premise about unity; certainly there must be some unity in a state, as in a household, but not an absolutely total unity. There comes a point when the effect of unification is that the state, if it does not cease to be a state altogether, will certainly be a very much worse one; it is as if one were to reduce harmony to unison or rhythm to a single beat. As we have said before, a city must be a plurality, depending on education for its common unity. And it is very strange that Plato, whose intention it was to introduce an education which he believed would make the city good, should think that he could obtain good results by such methods. It is going the wrong way about it; regulations about property are no substitute for the training of the character and the intellect or for using the laws and customs of the community to that end.*

There is another point that ought not to be overlooked; the immense period of time during which this form of communism has remained undiscovered, as it surely would not have remained had it been really good. Pretty well all possible forms of organization have now been discovered, though no collection of them all has been made, and many are known in theory only, not having been tried. The force of our arguments about unity would become clearer if we could see a Platonic city actually being put together; it

* For example, at Sparta and in Crete the legislator effected a certain sharing of goods *by means of* the custom of common meals, not the other way round.

would be impossible to construct such a city without keeping its parts separate, dividing it either into messing-groups, as at Sparta, or into brotherhoods and tribes, as at Athens. The only significant new feature would be that Plato's Guardians do not engage in agriculture; and this is exactly what the Lacedaemonians are now trying to introduce.

The economic and constitutional positions of the populace have not been clearly defined by Plato and, so far as they can be ascertained, appear to Aristotle to make for disunity.

But what of the bulk of the population? To what extent will they participate in membership of the state? In the absence of any positive statement in the text it is very hard to say. Certainly they will make up almost the entire population, but it is not stated whether the farming class are to have communal or private ownership, whether of property or of wives and children. Suppose that they too are to have these in common, what will there then be to distinguish them from the Guardians? And what good will it do them to submit to their government or what inducement will there be to accept it? (Perhaps recourse might be had to a Cretan device of allowing to the lower classes every privilege except those of physical education and carrying arms.) If on the other hand we assume that there is no communism among them but private ownership exactly as elsewhere, how will they participate in the state at all? The inevitable result would be two states within one, and these in some degree in opposition to each other. For on the one side he puts the Guardians, like an army of occupation, on the other the farmers, craftsmen, and the rest of the citizens. This can only lead to disputes and litigation and all the other evils that he speaks of. And yet Socrates says that thanks to good education, there will be no need for a large number of regulations such as those governing administration, trading, and the like, and this while giving education only to the Guardians. Again, he makes the farmers owners of their produce but requires them to pay rent; but in that position they are much more likely to be troublesome and discontented than the helots, serfs, slaves, and other lower classes that we know of.

In any case no final decision was reached about the need for such arrangements, nor yet about closely related questions, such as the type of constitution, and the nature of the education and laws which will be provided for them. This is not easy to discover; and yet these things will make all the difference to the maintenance of the communism of the Guardians. If he means to make wives shared and property privately owned, who will look after the house, as men tend the fields? And what if both the wives and the property of the farming class are held in common? To argue from an analogy with wild animals and say that male and female ought to engage in the same occupations is futile: men do not do housework. Risky too is Socrates's way of appointing the rulers; they are to be always the same people. This is a sure source of discontent, for there will be many who feel that they are getting no recognition of their merit – to say nothing of that class called 'warlike and spirited'. But clearly his principles make it unavoidable that the same persons should always rule; for that divine or 'golden' element in the soul, of which he speaks, does not vary in its incidence but is present always in the same people. It is, according to his own statement, immediately at birth that the admixture takes place, of gold in some cases, of silver in others, and, for those who are going to be craftsmen or farmers, of bronze and iron. Again, when he denies to the Guardians any right to happiness, he tries to justify it by saying that it is the duty of a lawgiver to make the whole city happy. But it is impossible for the whole to be happy, unless the majority, if not actually all, or at any rate some, parts possess happiness. The evenness of an even number is a very different thing from the happiness of a city; two odd numbers added together make an even number, but two unhappy sections do not add up to a happy city. And if the Guardians are not happy, who will be? Certainly not the craftsmen and the general run of menially employed people.

These are some, but by no means all, the drawbacks inherent in the kind of state described by Socrates in Plato's *Republic*.

Aristotle deals very summarily with the Laws *of Plato; he ignores many of the important differences between it and the* Republic *and forgets that there is no Socrates in it. On the other hand he sees clearly the economic impossibility of Plato's 'second-best' state.*

6

The case of Plato's *Laws*, which was written later than the *Republic*, is somewhat similar; it would therefore be advisable to look also at the constitution there depicted. We have seen that in the *Republic* Socrates came to definite conclusions only about very few matters – the common possession of wives and children and of property, the general organization of the state into classes (the bulk of the inhabitants being divided into two parts, a farming class and a fighting class, while out of the fighters a third group is formed which makes decisions and governs the city). But there are many things which Socrates left undetermined: are farmers and craftsmen to have no share in the government or are they to have a certain share? Are they or are they not to possess arms and join the rest in defending their country? He does say that he thinks women ought to fight and ought to receive the same education as the Guardians, but for the rest he has filled up his account with much extraneous matter, particularly about the way in which the Guardians are to be trained. Turning then to the *Laws* we find that the greater part of it is in fact 'laws', and there is very little about constitution. He is trying to make a kind of society which would be more generally acceptable to our cities than the *Republic*, but he gradually comes back again to the earlier constitution. For, apart from the sharing of wives and property, he constructs the two societies on very much the same pattern – the same kind of education, the same freedom from menial tasks, and the same arrangements for common meals, except that in the *Laws* women also are to have the common meals, and the number of those bearing arms is five thousand, not one thousand.

Now all the Socratic dialogues are marked by a certain exaggeration and playfulness, by a desire for novelty, and by an inquiring mind; but they can hardly be expected to be always right. For example these five thousand citizens just mentioned – it is quite obvious that it will require the territory of a Babylon or some other huge country to support so many men not engaged in productive work, to say nothing of still larger numbers of women and servants who would be attached to them. We can in our speculations postulate any conditions we like, but they should at least be within the limits of possibility. It is further stated that in framing the laws a legislator ought to have regard both to the territory and to the population; but surely he ought also to take note of the neighbouring territories. This is obvious if the state is to have the normal existence of a *polis* and not live in isolation; for in that case it must provide itself with such arms as it needs, not merely for internal use but also for defence against those beyond its borders. And in the other case, where there is no desire, either nationally or individually, for having dealings with neighbours, even so, I think, the need is just as great to appear formidable to potential enemies, whether they come or whether they don't.

Then there is the amount of property to be possessed by each man: this ought to be looked at to see whether there is not room for some clarification of Plato's proposals. He says that a man ought to have enough to live on *virtuously*. There are two objections to this: he uses 'live virtuously' as if it meant the same as 'live the good life', which is a far more comprehensive expression; also it is quite possible to live a virtuous life and yet be miserable. I suggest that a better formula would be 'virtuous and liberal'. We need both; taken separately the one leads to a life too easy, the other to a life too hard. And these are the only qualities that bear directly on the use of wealth; we do not say that a man uses his wealth gently or bravely, but that he uses it virtuously, that is with moderation, and liberally. These then are essentially the right attitudes towards the use of wealth.

Furthermore, there is no point in equalizing property, if we do nothing to regulate the number of citizens, but allow births to go on unhindered in the belief that, as appears to happen in cities that we know of, the population would be kept constant, however high the birth-rate, merely by the number of childless couples. But in Plato's state the balance would need to be maintained much more accurately. At present, with the practice of dividing the property among all the children however numerous, nobody is in actual want. Under the proposed arrangement the property becomes indivisible and all save the heir have to go without, whether there be few or many in the family. Indeed it may well be that we ought to limit the production of children more than the amount of wealth owned, ensuring that no more than a certain number are born. In fixing this number regard should be had to incidental factors such as the non-survival of some infants and the childlessness of some couples. To leave the number of births unrestricted, as is done in most states, inevitably causes poverty among the citizens; and poverty produces discontent and crime. Pheidon of Corinth, one of the earliest of the lawgivers, held that the *number* of houses and the *number* of citizens should be kept equal, even if to begin with they all had inherited property of varying *magnitude*. In the *Laws* it is the other way round.*

Again, when he allows a man's *whole* property to be increased up to five times the original amount, why should there not be a stated limit up to which *landed* property

* Our own view as to how these matters would be best regulated will be stated later. Here we add a further deficiency in the *Laws*. It concerns the rulers and how they are to differ from the ruled. He merely says that the warp is made of different wool from the weft, and that is what the relation between ruler and ruled ought to be.

may be increased? Consider also his separation of one household into two; I doubt if it is advantageous for working purposes. Plato was for giving two separate households to each man; but it is awkward to live in two houses.

In discussing the constitutional defects of Plato's Law-state Aristotle refers at the outset to the use of the word πολιτεία, constitution, to describe a particular type, as it were a 'constitutional constitution'. In order to avoid confusion the Greek term modernized as 'polity' is generally used to translate πολιτεία in this restricted sense. It was generally accepted in the fourth century B.C. that 'polity' was a good thing because it did not denote anything extreme. All else was a matter of debate, and Aristotle in Book IV describes his own particular brand of middle-class, middle-of-the-road polity. He is not here rejecting the notion of polity, merely arguing that as conceived in the Laws *it fails to do what Plato wanted it to do – be a good second best to the ideal state of the* Republic.

The whole constitutional set-up is intended to be neither democracy nor oligarchy but mid-way between the two – what is sometimes called 'polity', the members of which are those who bear arms. If he is framing his constitution on these lines because such constitutions are found in our cities more generally than any other type, we may perhaps accept his word. But we cannot do so if he means it to be the second best, inferior only to the ideal constitution. For in that case one might well prefer the Lacedaemonian or some other constitution with a more aristocratic basis. There are indeed some who say that the best constitution is one composed of a mixture of all types and who therefore praise the Lacedaemonian. Some of these say that it is made up out of oligarchy, monarchy, and democracy; its kingship is monarchy, its council of elders oligarchy, and yet it is also democratically ruled through the authority exercised by the ephors, who are chosen from the people. Others draw a different comparison, saying that the power of the ephors is a tyranny and that the democratic element is to be found in the common meals and the communal daily life of the Spartan citizens. But in Plato's *Laws* it is stated that the best constitution ought to be composed of democracy and tyranny; yet surely these two ought to be regarded either as not constitutions at all or as the worst of all. There is therefore a strong case for including a large number of different elements in any form of mixed constitution.

Considered in this light we find that the constitution of the *Laws* appears to have nothing monarchical about it at all, only oligarchy and democracy with a bias towards oligarchy. This is shown in the method of appointment of office-bearers. I do not mean the practice of selection by lot from a number chosen by election, for that is common both to oligarchy and democracy. But to impose upon the richer citizens and upon them only the obligation to be members of the Assembly, to vote for office-bearers and do any other duty that falls upon a citizen – that is oligarchical. So also is the attempt to secure that a majority of the office-holders come from among the wealthy and that the highest offices are filled by those with the highest incomes. Oligarchical also is the manner of election which he proposes for members of the Council. It is true that all take part in the election; but they elect first some from the class possessing the highest property-qualification, then an equal number from the class next below; then from the third class, but there was to be no general obligation to elect from the third class or the fourth class, and only the first two classes were to be obliged to elect from the fourth class. And after all that, he says that from each class an equal number is to be appointed to the Council. The result will be that those who elect from the highest property-class will be more numerous and more upper-class, because the lower classes, not being obliged to vote, will refrain from doing so. These considerations show that this kind of constitution, the mixed kind, ought not to be compounded out of monarchy and democracy; and this conclusion will be strengthened by what will be said hereafter when we come to consider our own view of a constitution of this type. And with regard to elections this idea of electing from the elected is a dangerous one. For if a number of persons, not necessarily a large number, are resolved to stand firmly by each other, the elections will always go according to their wishes. So much for the constitution of Plato's *Laws*.

Nothing is known of the egalitarian Phaleas apart from what we here learn of him.

7

There are other 'Republics' beside Plato's; their authors are sometimes professional politicians or philosophers, sometimes not professionals at all. These all sketch constitutions that come nearer than either of Plato's to existing constitutions, under which people actually live; for no other person has even introduced such novelties as the sharing of children and wives, or common messing for women. They prefer to start from essentials; for some that means getting the best possible distribution of wealth, for, they say, it is always about these basic necessities that disputes arise. This was the motive behind Phaleas of Chalcedon, who was the first to propose equalizing the property of all the citizens. He held that this was not difficult to do at the very beginning, and that, although it was more difficult in states already set up and working, still all properties could quickly be brought to the same level, simply by arranging that the rich should bestow dowries but receive none, and the poor give no dowries but only receive them. Plato, when writing the *Laws*, thought that there ought up to a certain point to be freedom from property-control, but that, as has been stated earlier, none of the citizens should have the right to own property more than five times as great as the smallest property owned. Those who legislate along these lines must not forget, as indeed they are apt to do, that while fixing the amount of property they ought also to fix the number of children; for if the number of children becomes too great for the size of the property, it becomes impossible to maintain the law as it stands. And if you do maintain it, many who were rich will become poor; this is a most undesirable consequence, since you can hardly prevent such persons from becoming bent on revolution.

That equality of property has considerable effect on the partnership which we call the state has, so we find, been realized by some long ago; it can be seen in the legislation of Solon; there are cities where there is a law against unlimited acquisition of land; laws likewise exist which prevent the sale of property, as for example in Locri, where the law is that property may only be sold where it can be shown that a misfortune has occurred to make the sale imperative. Other laws require the ancient lots of land to be maintained intact. It was the abrogation of such a law that rendered the constitution of Leucas over-democratic; it ceased to be possible to appoint to office only those possessed of the proper qualification. Equality of property may exist and yet the level be fixed either too high, with resultant excess of luxury, or too low, with inevitable discomfort. It is clear, therefore, that it is not enough for a legislator to equalize property-holdings; he must aim at fixing an amount mid-way between extremes. But even if one were to fix a moderate amount for all, that would still not answer the purpose; for it is more necessary to equalize appetites than property, and that can only be done by adequate education under the laws. Perhaps, however, Phaleas would say that this is exactly what he himself meant; for he holds that in states there ought to be equality of education as well as equality of property. But one must state what exactly the education is to be; it is no use simply saying that it is to be one and the same. 'One and the same' education might very well be of such a kind that it would produce men ambitious to secure for themselves wealth, or distinctions, or both. And dissension is caused by inequality in privilege no less than by inequality in wealth, though for opposite reasons on either side; that is to say, the many are incensed by the sight of inequality in wealth, the upper classes are incensed if honours are equally shared, for then, as the Homeric tag has it, 'good and bad are held in equal esteem'

Equality of wealth will not put an end to stealing.

It is held that equality of wealth, by ensuring that no one need resort to stealing clothes or food because he is cold or hungry, is a sufficient cure for such crimes. But to secure the necessities of life is not the only purpose for which men commit crimes against property. They also wish to enjoy things which they have long coveted; and if their desire goes beyond mere necessities, they will seek a remedy in crime. Nor is that the only motive; men also wish to enjoy pleasures that bring no pain. Thus there are three different sets of persons to be considered and three different cures: for the first set (those who steal in order to live) a modest competence and employment; for the second, self-control (they must learn to curb their desires). As for the third, if they wish to find enjoyment not in coveting anything but in themselves, philosophy alone, I think, will provide the answer; unlike the other two sets of people they stand in no need of a third party. As for major crimes, men commit them when their aims are extravagant, not just to provide themselves with necessities. Who ever heard of a man making himself a tyrant in order to keep warm? For the same reason, the magnitude of the crime, there is more credit in slaying a tyrant than slaying a thief. So we may conclude that the typical characteristics of Phaleas's constitution would be a protection only against minor crimes.

Where will the surplus wealth come from that will be needed to meet external dangers?

Moreover Phaleas is chiefly concerned to make the internal arrangements of his city work well, disregarding, as he ought not to do, relations with neighbouring and other foreign cities. In framing a constitution it is essential to have regard to the acquiring of strength for war; yet Phaleas has said nothing about this. A nation's wealth is part of its strength; for it is essential that there should be resources sufficient not merely for its internal needs but also to meet external dangers. For this purpose the total amount of property ought not to be so large that more powerful neighbours will covet it, and the owners be unable to repel the invasion; on the other hand it must not be so small that they cannot finance a war against an equal or similar foe. Phaleas of course fixed no limit and there is no denying that surplus wealth is very useful. But a limit there should be, and perhaps the best way of stating it would be to say that the total wealth should not be so great as to make it profitable for a stronger power to go to war attracted by its great size, but only such as might be wanted in a war not motivated by the attraction of huge wealth. For example when Autophradates was about to lay siege to Atarneus, its ruler Eubulus asked him to consider how long it would take him to complete the capture of the city, and then to count the cost of a war of that duration. 'For', he added, 'I am willing now to abandon Atarneus in return for a sum of money very much less than that.' These words of Eubulus caused Autophradates to think again and to abandon the siege.

So, while there is certainly some value in equality of wealth as a safeguard against civil strife, we must not exaggerate its efficacy, which is not really very great. In the first place discontent will arise among the upper classes, who will think they deserve something better than equality. (There are many instances of upper-class revolutionary conspiracy.) Secondly it is a defect of human nature never to be satisfied. At first they are content with a dole of a mere two obols; then, when that is well-established, they go on asking for more and their demands become unlimited. For there is no limit to wants and most people spend their lives trying to satisfy their wants. A better means, therefore, than equalizing property for securing a stable society would be to ensure that those who are by nature a superior class should not wish to get more than their share, and that the inferior should not be able to do so; and that means that they should be weaker but not downtrodden.

There are errors also in what Phaleas has said about equality of wealth in itself. For it is only possession of land that he makes equal, forgetting that wealth may consist also of slaves, cattle, coined money, and all that is generally called moveable property. Equality, or at least some moderate limit, should be aimed at in all these forms of property. Otherwise things must just be allowed to take their course. To judge from his own legislative proposals Phaleas appears to be framing a city with only a small number of citizens, at least if all the skilled workers are to be public slaves and not members of the citizen-body. But if there are to be slaves owned by the state, these should consist not of all the skilled workers but only of those employed in the public service. That is what takes place at Epidamnus, and at one time Diophantus tried to introduce it at Athens. These remarks on the Republic of Phaleas will put the reader in a position to judge what is good and what is bad in it.

The first town-planner.

8

Hippodamus, son of Euryphon, came from Miletus. Apart from those actually engaged in making a constitution Hippodamus was the first to discourse about the Best State. It was he who invented the division of cities into quarters and he laid out the street-plan of the Piraeus. His ambition always to be different from other people caused him to live a life that was peculiar in a variety of ways, and many thought that he was carrying his oddities too far with his long hair and expensive ornaments, wearing at the same time clothing that was cheap but warm, the same being worn in summer and winter alike. He also liked to be considered expert in natural science. Hippodamus planned a city with a population of ten thousand, divided into three parts, one of skilled workers, one of agriculturalists, and a third to bear arms and secure defence. The territory also was to be divided into three parts, a sacred, a public, and a private; the worship of the gods would be maintained out of the produce of the sacred land, the defenders out of the common land, the agriculturalists out of the private. He held the view that there were only three kinds of laws, each corresponding to a type of lawsuit – damage to the person, damage to property, manslaughter. He also wanted to establish a single and final court of appeal, to which were to be referred all cases that appeared *prima facie* to have been badly judged; this court was to consist of selected elder persons. Verdicts in law-courts he thought ought to be given not by simply voting for or against, but each member of the court was to have a tablet, on which he was to state in writing the penalty or damages, if it was a simple verdict of condemnation, and leave blank if a plain acquittal; and if it was neither one nor the other, he was to state this opinion on the tablet. He thought the present system bad in this respect that, by compelling judges to give a verdict either one way or the other, it might make them false to the oath which required them to vote according to their honest conviction. His next set of enactments was to the effect first, that all who made discoveries advantageous to their country should receive honours and rewards, and second, that the children of those who fell in war should be maintained at the expense of the state. (He seems to have been under the impression that this latter practice was something entirely new; but it certainly obtains today at Athens and elsewhere.) Then, too, officials of government were all to be elected by the people, the electors consisting of all three sections just mentioned. The duties of these elected officials would include public business and the interests of non-nationals and of orphans.

In the criticisms which follow now it is noteworthy that Aristotle takes it for granted that possession of arms is a prerequisite for full citizenship and full eligibility for office.

Such are the main features, and those most deserving of comment, of the constitution of Hippodamus. My first point of criticism is the division of the whole body of citizens into three. For they all, skilled workers, agriculturalists, and those who carry arms, share in full citizenship; the farmers have no arms, the workers have neither land nor arms; this makes them virtually the servants of those who do possess arms. In these circumstances the equal sharing of offices and honours becomes an impossibility. For it is an absolute essential that generals, and those whose duty it is to protect the citizens, and one might say all those who hold the highest offices, should be drawn from the ranks of those who possess arms. On the other hand, if they do not all share in full citizenship, how can they be expected to be content with the constitution? But, as I say, those who possess arms must be superior in power to both the other sections, and that is not easy unless they are numerous. And if they are numerous, what need is there for the rest to have full citizenship and be eligible to hold offices of government? Again, if farmers have to feed only themselves and their families, what use are they to the state? Skilled workers of course are essential; every state needs them and they can support themselves on the earnings of their craft as in other countries. But the farmers – if they were expected to provide maintenance for those possessing arms, only then would it have been reasonable for them to share in the state. But in Hippodamus's state that is not so; the land they work is their own and they work it for their own benefit. And the common or public land which is supposed to support the warrior class – who is going to work it? If the warriors are to do it themselves, there will be no difference, as Hippodamus intended there should be, between fighting men and agriculturalists. And if those who work the land of the fighting men are to be different from the farmers working for their own benefit, that means that there will be a fourth section of the community, one with no share in anything but quite extraneous to the whole. Or again, if one makes the same people cultivate the private and the common land, there will not be enough produce to enable each man to maintain two households, his own and a warrior's. And what then is the point of the land-division? Why should they not both get their own sustenance and provide for warriors directly out of the land in general, each working a single plot instead of a private one here and a public one there? There is much confusion here.

Not any better are his proposals relating to decisions given in courts of law. He thinks that even where the verdict demanded is a simple yes or no, the various judges should draw distinctions and make qualifications. But this is to turn dicast into arbitrator. Certainly that is what is done in arbitrations, and if there are several arbitrators, they discuss their decision among themselves. This is not possible in a court of law, and not desirable either; for most legislators make a point of preventing judges from having any opportunity to confer with each other. Again, surely confusion will arise from his suggestion that each judge should state the amount of damages to be paid; because it may be the opinion of a judge that damages ought to be awarded, but a lesser amount than the plaintiff demands. Suppose he demands twenty minae and one judge says ten (or the other way round), and another says five, another four (obviously this is the kind of splitting the difference that will go on): some will award the full amount claimed, others not a farthing. How then are the votes to be counted? Again, nobody is asking a judge to be false to his oath by requiring him to give a simple verdict for or against, provided that the plea is framed in simple terms, and he gives his decision honestly. For he who rejects the plaintiff's demands does not say that nothing at all is due to him, but just that the sum due is not twenty minae. The only person who would be false to his oath would be one who accepted the plaintiff's

demand for twenty minae while believing this sum not to
be due to him.

*Aristotle next objects to the proposal of Hippodamus for awards
for new ideas. Aristotle is not thinking of technological discoveries,
but if he had known of any, he would probably have been suspicious
of them; certainly the nineteenth and twentieth centuries have shown
how new inventions very soon alter the whole* politeia. *He is
thinking rather of new social and political ideas; and these in a
settled régime of any type are always suspect. To mention such a
topic is to raise one of the most important and difficult questions of
politics. So long as constitutionalism and adherence to tradition act as
safeguards against arbitrary and tyrannical government, so long
must they be respected; and the political memory of the Greeks helped
to make this conservative attitude very general. Aristotle admits
that there have been improvements in the past and that there may
be need for improvement at any time; but he counsels extreme caution
and reluctance.*

And now for his suggestion that there should be a reward
for those who discover something advantageous to the
state: this sort of law looks well and sounds well but it is
very risky. It would lead to backstairs intrigue and in some
cases also to upsetting the constitutional way of life. This
being so, we cannot separate it from another and wider
question: Is it a good thing or a bad thing for cities to
alter their traditional and ancestral laws and customs whenever some better way is found? If the answer to this question
is that all such alteration is bad, then one can hardly give
ready assent to Hippodamus's proposals. It is possible for
people to bring in proposals for dissolving society and its laws
on the ground that such proposals are for the public good.

Now that we have touched upon this matter it might be
as well to say a little more about it, especially as there is a
case to be made out also in favour of change. Certainly if we
look at the other sciences, we can say definitely that changes
have been beneficial – the abandonment by medicine of

certain old-fashioned methods, improvements in physical training and generally in the skill and methods of every professional activity. Now since we regard politics as one of these, we expect to find some improvement there too. And so indeed we do find some, if we look at the facts and observe how uncivilized, how rough-and-ready, were the old laws and customs. Greeks used to go about carrying arms; they used to buy their brides from each other; and traces survive of other practices once doubtless habitual, which merely make us smile today; such as the law relating to homicide at Cyme, by which, if the prosecutor can produce a sufficient number of witnesses, members of his own family, then the defendant is guilty of murder. Generally of course it is the good, and not simply the traditional, that is aimed at. It would be foolish to adhere to the notions of our first ancestors, born of earth or survivors of some great catastrophe; we may reasonably suppose that they were on a level with ordinary, not very intelligent, people today, and lack of intelligence was said to be one of the marks of the Earth-born. We might go further and say that even those customs and laws which have been written down are best regarded as not unchangeable. On the analogy of other sciences we would certainly have to say that to set down in writing the whole organization of the state down to the last detail would be quite impossible; the general principle must be stated in writing, the action taken depends upon the particular case. From these considerations it is clear that there are occasions that call for change and that there are laws which need to be changed. But looking at it in another way we must say that there will be need of the very greatest caution. In a particular case we may have to weigh a very small improvement against the danger of getting accustomed to easy changes in the law; in such a case we must tolerate a few errors on the part of law-makers and rulers. A citizen will receive less benefit from a change in the law than damage from becoming accustomed to disobey authority. And the analogy with the professions is false; there is a difference between altering a professional method and altering a law. There is every inducement to adopt an improved method, but the law in itself has no power to secure obedience save the power of custom, and that takes a long time to become effective. Hence easy change from established laws to new laws means weakening the power of the law. Again, if changes in laws are to be permitted, it will have to be decided whether they may all be changed or only some, and whether this applies to every type of constitution. And who is to propose changes? Anybody or only certain persons? That will make a considerable difference. We will now give over this discussion; it can be resumed on other occasions.

Having finished examining the proposals of the theorists, Plato, Phaleas, Hippodamus, Aristotle now turns to constitutions that are or have been actually in operation, Lacedaemonian, Cretan, Carthaginian, choosing these, he tells us at the end, because they are rightly admired. He has much fault to find with Spartan ways but in the fourth book he notes that in its balance between different principles the Lacedaemonian constitution resembles his own brand of 'polity'.

About the standards of value which Aristotle now applies to constitutions two points should be noted, because they are characteristic of his whole approach: first, the very best or ideal constitution may well differ from the type best suited to a particular place or time; and second, it is taken for granted that a citizen, if he is to develop the qualities worthy of a citizen, must not do work that is felt to be degrading. But it is recognized that if the citizens are not going to do their own dirty work, there must be a subordinate class to do it for them; and this class is bound to be a source of trouble. It is surprising that Aristotle has not more to say about this problem; he can think of no answer except repressive legislation.

9

About the constitution of the Lacedaemonians, and about that of the Cretans, and generally about others too, there are two questions to be asked: first, are its arrangements good or bad, judged by the standard of the absolute best; second, does it contain anything that is not in keeping with the principles and character of the constitution which they have set out to achieve. Now it is agreed that a first necessity for any properly run city is that its citizens should be free of all menial tasks, but how that condition is to be secured is not so easy to say.

For example in Thessaly the serfs often attacked the Thessalians, just as helots attack the Spartans, always on the look-out for any mischance that may befall their masters. But nothing of the kind has so far occurred among the Cretans. The reason for this is perhaps that the neighbouring cities, though they might well be at war with each other, never joined up with the rebels; it was not in their interest to do so, since they too had a subservient class living among them. Sparta's neighbours on the other hand, Argives, Messenians, Arcadians, were all hostile to her. Similarly there were from the start risings against the Thessalians, because they were still constantly at war with their neighbours, Achaeans, Perrhaebians, and Magnesians. And even if there is no other source of trouble, there is always the need to be on the alert about how best to live with a subject population; if they are allowed too much licence, they become full of themselves and begin to claim equal rights with their masters; if they are badly treated, they become resentful and rebellious. It is clear therefore that those who find themselves in such relations with their helotry have not yet found a solution to their problem.

Again, the licence accorded to Spartan women is detrimental both to the attainment of the aims of the constitution and to the happiness of the city. For just as man and wife are each part of a household, so we should regard a city also as divided into two parts approximately equal numerically, one of men, one of women. So, in all constitutions in which the position of women is ill-regulated, one half of the city must be regarded as not properly legislated for. And that is what has happened at Sparta.

For there the lawgiver, whose intention it was that the whole state should be firm in character, has certainly taken some pains as far as the men are concerned, but he has failed and been negligent over the women. For at Sparta women live without restraint, enjoying every licence and indulging in every luxury. One inevitable result of such a way of life is that great importance is attached to being rich, particularly in communities where the men are dominated by the women; and this is a common state of affairs in a military and warlike community, though not among the Kelts and other peoples among whom male homosexuality is openly approved. Indeed it seems as if there was a rational basis for the myth of a union between Ares and Aphrodite; certainly all soldiers have a strong urge towards sexuality, whether directed towards the male or the female. Hence the condition of affairs at Sparta, where in the days of their supremacy a great deal was managed by women. And what is the difference between women ruling and rulers ruled by women? The result is the same. Boldness is not a quality useful in the affairs of daily life, but only, if at all, in war. Yet even here the influence of Spartan women has been harmful. This was demonstrated when Laconia was invaded by the Thebans; instead of playing a useful part, like women in other states, they caused more confusion than the enemy. Now it is not surprising that from the earliest times lack of control of women was a feature of Laconian society; there were long periods when the Spartan men were obliged to be absent from their own land on military service fighting against Argives, or again against Arcadians or Messenians. When they returned to a life of ease, predisposed to obedience by military life, which offers scope for many kinds of virtue, they readily submitted themselves to the lawgiver Lycurgus. But not so the women. It is said that Lycurgus endeavoured to bring them under his regulations, but that when they resisted, he gave up the attempt. These then are the causes of what took place, clearly therefore also the causes of the defect which we have been discussing. But our present inquiry is about what is right or wrong, not an attempt to apportion praise or blame. And, as has been said earlier, the position of women at Sparta is wrong; it offends against the principles of the constitution itself and it contributes largely to the existing greed for money.

Next one might go on to attack the Spartan inequality of property-ownership. For we find that some Spartans have far too much property, others very little indeed; the land has come into the possession of a small number. This too, like the position of women, is due to errors in framing the constitution. For their lawgiver, while he quite rightly did not approve of buying and selling existing estates, left it open to anyone to transfer land to other ownership by gift or bequest; and this of course leads to the same result. Moreover, something like two-fifths of all the land is possessed by women; there are two reasons for this, heiresses are numerous and dowries are large. It would have been better to have regulated dowries by law, prohibiting them altogether or making them very small or at any rate moderate in size. And as for the heiresses, under the constitution as it is they may be given in marriage to any person whatever. And if a man dies without leaving directions in the matter, the person named as administrator of his estate gives her to whom he likes.

This decline in the number of male property owners had the effect of reducing the number of full citizens to below a thousand, although the land was sufficient to support 1,500 cavalry and 50,000 heavy infantry. And history has shown that these arrangements were bad; the impact of one single battle [Leuctra, 371] was too much for Sparta; she succumbed owing to the shortage of manpower. It is said that in the time of their early kings the Spartans shared their citizenship with others, so that in spite of long continuing wars there was not then any shortage of men. It is also said that at one time the Spartiatae numbered ten thousand. However, whether these statements are true or false, it is far better to keep up the numbers of male citizens in a state by a levelling of the amount of property. But at Sparta there is also a law encouraging the begetting of children; and this operates against any such method of keeping a proper balance in the ownership of property. For the law-giver, intending that the Spartiatae should be as numerous as possible, encourages the citizens to beget many children. For example there is a law by which the father of three sons is exempt from military service and the father of four from service of any kind. But it is obvious that if many sons are born and the land distributed accordingly, many must inevitably become poorer.

Another defect in the Lacedaemonian constitution is seen in connexion with the office of ephor. The ephorate in-dependently controls much important business. Its five members are chosen from among all the people, with the result that very often men who are not at all well-off find themselves holding this office, and their lack of means makes them open to bribery.* And just because the power of the ephors is excessive and dictatorial, even the Spartan kings have been forced to curry favour with them. And this has caused further damage to the constitution; what was supposed to be an aristocracy has become more like a democracy. In itself the ephorate is not a bad thing; it certainly keeps the constitution together; the people like it because it gives them a share in an office of power. So whether this is due to the lawgiver Lycurgus or to good fortune, it suits the circumstances very well.† But while it was necessary to elect ephors from among all the citizens the present method of election strikes me as childish. The

* There have been many examples of this in the past; and in our own day we have the affair of Andros, in which certain ephors have been so corrupted by gifts of money that it is no thanks to them if their city is not utterly ruined.

† The point is that if a constitution is to have a good prospect of maintaining itself, it must be such that all sections of the community accept it and want it to go on. At Sparta the kings have this feeling about the constitution because it confers dignity and profit on themselves; the best people have it because membership of the council of elders, the gerousia, is something to which they are entitled as a reward for being 'best', the people because of the universal basis of the ephorate.

ephors have powers of jurisdiction also and decide cases of importance; but considering that anybody at all may hold the office, it would be better that they should not have power to give verdicts on their own, but only to decide in accordance with stated rules and regulations. Nor does the way in which ephors live conform to the aims of the constitution. They live a life of ease, while the rest have a very high standard of strictness in living, so high indeed that they really cannot live up to it but secretly get round the law and enjoy the more sensual pleasures.

Reference is made in what follows to the practice of requiring outgoing officials and committees to render an account of themselves and their conduct. It is interesting also to note Aristotle's disapproval of those who have political ambitions.

There are objections also to the authority exercised by the board of elders, the 'gerousia'. One might suppose that, so long as it consists of good men well-trained in all manly virtues, this institution is a good thing for the state. But they remain members for life; and the mind grows old no less than the body; so it is very questionable whether they ought to continue to have power to decide important cases. And when we find that their upbringing has been of such a kind that even the lawgiver has no confidence in their being good men, the situation becomes dangerous. It has been noticed that those who serve on this board allow the conduct of public business to be corrupted by bribery and favouritism. For this reason it would be better that their proceedings should not, as they are at present, be exempt from any scrutiny. It may be thought that the committee of ephors acts as a check on all other authorities; but that is to put far too much power into the hands of the ephorate and is not in the least what we mean by requiring an authority to give an account of its proceedings. And as for elections to the gerousia, the way in which the choice of candidate is made is silly; and it is all wrong that a person deemed worthy to become a member should himself solicit the honour of membership. Whether he likes it or not, the man fit to hold office should be made to accept it. But at Sparta the lawgiver, in a way that is typical of his whole approach to the making of a constitution, begins by making the citizens ambitious and then uses their ambition as a means of getting people elected to the gerousia; for no one not ambitious would ask to be elected. Yet the truth is that mens' ambition and their desire to get on and make money are among the most potent causes of calculated acts of injustice.

From very early times down to 219 B.C. there were always two hereditary kings at Sparta, reigning simultaneously. Men taking their meals not at home but in a common mess is a necessary feature of army life, which at Sparta was made obligatory at all times.

Now as to the Spartan kingship, we are not now saying whether cities are better with or without kings, but we are saying that they would do better not to have kings after the present Spartan fashion. We say that in every case a king should be chosen in the light of his personal life. It is clear that even the Spartan lawgiver himself does not believe it possible to produce good men of first quality. He certainly has no confidence in kings reaching that standard. This explains why they used to send their personal enemies to accompany them on important missions, and why they regarded disagreement between the two kings as a healthy sign. Unsatisfactory also are the arrangements made by him who first established the system of common meals, called by the Lacedaemonians 'phiditia'. The mess ought to be run at public expense, as in Crete. At Sparta every individual has to contribute, and as some of them are quite poor and unable to meet this heavy expenditure, the result is the opposite of what the legislator intended. For messing in common is intended to be a democratic practice, but under the rules such as those obtaining at Sparta it is anything but democratic. For it is not easy for those who cannot afford it to join in, yet this is their traditional way of determining citizenship – to exclude anyone who is unable to pay this particular due.

Some have objected also to the law about naval commanders. The objections are well founded, for the arrangement is the cause of much serious dissension. This is because over and above the kings, who are perpetual commanders of the forces, a naval command is set up which is almost another kingship. Another way in which the Spartan system fails to live up to the principles of its founder is one which Plato has criticized in his *Laws*: the whole structure of their society is directed to securing one part only of virtue, military prowess, as being valuable in the acquisition of power. Hence the Spartans prospered while at war but began to decline once they reached a position of supremacy; they did not understand what being at peace meant and never attached any importance to any other kind of training than training for war. Another, and equally serious, error is that, while they rightly hold that all that men strive for is to be won more by virtue than by vice, they wrongly suppose that the objects striven for are greater than the virtue. Public finance is another thing that is badly managed by the Spartans. They are obliged to undertake large wars, but there is never any money in the treasury. Also they are very bad at paying taxes; as most of the land is the property of the Spartiatae themselves, they do not inquire too closely into each other's contributions to the treasury. And so a state of affairs has come about which is just the opposite of the happy conditions envisaged by Lycurgus; he has produced a city which has no money but is full of citizens eager to make money for themselves.

These are the main defects of the constitution of the Lacedaemonians; so let that suffice for the topic.

Property-owning, inheritance, heiresses, power, and influence of women – Aristotle has found fault with Sparta on these counts, but ignores them in dealing with Crete, although the conditions were from Aristotle's point of view even worse there. In any case he has in

mind the contrast with Athens, where the law had long ago
strengthened the hand of the male property owner. Crete had many
cities but they appear to have had a common pattern of constitution.

10

The type of constitution to be found in Crete is very similar
to the Lacedaemonian; in some particulars it is certainly
no worse but in general it is less finished. It is said, and
appears to be true, that to a very great extent the Cretan
constitution was taken as a model by the Lacedaemonian.
(Generally later forms of constitution are more fully
developed than earlier.) Tradition tells that Lycurgus after
laying down his guardianship of King Charillus went
abroad and on that occasion spent most of his time going
about in Crete. He chose Crete because the two peoples
were akin, the Lyctians being colonists from Laconia; and
when the colonists came, they found the inhabitants at that
time living under a constitution which they then adopted
and still retain. And to this day the dwellers in the countryside round about the cities use these laws unchanged,
believing Minos himself to have laid them down in the first
place. The island of Crete appears to be both very well
placed and naturally suited to dominate the Hellenic world.
It lies right across our sea, on whose coasts all around dwell
mostly Greeks. At one end the Peloponnese is not far away,
and at the Asiatic end lie Triopium and Rhodes. This
enabled Minos to build up a maritime empire; he made
some of the islands subject to himself, to others he sent
settlers; in the end he even attacked Sicily, where he met his
death near Kamikos.

Here are some of the ways in which the Cretan constitution resembles the Laconian. To the Lacedaemonian helots
correspond the Cretan serfs. Both countries have a system of
common meals, for which in ancient times the Spartans
used not their present name phiditia, but the same name
as the Cretans – 'andria'. This is an indication of its Cretan
origin. Similarly as regards the political set-up; the Cretans

have officials called 'kosmoi', whose powers are the same as those of the Spartan ephors; but there are ten of them, while the ephors number five. The elders, who in Crete make a body known as the Council, are similar in function and number in both countries. The Cretans used to have the office of king, but they did away with it and the kosmoi exercise leadership in war. All are members of the citizen-assembly but this body has no power to do anything except give its assent to measures decided upon by the elders and the kosmoi. The arrangements for the common meals are better among the Cretans than in Laconia. At Sparta each man contributes a specified *per capita* amount; failure to pay involves loss of citizenship, as has been said earlier. In Crete the basis is more communal: out of the entire revenue, both agricultural produce, whether stock or crop, yielded by public land, and the taxes paid by the serfs, one sum is set aside for the gods and for public services generally and another sum for the common meals. In this way all, men, women, and children alike, are maintained at the public expense. The Cretan lawgiver regarded abstemiousness as beneficial and devoted much thought to securing economy in the common meals, as also to keeping down the birth-rate by keeping men and women apart and by instituting sexual relations between males; whether he acted wisely or not will be discussed on another occasion. It is clear then that the arrangements for communal meals are better among the Cretans than among the Laconians.

On the other hand their kosmoi operate in a more detri-mental manner than the ephors; the chief defect of the ephorate, its indiscriminate composition, is there too, but its chief merit, its contribution to the stability of the constitution, is absent. For at Sparta the people, because the ephors are chosen from among all, have a share in the most powerful office and are therefore disposed to keep the constitution as it is. But in Crete they choose the kosmoi not from all but from certain families only.* The fact that the

* They also select members of the Council of Elders from among those who have held the office of kosmos. And about that body one might

people are content not to have any share in the office of
kosmos must not be taken as evidence of a sound constitution. For there is no profit to be made out of the
office of kosmos, as there is out of the ephorate, and, Crete
being an island, they are farther away from the danger of
corruption by foreign gold.

There appears to be no constitutional way of removing unsatis-
factory officials unless they choose to resign of their own accord.

The methods employed to cure the defects of this institution are outlandish, arbitrary, and unconstitutional. It
often happens that kosmoi are turned out of office by a
conspiracy, which may be engineered partly by some of
their own number or wholly by persons outside. It is actually
possible for kosmoi to resign office during their tenure; but
matters such as tenure of office are better regulated by law
and not left to the personal decision of individuals; a rule
is not liable to fluctuate. But worst of all is the condition
where there are no kosmoi at all; and this often occurs,
being brought about by the action of powerful people who
try to escape the consequences of the law. All this makes it
pretty clear that in Crete, while there is a certain amount of
constitutional arrangement, there is really no constitution
properly so called, but only a *dynasteia*, a system based on
violence. The powerful men have a habit of taking bands
of their friends and of the people, using these in quarrels
and fights with each other, and so causing suspension of all
government. And that surely is nothing less than the cessation of the state and the break-up of what we have called
the 'political association'. It is indeed a dangerous state of
affairs when those who wish to attack the state are also
those who have the power. However, as we have already

---

make the same comments as about the Spartan elders: their freedom
from outside scrutiny and their life-tenure are privileges in excess of the
merits of the institution, and their power to make decisions on their own,
and not simply in accordance with rules, is dangerous.

remarked, Crete is preserved by its geographical situation; its distance has kept foreigners away as effectively as the expulsion of foreigners practised at Sparta. For this reason also the Cretan serfs remain settled, while the Lacedaemonian helots are often in rebellion. And the Cretans do not participate in any dominion overseas. The weakness of their constitutional position is thus kept concealed. But when, as happened recently, a foreign war reached the island, this weakness became apparent. So much for the Cretan constitution.

Little detail is given, and that very obscurely, about the constitution of Carthage, the only non-Greek state here examined. Aristotle compares it with the Spartan and therefore thinks he can describe it using Greek terms – kings, elders, generals. The Romans used the native word for the supreme Carthaginian magistrates, latinizing it as sufetes. *Aristotle is well aware that 'the characteristic and vital force in Carthaginian politics was before all things money' (W. E. Heitland) and this constitutes for him a serious deviation from the standards of excellence and ability demanded by the aristocratic principle. What counted in favour of the Carthaginian way of government was that it was generally acceptable and continued to work.*

11

The Carthaginians also have been regarded as very successful in managing their political affairs, more so than most. In some particulars they closely resemble the Lacedaemonians; indeed these three constitutions, Cretan, Laconian, and Carthaginian, present a number of resemblances to each other and many differences from the rest. Many of the Carthaginian institutions are good; it is an indication that a constitution is well constructed when the people are content to remain in their allotted status, when there is no serious internal strife, or virtually none, and no dictator makes himself master.

The common messes of the clubs are like the Spartan

phiditia; their board of 104 members corresponds to the ephorate, but it is better; its members are chosen as belonging to the best people and not from all indiscriminately as are the ephors. Their kings and elders are the counterpart of the Spartan kings and gerousia; they are chosen on a basis that is neither too wide nor too narrow; the kings are not drawn from one family alone, nor yet from any and every family. Choice depends more on eminence than on age. This is important; persons of low degree appointed to have control of weighty affairs can do a lot of damage, as we have seen happen in the Lacedaemonian state. The Carthaginian state could indeed be criticized on formal grounds for its departures from a proper norm, but most of the objections brought on that score are applicable to all the three states here mentioned. In relation to a norm of aristocracy, or what I call 'polity', some features are objectionable because they deviate into oligarchy, others because they deviate into democracy. An example of the latter is the fact that at Carthage, when the kings and the elders agree that certain matters are to be referred to the people, that is done; but it is also done when they do not agree! Moreover when a matter agreed upon by kings and elders is referred to them, they have the right not merely to listen to the decisions of the higher bodies but to give independent judgement; and it is open to all and sundry to oppose and speak against the proposals that have been laid before them. This right does not exist in the other two constitutions. Then there are oligarchical features: the committees of five, the Pentarchies, which have control over many important matters, not only fill up vacancies on their own by co-option but appoint members of the Hundred, the highest constitutional authority. Moreover they enjoy a longer tenure of office than the rest; they begin to exercise authority before they become members of the committee and continue to do so after they have ceased to be members. On the other hand we must allow as aristocratic the fact that they receive no pay and are not chosen by lot, and one or two other features of that kind; for example all law-suits are decided by these committees, not, as at Sparta, some by one set of persons, others by another.

The most conspicuous divergence of the Carthaginian constitution from the aristocratic towards the oligarchical is one which is quite in accord with the mentality of the Carthaginians in general: they believe that rulers should be chosen not merely from the best people but also from the wealthiest. It is impossible, they argue, for a man without ample means either to be a good ruler or to have the leisure to be one. Now if it is accepted that election according to wealth is oligarchic, according to merit aristocratic, this then must be a third principle and one which is constitutionally imposed on the Carthaginians. For they have both these in mind, merit and wealth, when they elect, particularly when they elect the highest officers, kings and generals. But this deviation from aristocracy cannot be regarded as anything but an error on the part of the Carthaginian lawgiver. For it is most essential that from the very start provision shall be made for the best people to have leisure and not in any way to depart from standards of propriety either in behaviour or in their occupations, not only while in office but also as private citizens. But while we must look to wealth for the purpose of securing leisure for the discharge of duties of office, it is a very bad thing that the highest offices themselves should be for sale, as are the offices of king and general at Carthage. Where this practice is legal and customary, wealth becomes of more account than merit and causes the whole nation to become bent on making money. Whatever is most valued by the highest authority, that inevitably becomes the aim of the rest, whose opinion simply follows suit. And wherever merit is not the most highly prized thing, there a firmly aristocratic constitution is an impossibility. People who lay out large sums of money in order to secure office look, not unreasonably, for some return. Even the poor but honest man will want his profit, so it could hardly be expected that the not so honest, who has already put his hand in his pocket, should not want his profit too. Therefore it should be those who are best able to do the work of the office that should be appointed to that office. And even if the lawgiver has abandoned the idea of making all the honest men wealthy, at any rate he ought to secure leisure for those in office.

Another feature, which would strike most people as objectionable, though the Carthaginians think highly of it, is plurality of office, the same man holding more than one. Surely work is best done when one task is performed by one man. The legislator ought to ensure this, and not require one and the same man to be a professional musician and a shoemaker. So too in the work of government, where the city is not too small to allow of it, it is more statesmanlike, as well as more democratic, that a variety of people should share in the offices. For, as we have said, in this way the work is more widely distributed and each individual task is performed more efficiently and more expeditiously. This can be illustrated from the sphere of the army and the navy; for in both these one might say that commanding and being commanded run right through all ranks.

Of course this would be impossible at Carthage so long as the richest men hold all the offices. How then do they manage to carry on? The answer is that it can be done if the general standard of living is maintained at a high level.

But when the constitution is an oligarchy they escape the consequences simply by being wealthy. From time to time they remove a section of the people to outlying cities. That is the way in which they cure the trouble and make their society stable and continuing. But all that is a matter of luck not of policy; and it ought to be the policy of a legislator to avoid all discontent. As it is, if any serious outbreak were to occur and the mass of the subject population rebel, the laws provide no means of restoring peace.

So much for my account of the Lacedaemonian, Cretan, and Carthaginian constitutions, all of which have a just claim to our respect.

*Some miscellaneous notes on lawgivers, especially the Athenian
Solon, and two widely different estimates of the value of his work.*

12

Those who have voiced opinions on political constitutions
fall into two classes. We have already given some account,
so far as it is relevant to our purpose, of the first class, that is
those who took no part in public life but remained private
citizens all their lives. The others, after personal experience
of politics, have become lawgivers either in their own or in
foreign cities. Some of these merely drafted laws, but others
like Lycurgus and Solon made constitutions, establishing
both the laws and the social structure. Of Lycurgus and the
Spartan constitution I have already spoken; about the
merits of Solon's constitution there is divergence of opinion.
Those who say that he was a good lawgiver put forth the
following reasons: (1) he broke up the absolute and un-
diluted oligarchy; (2) he put an end to the enslavement of
the people; and (3) he set up the traditional Athenian
democracy by mixing well the constitution. They explain
that the mixture contains an oligarchical element – the
Council of the Areopagus, an aristocratic element – the
selection of officials, and a democratic – the judicial system.
As a matter of fact it would seem that Solon found the first
two of these already in existence, the council and the
selection of officials, and merely refrained from abolishing
them. On the other hand by setting up a judicial system,
the personnel of which was drawn from the entire body of
citizens, he did establish democracy at Athens. It is just
here that those who hold the other view find Solon at fault;
they say that by giving power over all matters to the jury-
courts, appointed by lot, he ruined the other half of his
work. As soon as these courts became powerful, they began
to do everything with a view to pleasing the people, just
as if they were humouring a tyrant, and in this way brought
into being the democracy as we now have it. Ephialtes and
Pericles reduced the power of the Council of the Areopagus,

and Pericles introduced payment for service in the jury-courts; in this way each successive leader of the people made the constitution more and more democratic. But it seems to me that all this took place not according to Solon's intention but as a result of circumstances. For instance the Athenian sea-power in the Persian wars was due to the whole Athenian demos and this gave them a great opinion of themselves; they chose inferior types for their leaders, the better sort opposing. Certainly Solon himself seems to have given only a minimum of power to the people – the right to elect officials and to require an account of them, without which the people would be no better than slaves or foes. Under his constitution officials were to be elected from among the notables and men of substance, that is to say he excluded only the lowest property-class.*

Other lawgivers were Zaleucus, who made laws for the Epizephyrian Locrians and Charondas of Catana, who made laws both for his own citizens and for other cities of Italy and Sicily that were of Chalcidic origin.† Then there was Philolaus the Corinthian who made laws for the Thebans. He was of the Bacchiad family. He became the lover of Diocles who was a victor in the Olympic Games. This Diocles in disgust at the amorous passion of his mother Alkyone left Corinth for Thebes. Here he was joined by Philolaus and the two friends ended their days there. Visitors are still shown their two tombs which are visible one from the other; but one can be seen from Corinthian territory, the other not. The story is that they planned the sites of the two tombs themselves, Diocles so that the land of Corinth with its bitter memories of incestuous passion should be invisible from his grave, Philolaus that it might be visible from his. That is how they came to be living at

---

* Called Thetes. The three upper classes were Pentacosiomedimni, Zeugitae, and Knights, and from these officials were chosen.

† Some wish to include Onomacritus as the first skilled expert in law-making, saying that he was a Locrian, that he trained in Crete as a seer and there practised this art, that Thales the Cretan was his friend, that Lycurgus and Zaleucus heard Thales lecture and Charondas heard Zaleucus. But all that is to disregard chronology.

Thebes. Philolaus became their lawgiver; and among his enactments the most noteworthy are those relating to the begetting of children. These the Thebans called 'laws of adoption'. They constituted an arrangement peculiar to Philolaus which was designed to keep fixed the number of parcels of land. As for Charondas there is nothing particular to be said about his laws except those concerning false witness; he was the first to make perjury an indictable offence. In the careful detail of his legislature he is more precise even than modern legislators. The special features of Phaleas is his equalization of property; about Plato we note communal ownership of property, wives, and children, common messing for women as well as men; also his law about intoxication, that the sober preside at drinking parties, and again that soldiers in their training should learn to become ambidextrous in their use of weapons, instead of having one hand useful, the other useless. There were the laws of Draco, but these were additions to an existing constitution. There is nothing worthy of special mention in them except the severity of their punishments. Pittacus too was a maker of laws not of a constitution; a law peculiar to him states that if drunk men commit acts of violence they should pay a larger fine than sober men. This seemed to Pittacus to be a far more practical expedient than to regard a state of intoxication as 'an extenuating circumstance'. The inhabitants of the Chalcidian peninsula in Thrace had as lawgiver Andromas of Rhegium, whose laws related to manslaughter and heiresses, but I cannot think of anything particular to say about them.

Let this suffice for our survey of constitutions, actual and supposed.

BOOK III

*The third book contains much of Aristotle's best work on politics
and much that is of permanent interest. The major part of it is
devoted to constitutions – democratic, oligarchic, monarchic – a
topic which had long been the kernel of Greek political thought. It
opens with a difficult passage, some of which looks more like notes
for a lecture than continuous discourse. He has hardly mentioned
that he is about to discuss the constitution of a state, when he makes
a series of observations about the* polis *or state, the* polites *or
citizen, and the* politeia *or constitution. The connexion between
these observations is not clear, but the argument may have been
something like this: One ought, before discussing* politeia, *to define*
polis; *there is no unanimity about its definition, but, since a city is
made up of its citizens, we should rather begin by defining citizen;
there is just as much dispute about this definition, but it must be
attempted, as a preliminary to discussing constitution, which is a
kind of system of relationships governing the state and the citizen.*

*Aristotle accordingly discusses the definition of a citizen. It may
seem odd to us thus to make the citizen prior to the city, but we
should remember, first, that merely to say 'a citizen is a member
of a city' involves asking 'what constitutes membership of a city?',
which is just the question now to be discussed; and second, that
Aristotle's outlook is here, as so often, coloured by his biological
studies; he is inclined to think of citizen as a kind of species and to
look for the marks by which it may be recognized.*

*For the rest, the material of this book is greatly diversified; it
looks as if Aristotle had assembled and utilized parts of some earlier
work.*

I

In considering now *Constitution* in its various kinds and
forms, we must begin by looking at the state and seek a
definition of it. There is no unanimity about this; for
example, in regard to its functioning, some say that action is

taken by the state, others that the action is taken not by the state, but by the oligarchy or by the dictator or whatever it may be. Obviously the activities of statesman and legislator closely concern the state. The constitution is a way of organizing those living in a state. Like any other whole that is made up of parts the state must be analysed into those parts; and we must first consider the citizen, for a state is the sum total of its citizens. So we must ask Who is a citizen? and What makes it right to call him one? Here too there is no unanimity, no agreement as to what constitutes a citizen; it often happens that one who is a citizen in a democracy is not a citizen in an oligarchy.* One suggested definition is 'those who have access to courts of law, who may sue or be sued'. But this is too wide; this access is open to any person who has entered into a commercial contract, or at any rate partially open, for a resident foreigner may be obliged to appoint someone to act for him, so that his participation in the state is incomplete.†

I suggest that what effectively distinguishes the citizen from all others is his participation in Judgement and Authority, that is, holding office, legal, political, administrative. Some offices are distinguished in respect of time of tenure, some not being tenable by the same person twice under any circumstances, others only after an interval of time. Others, such as membership of a panel of judges or of a citizen-assembly, have no such limitation. It might be objected that such persons are not really 'ruling' and therefore not participating in authority. But they have the power and it would be ridiculous to deny their participation

* I think we may leave out of account those who merely acquire the title, those who are made citizens. Nor does mere residence confer citizenship; foreigners and slaves are not citizens but they can dwell in the country.

† Boys not yet old enough and old people who have retired from duty may be termed citizens in a sense, but only with the addition of 'not fully' or 'superannuated' or some such word clear in its context. What we are looking for is the citizen absolute, without any qualifying word. Questions about persons exiled or disfranchised do not really present any difficulty.

in authority. In any case it need not make any difference; it is just that there is no word covering that which is common to judge-juror on the one hand and member of legislative body on the other. For the sake of a definition I suggest that we say 'unspecified authority'. We therefore define citizens as those who participate in this. Such a definition seems to cover, as nearly as may be, those to whom the term citizen is in fact applied.

On the other hand we must remember that the state is one of those things in which the substrata may differ in kind and that one may be primary, another secondary, and so on, there being nothing, or scarcely anything, which is common to them all, which makes them what they are. Thus we see the various forms of constitution differing from each other in kind, some logically prior to others, since those that have gone wrong or diverged must be subsequent to those which are free from error.* The meaning of citizen, therefore, will vary according to the constitution in each case. For this reason our definition of citizen is best applied in a democracy; in the other constitutions it may be applicable but it need not necessarily be so. For example in some constitutions there is no body corresponding to the demos, no Assembly with definite membership but only an occasional rally. Again, justice may be administered not by citizens in turn but by a section. For example at Sparta contract cases are tried by the ephors, one or other of them, cases of manslaughter by the elders, other cases doubtless by other bodies. Similarly at Carthage all cases are tried by official bodies. But our own definition of a citizen need not be abandoned; it can be amended so as to apply also to non-democracies. We simply replace our 'unspecified authority' of juror or member by 'officially determined'. For it is to all or some of these that the task of decision, legal or political, is assigned in whole or in part. From these considerations it has become clear who is citizen: as soon as a man becomes entitled to participate in authority, deliberative or judicial, we deem him to be a citizen of that

* I will explain later what I mean by divergent.

state; and a number of such persons large enough to secure a self-centred existence we may, by and large, call a state.

2

For practical purposes a citizen is often defined as one of citizen birth on both his father's and his mother's side; others would go further and demand citizen descent for two, three, or even more generations. But, while definition by descent provides a quick and practical method, some object to going back three or four generations, asking how a great grandfather's citizenship can be determined.* The answer to such objectors is simple: if they participated in the manner prescribed in our definition, they were citizens. Of course the criterion of citizen-descent cannot be applied in the case of colonists or original founders. I think however that there is a more important question here, namely the determination of citizenship after a change in constitution: as for example after the expulsion of the tyrants from Athens, when Cleisthenes made many foreigners and slaves citizens by enrolling them in the tribes. The question here is not 'Are these persons citizens?', but whether they are rightly or wrongly so.†

3

This question cannot be separated from the larger question already mentioned – the nature of state-action and its continuing validity; for example when a change takes place

---

* Gorgias of Leontini, partly in earnest partly in jest, said that, as mortars are what mortar-makers make, so Larissaeans, citizens of Larissa, are those made by the 'people-workers', that being the title of the chief magistrates at Larissa, and 'Larissaean' being a type of kettle or pot.

† Some would go further and question whether anyone can truly be a citizen unless he is rightly so, on the ground that wrong and false mean the same thing. But when persons exercise their authority wrongly or unjustly, we continue to say that they rule, though unjustly; and as the citizen has been defined by his participation in that kind of authority, we cannot deny the propriety of using the term.

from oligarchy or tyranny to democracy. There are those who after such a change claim that they are no longer obliged to fulfil the terms of a contract; for it had been entered into, so they say, not by the state but by the tyrant. Similarly they would disown other obligations, if these have been incurred under one of those types of government which rest on force and disregard the common weal, such as oligarchy and tyranny. It follows that if there is a democracy of this type, based on force, we must say that its actions, like actions of oligarchy or tyranny, are actions of the democracy not of the state. And this seems to me to be part of yet another question – how are we to tell whether a state is still the same state or a different one? We might try to answer this question using territory and inhabitants as criteria; but this would not carry us very far, since it is quite possible to divide both territory and population into two, putting some people in one part and some into the other, calling them two states. That perhaps is not a very serious matter: it arises from our use of the word *polis* to mean both the state and its territory. Another factor is size: with a population living in the same place, what is the limit which determines the one-ness of the city or state? It cannot be the walls, for it would be possible to put one wall round the whole Peloponnese. Babylon is perhaps a similar case and any other that embraces a nation rather than a city.*

But the main question of continuity of the state still remains even when we assume that the same population continues to dwell in the same territory. On the one hand we may say that the identity of the state remains the same so long as there is continuity of race; for, as we call a river by the same name, although different water passes into and out of it all the time, so we ought to speak of the state as the same state, although one generation of people dies and

---

* It was said of Babylon that its capture was, two days later, still unknown in a part of the city. This question of size and the question of the numbers and racial variety of the population are important matters to which we shall return later (Book VII).

another is born. On the other hand it might be said that
while we speak of the population as being the same for the
reasons stated, we ought to say that the state is different.
For, since the state is an association of citizens in a constitution, when the constitution of the citizens changes and
becomes different in kind, the state also does. We may compare this with a chorus, which may at one time perform in a
tragedy and at another in a comedy and so be different in
kind, yet all the while be composed of the same persons.
And the same principle is applicable to other combinations;
the same musical notes may be used to produce either the
Dorian or the Phrygian mode. If this is right, it would seem
that the criterion of continuity or continued identity ought
to be *constitution* rather than race. This leaves it quite open
either to change or not to change the *name* of a *polis*, both
when the population is the same and when it is different.

*This decision to make the form of constitution the criterion of con-
tinuity has lent colour to the claim that a new form of government
is not bound by all the contractual obligations of an old. But
Aristotle does not want us to jump to this conclusion, for he adds:*

But whether, when a constitution is changed, the obligation to discharge debts continues or does not continue – that
is another question.

*Aristotle has discussed, but has not really finished discussing,
citizen and state in relation to constitution. He has had difficulty
in defining citizen in such a way as to be applicable to all forms of
constitutions. This same difficulty now reappears in another form;
in attempting to find out what a good citizen is he finds that here
too the answer depends largely on the* politeia *in connexion with
which the citizenship is held.*

*Here it may be well to remind ourselves of the inadequacy of
'constitution' as a translation of* politeia *and also that 'goodness'
or 'virtue' is often conceived in terms of function rather than*

106

character; 'what I can do' as well as 'what I am'. What follows now, about the good man, good citizen, and good ruler or official, will be clearer if these points are borne in mind.

4

Connected with the matters just discussed is the question whether we ought to regard the goodness of a good man and the goodness of a serious and dutiful citizen as the same goodness or not. In this connexion we must first try to form some conception of the goodness of a citizen. A citizen is one of a community, as a sailor is one of a crew; and although each member of the crew has his own function and a name to fit it – rower, helmsman, look-out, and the rest – and has therefore his goodness at that particular job, there is also a type of goodness which all the crew must have, a function in which they all play a part – the safe conduct of the voyage; for each member of the crew aims at securing that. Similarly the aim of all the citizens, however dissimilar they may be, is the safety of the community, that is, the constitution of which they are citizens. Therefore the goodness of the citizen must be goodness in relation to constitution; and as there are more kinds of constitution than one, there cannot be just one single perfect goodness of the good citizen. On the other hand we do say that the good *man* is good in virtue of one single perfect goodness. Clearly then it is possible to be a good and serious citizen without having that goodness which makes a good man good.

Look now at the matter from another angle and consider the goodness of the best constitution, that is to say, suppose it to be possible for a state to consist entirely of good and dutiful men; each must then do and do well his proper work, and doing it well depends on his goodness at it. But since it is impossible for all the citizens to be alike, there cannot even then be one goodness of citizen and good man alike. For the goodness of the good citizen must be within the reach of all; only so can the state itself be really good.

But it is impossible for all to have the goodness of the good man, unless it be an essential condition for a good city that all its citizens be good men.

Again, a city is made up of unlike parts. As an animate creature consists of body and mind, and mind consists of reasoning and desiring, and a *ménage* consists of husband and wife, and a business of owner and slaves, so also a city is made up of these and many other sorts besides, all different. The goodness of all the citizens cannot therefore be *one*, no more than in a troupe of dancers the goodness of the leader and that of the followers are one.

At this point one might wish to interpose the question ' Is there then no place for moral virtue in the qualifications for citizenship?' And indeed there follows something like an answer to that question. Moral virtue is certainly demanded of a ruler, and in many excellent constitutions the citizens take turns at ruling. Hence moral virtue will be expected of a citizen, at any rate in so far as he is a potential ruler. But that is not to say that normally the virtues of good man and good citizen are identical.

Now while this is all perfectly true in general, the question may be asked whether it is not possible in a particular case for the same goodness to belong both to the good citizen and the good man. We would answer that there is such a case, since we take it for granted that a good ruler is both good and wise, and wisdom is essential for one engaged in the work of the state.* But though we may say that the goodness is the same of good ruler and good man, yet, since he that is ruled is also citizen, we cannot say absolutely that the goodness of citizen and man are one, but only

* Some say that this is a matter of education and that from the very start there should be a different kind of education for rulers. They instance (1) the training of the sons of royalty in horsemanship and war and (2) a saying of Euripides which is supposed to refer to the education of a ruling class – 'No frills in education, please; only what the nation needs.'

that they may be in the case of a particular citizen. For certainly the goodness of ruler and citizen are not the same. And that doubtless is the reason why Jason of Pherae said that he went hungry whenever he ceased to be sole ruler, that being the only kind of job he was good at.

But it is surely a good thing to know how to obey as well as how to command, and I think we might say that the goodness of the citizen is just this – to know well how to rule and be ruled. If then we say that the goodness of the ruler is to be good at ruling and that of the citizen to be good at both ruling and obeying, the two virtues cannot be on the same level.

Next come two obscure lines ending cryptically with 'one can see from what follows'. And what follows concerns the master-and-servant type of rule in which there is never any 'ruling and being ruled by turns'.

There is such a thing as despotic rule. Work done under such conditions is necessary but servile; the master needs to know no more than how to use such labour. Anything else, I mean to be able to perform, and actually to perform, the work of servants, is simply servile. This applies to various kinds of work, including all kinds of manual labour skilled and unskilled; only in extreme democracies have the craftsmen attained to participation in office. The work then of those who are subject to a master is not work which either good man or statesman or good citizen needs to learn, except for what use he may require to make of it. Otherwise the distinction between master and servant just ceases to exist.

And that, of course, would be unthinkable. We return now to a kind of ruling which has closer relevance.

But there is another kind of rule – that exercised among men who are free and equal in birth. This we call 'constitutional' or 'political'. It is this that a ruler must first learn through being ruled, just as in any arm of the services one learns to command by being at first a junior officer. This is a sound principle; it is not possible to be a good commander without first learning to obey. Not that good ruling and good obedience are the same, only that the good citizen must have the knowledge and ability both to rule and be ruled. That is what we mean by the goodness of a citizen – understanding the governing of free men by free men.

Returning now to the good *man*, we find the same bivalence; he is *good* whether ruled or ruling. And this is true even though good behaviour and justice are not the same in a subject as they are in the sphere of government. For clearly the goodness of the good man, who is free but governed, for example his justice, will not be always one and the same; it will take different forms according to whether he is to rule or be ruled, just as standards of good behaviour and courage vary as between men and women. A man would seem a coward if he had only the courage of a woman, a woman a chatterbox if she were no more reticent than a good, well-behaved man. Men and women have different parts to play in the home; his to win, hers to keep. But for a ruler the only special quality or goodness is intelligence; all the others belong, essentially so it seems to me, both to rulers and to subjects. The quality needed for being a subject is not intelligence but correct information; he is rather like a person who makes flutes, while the ruler is one who can play a flute.

The differences, and the nature and extent of the differences, between the goodness of the good man and that of the good citizen are now clear.

Aristotle now returns to citizenship. He is aware that in some states the banausoi, *or workers, have full citizenship; but in his view they cannot by the nature of their occupation possess the qualities and abilities necessary for a citizen. Does this call for a new definition? Aristotle does not think so. He holds that citizens are a particular class of men, to which no one who is constantly engaged in commercial or manual labour can possibly belong.*

5

There remains still a question about the definition of a citizen. Is a citizen really 'one who has the ability and the chance to participate in government' or are we to count workers as citizens? If we do the latter – give them the title citizen though they cannot share in government, then the goodness of the citizen ceases to be that of every citizen, since the worker does not possess it, and he too is a citizen. On the other hand, if he is not a citizen, where does he belong? He is not a foreign resident or a visitor; in what category are we to put him? Perhaps this kind of reasoning does not really result in any absurdity. After all, slaves do not belong to any of the above-mentioned categories, nor do freed slaves. And we do not for a moment accept the notion that we must give the name citizen to all persons whose presence is necessary for the existence of the state. Children are as necessary as grown men but, as we have already remarked, they can be called citizens only in a qualified sense. In ancient times in certain countries the working class did rank as slaves or foreigners and in most cases the same is still generally true. But the best state will not make a worker a citizen. If even the worker is to be a citizen, then what we have called the goodness of a citizen cannot be ascribed to everyone or to free men alone, but simply to those who are in fact relieved of all menial tasks.*

A little further examination will show how it stands with these people and a statement of the actual position will suffice: as there are different constitutions, so there must be different kinds of citizen, particularly of citizen under government or ruler. Thus in one constitution it will be necessary, in another impossible, for the labourer or employed person to be a citizen. It would, for example, be

* These tasks may be discharged by the personal slaves of an individual, or by workers and labourers in public service.

impossible in any constitution called aristocratic or any other in which advancement depends on merit and ability; for it is quite impossible, while living the life of worker or employee to possess all the necessary merit and ability. In oligarchies it is not possible for a labourer to be a citizen because of the high property-qualifications required for holding office; but it may be possible for a workman, since many skilled workers become rich.

The view that constant paid employment, even in what we might call 'the high-grade executive class', is a bar to citizenship and to the holding of office was not peculiar to Aristotle. But numbers must be maintained.

In Thebes there was a rule requiring an interval of ten years to elapse between retiring from business and holding office of government. In many constitutions the custom is to admit to citizenship a certain number even of foreigners; in some democracies the son of an alien father and a citizen mother is a citizen, and in many the same applies to illegitimate children. Lack of population is the usual reason for customs such as these. But when, after admitting such persons because of a dearth of genuine citizens, the state has filled up its numbers, it gradually reduces the number of admissions, dropping first the sons of slave father or slave mother, then sons of citizen mother but not father, and finally they confine citizenship to those of citizen birth on both sides.

From all this two points clearly emerge; first, that there are different kinds of citizen, but, second, that a citizen in the fullest sense is one who has a share in the privileges of rule. We are reminded of Homer's 'Like some interloper of no standing'. For he whose standing gives him no share in these privileges is no better than an alien.*

We have now answered the question whether it is the same or a different goodness that makes a good man and a

* Sometimes it is not publicly stated what practice is being followed so that a section of the population is kept in ignorance of its own rights and status.

good citizen, and have shown that in one state it will be the same and in another different, and that where it is the same, not every citizen will possess it, but only the 'statesman', that is one who is in control, or capable of being in control, either alone or in conjunction with others, of the conduct of a nation's affairs.

Aristotle now leaves citizenship and turns to constitutions, as promised at the beginning of Book III. In his search for a single description of polites *Aristotle was not really successful and was obliged to concede that citizens differ according to the differences in the societies in which citizenship finds its expression. He now asks a similar question about* politeia, *but there is no need to answer it, the plurality of constitutions has already been taken for granted. But what is important is to know in what the difference consists and so to classify them. The main criterion is the* politeuma, *the totality of the citizen-body. This was the view generally held; in an oligarchy, for example, the 'few' are the entire citizen-body. A second criterion is* cui bono? *in whose interests is government carried on? The reference back is to Book I, Chapter 3.*

6

Having settled these questions we must proceed to our next and ask whether we are to posit only one constitution or more than one; and if more than one, ask what they are and how many and what are the differences between them. By the 'constitution' we mean the organization of the various authorities and in particular the sovereign authority that is above all the others. Now in every case the citizen-body is sovereign; the constitution *is* the sum total of the *politeuma*. Thus in democratic constitutions the people or demos is supreme, in oligarchies the few. *That* is what makes one constitution differ from another – the composition of the citizen-body; and the same criterion can be applied to the others also.

We ought at the outset to state the purpose for which the

state has come to be, as well as the nature and number of kinds of rule or authority controlling the men of the city and their life as members of a common society. At the beginning of this work, when we drew a distinction between ruling a household and despotic rule, we also stated that by nature man is a political animal. Men have a natural desire for life in society, even when they have no need to seek each other's help. Nevertheless common interest is a factor in bringing them together, since the interest of all contributes to the good life of each. The *good* life is indeed the chief end of the state both corporately and individually, but men form and continue to maintain this kind of association for the sake of life itself. Perhaps we may say that there is an element of value even in mere living, provided that life is not excessively beset with troubles. Certainly most men, in their desire to keep alive, are prepared to face a great deal of suffering, finding in life itself a certain comfort and a feeling that it is good to be alive.

But to return to authority, it is not difficult to distinguish the named varieties of it – I often speak about their definition in my public lectures. First the authority of master over slave; this is exercised primarily for the benefit of the master and only incidentally for the benefit of the slave; strictly speaking, one whose nature is to be a slave has no other interest than that of his master by nature. But the master has an interest in maintaining the relationship; which cannot be done unless the slave is alive and able to work. Then there is the authority of a man over his wife, his children, and his household, to which form of government we give the name 'household management'. This is exercised either for the benefit of those subject to the authority or for the common benefit of both parties. Properly and in itself it is for the benefit of the subjects as we see by the analogy of other skilled activities, such as the work of a doctor or of an athlete's trainer, who are only incidentally concerned with their own interests.*

* Of course there is nothing to prevent a trainer on occasion being himself a member of the team in training, as the man who steers the ship

Thirdly the political authority: whenever it is constituted on a basis of equality and similarity between citizens, these claim the right to take it in turns to exercise authority, to govern.* It is clear then that those constitutions which aim at the common good are *right*, as being in accord with absolute justice; while those which aim only at the good of the rulers are *wrong*. They are all *deviations* from the right standard. They are like the rule of master over slave, where the master's interest is paramount. But the state is an association of free men.

7

Having drawn this distinction we must next consider what constitutions there are and how many. We begin with those that aim at securing the good of all, which we have called 'straight' constitutions, since, when these have been defined, it will be easy to see the deviation-types. As we have seen, constitution and *politeuma* are really the same; the citizen body is the sovereign power in states. Sovereignty must reside either in one man, or in a few, or in the many. Whenever the One, the Few, or the Many rule with a view to the common weal, these constitutions must be right; but if they look to the advantage of one section only, be it the One or the Few or the Mass, it is a deviation. For either we must say that those who participate are not citizens or they must share in the common good. The usual names for right constitutions are as follows:

---

is always a member of the ship's company. Trainer and pilot alike look to the good of those under their direction, but when he too is one of these he gets the same good out of it *per accidens* as they do.

 * This principle is very old but in earlier times it was applied in a natural and proper manner; men thought it their duty each to take a turn at public service and, during tenure of office, look after the interests of someone else, who would do or had done the same for him. But nowadays there is more to be gained out of public services and offices; so instead of being content to take their turn, men want to be continually in office. They could hardly be more zealous in their place-hunting if they were ill and their recovery depended on securing office.

(1) One man rule aiming at the common good – Kingship.

(2) Rule of more than one man but only a few – Aristocracy.*

(3) Rule exercised by the bulk of the citizens for the good of the whole community – Polity.†

The corresponding deviations are: from kingship, tyranny; from aristocracy, oligarchy; from polity or constitutional government by the many, democracy. For tyranny is sole rule for the benefit of the sole ruler, oligarchy for the benefit of the men of means, democracy for the benefit of the men without means. None of the three aims at the advantage of the whole community.

Further consideration shows that the distribution of political power is not the only thing that determines the character of a politeia; *the distribution of wealth is equally effective.*

8

We must however go into a little more detail about the nature of these various constitutions. Certain questions are involved which one whose aim was strictly practical might be allowed to pass over, but which we, looking at each subject from a philosophical standpoint, cannot neglect. We must state the true nature of each.

Tyranny as has been said, is that form of monarchical rule which is despotically exercised over the political

---

* So-called either because the *best* men rule or because it aims at what is *best* for the state and all its members.

† This is the same word as constitution. But it is reasonable to use this term, because, while it is possible for one man or a few to be of outstanding ability, it is difficult for a larger number to reach a high standard in all forms of excellence. But it may be reached in fighting qualities by the general run of people. And that is why in this 'constitutional constitution' the citizen-army is the sovereign body and only those who bear arms are members of it.

association called the state; oligarchy occurs when the sovereign power is in the hands of those possessed of property, democracy when it is in the hands of those who have no accumulated wealth, who are without means. The first of this set of questions concerns definitions of oligarchy and democracy: suppose the majority to be well-off and to be the sovereign power in the state, then we have a democracy, since the mass of the people is sovereign. So too, if it should occur that those who had no property, while fewer in number than those who had, were yet more powerful and in control of government, then that is an oligarchy since the few are in power. It looks therefore as if there were something wrong with our way of defining constitutions. Even if we try to include both criteria, combining wealth with fewness of numbers in the one case, lack of wealth with large numbers in the other, even then we are only raising a fresh difficulty. For if there is not in fact any other constitution than the six with which we have been dealing, what names can we give to the two just mentioned, one in which the wealthy are more numerous and one in which the non-wealthy are less numerous, each class being in the case in control of government? The argument seems to show that the real criterion should be property, that it is a matter of accident whether those in power be few or many, the one in oligarchies, the other in democracies. It just happens that way because everywhere the rich are few and the poor are many. So the basis of the difference has been wrongly given; what differentiates oligarchy and democracy is wealth or the lack of it. The essential point is that where the possession of political power is due to the possession of economic power or wealth, whether the number of persons be large or small, that is oligarchy, and when the unpropertied class have power, that is democracy. But, as we have said, in actual fact the former are few, the latter many. Few are wealthy but all share freedom alike: and these are the bases of their claim to a share in the *politeia*, property in the one case, free status in the other.

Another criterion is Justice, or Right. Certainly the differences in ethical standards provide an excellent way of classifying and of comparing one form of society with another. Unfortunately Aristotle does not use the new criterion thus. He ties it firmly to the old classification and narrows justice to distributive justice; fair shares for all. He accepts the notion that the state should confer benefits in proportion to value received, but objects to the oligarchic principle by which value is assessed only in terms of money. He is led on to consider the ethical basis of the state more generally and what differentiates it from other forms of partnership. – The reference is to Ethics, *1131 a 15.*

9

First we must ask what are the defining marks of oligarchy and democracy, and in particular what is the oligarchic and what is the democratic view of *Justice*. For all aim at justice of some kind, but they do not proceed beyond a certain point and are not referring to the whole of absolute justice when they speak of it. Thus it appears that the just is equal, and so it is, but not for all persons, only for those that are equal. The unequal also appears to be just; and so it is, but not for all, only for the unequal. We make bad mistakes if we neglect this 'for whom' when we are deciding what is just. The reason is that we are making decisions about ourselves, and people are generally bad judges where their own interests are involved. So, as justice means just for certain persons and also just in relation to certain things (a distinction pointed out in my *Ethics*), these people, while agreeing as to equality of the thing, disagree about the persons for whom; and this chiefly for the reason already stated of judging from their own case, and therefore judging badly. There is also this further reason that they imagine themselves to be talking about absolute justice simply because they have, both parties of them, a certain amount of right on their side, justice in a limited sense. Thus it is an error to suppose that men unequal in one respect, e.g. property, are unequal in all, just as it is an error to suppose that men equal in one respect, e.g. that they are free men, are equal in every respect. To argue thus is to neglect the essential: if persons originally come together and form an association based on ownership of property, then they share in that association, the state, in proportion to their ownership of property.

This is the basis of the oligarchs' view of the state and of justice; and in its favour it can certainly be said that it is not just that out of a sum of a hundred pounds he that contributed one pound should receive equal shares with him who found the remaining ninety-nine, and this applies equally to the original hundred pounds capital and to any profits subsequently made. But a state is something more than an investment; its purpose is not merely to provide a living but to make a life that is worth while. Otherwise a state might be made up of slaves or animals, and that is impossible, because slaves and animals are not free agents and do not participate in well-being.

A state is also something more than a pact of mutual protection or an agreement to exchange goods and services; for in that case Etruscans and Carthaginians, and all others with contractual obligations to each other, would be taken as citizens of a single state. Certainly they have trade-agreements, non-aggression pacts, and written documents governing their alliance. But this is very different from being one state with one citizenship; for in the first place each has its separate government and there are no official bodies to which they are both equally subject. Secondly neither is concerned with the *quality* of the citizens of the other, or even with their behaviour, whether it is honest or dishonest, except in dealings with members of the other state. But all who are concerned with lawful behaviour must make it their business to have an eye to the goodness or badness of the citizens. It thus becomes evident that that which is genuinely and not just nominally called a state must concern itself with virtue. Otherwise the state-partnership is a mere alliance, differing only in location and extent from alliance in the usual sense; and under such conditions Law becomes a mere contract or, as Lycophron the sophist put it, 'a mutual guarantee of rights', and quite unable to make citizens good and just, which it ought to do.

That this is the essential quality in a state will be clear from some further illustrations. Suppose you merge the territories into one, making the walls, say, of Corinth and Megara contiguous, that does not make a single state of them; nor would it, even if they established rights of marriage between the two, though this is one of the closest possible ties. Or again, suppose you had ten thousand people living at some distance from each other, but near enough not to lose contact; carpenter, farmer, leather-worker, and other necessary craftsmen are there, and furthermore they all accept laws and regulations prohibiting dishonesty in their dealings with each other; yet, so long as their associations with each other do not go beyond commercial exchanges and defence, that is still not a state. And why not? you may ask. The reason is certainly not that it is a loosely knit community. For even if they lived closer together, while otherwise maintaining only such contacts as I have described, except that each governed his own household like a state, and mutually supported each other in alliance against wrongdoers only, even then that is not a state, not at any rate in the strict sense, since the nature of their association is the same whether they live close together or far apart.

It is clear therefore that the state cannot be defined merely as a community dwelling in the same place and preventing its members from wrong-doing and promoting the exchange of goods and services. Certainly all these must be present if there is to be a state, but even the presence of every one of them does not *ipso facto* make a state. The state is intended to enable all, in their households and their kinships, to live *well*, meaning by that a full and satisfying life. This will not be attained unless these family-groups occupy one and the same territory and can inter-marry. It is indeed on that account that we find in various cities associations formed of relatives by marriage, brotherhoods, family reunions for sacrifices to the gods, and other ways of social intercourse. All these activities are an expression of affection, for it is our love of others that causes us to prefer life in a society; and they all contribute towards that good life which is the purpose of the state;* and that, we hold, means living happily and nobly. So we must lay it down that the political association which we call a state exists not simply for the purpose of living together but for the sake of noble actions. Those who do noble deeds are therefore contributing to the quality of the political association, and those who contribute most are entitled to a larger share than those who, though they may be equal or even superior in free birth and family, are inferior in noble deeds and so in the essential goodness that belongs to the *polis*. Similarly they are entitled to a larger share than those who are superior in riches but inferior in goodness.

All this makes it more clear than ever that those who speak of *justice* in connexion with various types of constitution are using the term in a limited and relative sense.

There is no very obvious connexion between this conclusion and the next chapter which implicitly goes back to the beginning of Chapter 6.

10

Another question is 'Where ought the sovereign power of the state to reside?' With the people? With the propertied classes? With the good? With one man, the best of all the good? With one man, the tyrant? There are objections to all these. Thus suppose we say the people is the supreme authority, then if they use their numerical superiority to make a distribution of the property of the rich, is not that unjust? It has been done by a valid decision of the sovereign power, yet what can we call it save the very height of injustice? Again, if the majority, having laid their hands on everything, distribute the possessions of the few, they are

* One could also make a *polis* out of an association of clans and villages, so long as the aim was a full and satisfying life.

obviously destroying the state. But that cannot be goodness which destroys its possessor and justice cannot be destructive of the state. So it is clear that this process, though it may be the law, cannot be just. Or, if that is just, the actions taken by a tyrant must be just; his superior power enables him to use force, just as the masses force their will on the rich. Thirdly, if it is just for the few and wealthy to rule, and if they too rob and plunder and help themselves to the goods of the many, is that just? If it is, then it is just in the former case also. The answer clearly is that all these three are bad and unjust. The fourth alternative, that the good should rule and have the supreme authority, is also not free from objection; it means that all the rest must be without official standing, debarred from holding office under the constitution.* The fifth alternative, that one man, the best, should rule, is no better; by making the number of rulers fewer we leave still larger numbers without official standing. It might be objected too that it is a bad thing for any human being, subject to all possible disorders and affections of the human mind, to be the sovereign authority, which ought to be reserved for the law itself. But that will not make any difference to the cases we have been discussing; the law itself may have a bias towards oligarchy or democracy, so that exactly the same results will ensue.

These short arguments, as far as they go, suggest that the number of persons eligible to hold office and share in sovereign power ought not to be unduly restricted, or, in the language of Chapter 6 above, the politeuma *should not be too small.*

11

The other points connected with sovereignty will be discussed elsewhere; at the moment it would seem that the most defensible, perhaps even the truest, answer to the

* We regard the offices as conferring honour, standing, *timē;* and if the same persons always hold office, the rest are without honourable standing.

question would be to say that the majority ought to be sovereign, rather than the best, where the best are few. For it is possible that the many, no one of whom taken singly is a good man, may yet taken all together be better than the few, not individually but collectively, in the same way that a feast to which all contribute is better than one given at one man's expense. For where there are many people, each has some share of goodness and intelligence, and when these are brought together, they become as it were one multiple man with many pairs of feet and hands and many minds. So too in regard to character and powers of perception. That is why the general public is a better judge of works of music and poetry; some judge some parts, some others, but their joint pronouncement is a verdict upon the whole. And it is this assembling in one what was before separate that gives the good man his superiority over any individual man from the masses. Handsome men differ from ugly, paintings from actual objects, just because they draw together into one what was previously scattered here and there, since any one of the features taken separately, the eye of one man, some other part of another, might well be more handsome than in the picture. But it is not at all certain that this superiority of the many over the good few is to be found in every people and every large majority, indeed there are some among whom it would be impossible; think of the effect of trying to apply this to animals – and some men are hardly any better than wild animals. But there is no reason why in a given case we should not accept and apply this theory of the collective wisdom of the multitude.

It does not necessarily follow that all sovereignty should belong equally to all members. But attempts to formulate a division of power soon run into difficulties and complications.

These considerations enable us to answer the question where sovereignty should be and also another and related question – in what spheres of work and over what persons is this sovereignty of the majority, the free men, to be exercised? We must remember that these men, though free, are not men of wealth and standing, have no claim to goodness or excellence in anything. To let them share in the highest offices of government is to take a great risk; their low standards will cause them to do wrong and their lack of judgement will lead them into error. On the other hand there is a risk in not assigning any duties or any status to them; for when there are many in a city who have no property and no official standing, they inevitably constitute a hostile element in the state. But even if we exclude them from the highest office it will still remain open to them to participate in deliberative and judicial work.

It was to avoid this hostile element in the state that Solon and some of the other lawgivers gave to the people power to elect officers of government and to demand an account from them at the end of their tenure, but no right individually to hold such offices. This was in accord with our principle that the whole body of citizens acting together have the necessary understanding, even though each is individually not qualified to decide. By thus cooperating with the better sort of citizen the people can render good service in their cities, in something like the same way that a combination of coarse foods with refined renders the whole diet more nutritious as well as more bulky.

But such a distribution of constitutional powers raises a number of difficulties. First, this matter of officials being required to give an account before the people of their conduct; the proper person to decide whether a piece of medical work has been properly done is the same sort of person as is engaged on such work, on curing the patient of his present sickness, in other words the medical practitioner himself. And this is equally true of other kinds of skilled activity. As then it is among doctors that a doctor should give an account of himself, so also other professional men among their peers. By physician I mean not only the ordinary practitioner and his more scientific counterpart, the specialist, but also the amateur who has been trained in the art, such as are to be found in pretty well all professions. And to the verdicts of these trained amateurs we attach equal importance as to those of the professionals. Second, in the matter of elections the same would seem to apply. Choosing aright is a task for those who have knowledge of the matter in hand, the land-surveyor of land-measurement, the navigator of navigation, and so on. Admittedly in some jobs and some kinds of skill you will find amateurs who know a good deal, but not more than the experts. So it would seem that by these arguments the mass of the people should not be given the power either of choosing officials or of calling them to account.

Perhaps, however, these are not the only arguments, or the right ones. First there is the argument which we used a while back – the argument of the collective intelligence of the masses, so long as they do not fall below a certain standard. Each individually will be a worse judge than the experts, but when all work together, they are better, or at any rate, no worse. Secondly, there are tasks of which the actual doer is not either the best or the only judge, cases in which even those who do not possess the operative skill pronounce an opinion on the finished product. An obvious example is house-building; the builder certainly can judge a house, but the user, owner or tenant, will be a better judge. So too the user of a rudder, the helmsman, is a better judge of it than the carpenters who made it; and it is the diner not the cook that pronounces upon the merits of the dinner. I think perhaps these two arguments are sufficient to resolve the question.

Thus the 'experts only' argument is outweighted and the critical ability of the people collectively is allowed to stand. It is however directly contrary to what Plato taught, but after one further objection is stated and disposed of by a reference to Athenian practice, we have a restatement of the doctrine of collective judgement.

But there is another objection connected with this. It is considered wrong that inferior persons should have control over greater matters than the better sort. Certainly the choice of officials and the reviewing of their work are very important matters. But they can be carried out by the mass of the people, and, as we have said, are assigned to them in some constitutions, the citizen-assembly having full control of such matters. It makes no difference that many of the members of the assembly, and also of the smaller body, the council, and of the panels of jurymen, are people of low property qualification and of almost any age; only for treasury officials, generals, and other very high offices is a high property qualification demanded.

The objection can be met and our position justified by arguments similar to those which we have just used: it is not the individual juryman, councillor, or member of assembly who is in control, but the court, the council, and the people; and of each of these the individual councillor, member, and juryman is a part. So it is quite right that the mass of the citizens be in control of important things, since people, council, and law-court are all formed from among the many. And as for property-qualification, the sum total of property owned is larger than that of the holders jointly or individually of the highest offices.

A summing up on law and sovereignty.

These matters may be regarded as settled in that way; but we must look back at our original question. From what we observed about sovereignty nothing emerges so clearly as the fact that the laws rightly framed ought to be sovereign, also that officials of government, whether individually or in committee, have sovereign power to act in all those various matters about which the laws cannot possibly give detailed guidance; for it is never easy to frame general regulations covering every particular. We said 'laws rightly framed', but we have not yet discovered what these are, so the question is not fully answered. But this much we can say, that, as constitutions vary, so in like manner must laws vary, good or bad, just or unjust; but clearly too the type of constitution comes first and sets the pattern for the laws; and that being so, laws framed in accordance with one of the 'right' types of constitution will be just, but if according to one of the 'deviations' unjust.

What follows now looks like a fresh start, so reminiscent is it of the opening of the Ethics, *but it soon links up with Chapter 9 and the subject of distributive justice. Every state must be an expression of some idea of what is fair and just, not absolutely but in the given circumstances and for the persons concerned. The Greek word* isos *means 'equal' as well as 'fair'; and this causes the same puzzlement as before, and the fifth book of the* Ethics *(V, 3) is again referred to.*

Justice in the present connexion means fair distribution of political power, privilege, and status. It starts from the assumption that if A is better than, i.e. superior to, B, then A is entitled to a larger share. So the question is what kind of superiority is to be regarded as constituting a claim to office and privilege. Aristotle, as we would expect, puts good birth and ownership of property on the list, also moral qualities, justice and courage; a high level of culture and education too will be a token of merit in one who is to take part in the working of a state which is aimed at securing the good life. Men are not equal in these respects and any state which ignores this fact and thinks in terms of absolute equality must be one of the wrong types of 'deviations'. (This is not how deviation was defined previously; wrong types of constitution are those in which the interests of one section of the community take precedence over all the rest; and the 'good of all' criterion of a right constitution is still adhered to.) The upper classes will always be superior in education and ability but numerical superiority may also be taken into account.

12

In every kind of knowledge and activity the end which is aimed at is *good*. This is especially true of the greatest of these, the activities of the state and citizens. In the state the good aimed at is justice; and that means what is for the good of the whole community. Now it is pretty clear that justice in a community means equality for all. This is not inconsistent with the theory of justice which I explained in my *Ethics*, for it involves the same principles – that justice is related to persons and that equality must be equal for equals. What we now want to find out is the kind of equality or inequality; in what sort of matters is this notion of 'equal' relevant to political theory?

It is possible to argue that it is relevant in every matter and say that superiority of any kind whatever justifies unequal distribution of offices of state, assuming that in all other respects than this the men are equal and similar, for any general differences in the persons would mean different justice and different deserts. But surely, if that be granted, we shall have to allow that superiority in height or complexion or any other good thing confers an advantage in the distribution of political rights. Is not the fallacy here pretty obvious? A comparison with other kinds of knowledge and ability shows that it is. For if, say, the flute players are equal in skill, we do not give the better instruments to those of better birth, for that would not enable them to play any better. The right to use the better instruments belongs to him who is the better performer on that instrument.

If this is not sufficiently clear it will become so as we proceed. If one man is outstandingly superior in flute-playing, but far inferior in birth or good looks (even supposing that birth and good looks are a greater good than flute-playing, and greater in proportion than the superiority of this player over the rest), even then, I say, the good player should get the best instrument. For superiority is only relevant when it contributes to the quality of the performance, which wealth and good birth do not do at all. Moreover, according to that way of reasoning every good thing would be commensurable with every other. For if in political justice marks are given for tallness, then tallness would be in constant competition with wealth and free birth. And if we say that X has greater superiority in height than Y has in virtue, then, even if in general virtue is of greater importance than height, we are making everything commensurable with everything; since if one amount is greater than p, there must be another which is equal to p. But such mensuration is quite impossible here and it is clear that in matters relating to the state men are quite right not to take any and every kind of inequality into account in discussing distribution of offices, but only those which are relevant, that is to say, those which contribute to making up the state as a whole, not such qualities as swiftness of foot, however important that may be in athletic contests. Qualities which have importance in a society, and have therefore a right to be considered, are noble birth, free birth, and property; since the members must be free and must be taxpayers, and you could no more make a city out of paupers than out of slaves. But something more is needed besides these; I mean the virtues of justice and military prowess. Without these it is not possible for the life and work of a city to go on; without free population and wealth there cannot be a city at all, without justice and valour it cannot be well managed.

13

To some or all of these points men have rightly paid attention in discussing the fabric of the state, but I must repeat that, in order to secure the good life, education and virtue and ability would have the highest claim to consideration. But since those who are equal in one particular need not be equal in all, nor those who are unequal in one respect unequal in all, it follows that constitutions in which such absolute equality prevails must be classed as crooked or deviations. It has already been stated that all men have some kind of justice in their claims but they cannot all claim to have an absolute right.

The rich argue that they have a greater share in the land

and the land is common, and further, that they are more to be relied upon to keep their word. The claims of the free-born and well-born are closely related, both being based on birth; the more nobly born are more fully citizens than the non-noble, good birth being held in esteem in every community, and the offspring of the better sort are likely to be better men, for being well-born is being sprung of good stock. Next, and equally rightly, we shall mention the claims of excellence or goodness; we always speak of justice as a good quality in a community and one which is sure to bring with it all the other virtues. And surely we ought to add numerical strength to this list; the majority have a better claim than the minority, as being stronger, richer, and better if we take numbers into account.

How then are these claims to a share in governing to be reconciled? None of them would seem to have anything more than a partial or relative validity.

Now suppose all these three classes to be present in a single city – that is to say, the good, the rich, and the well-born, and beside them the rest of the citizen body – will there or will there not be dispute as to which class shall hold office and govern? Of course, in the three types of constitution of which we spoke earlier no question arises; they differ from each other in just this respect, power being exercised in oligarchy by the rich, in aristocracy by the good, and so on. But we have to ask ourselves how a decision is to be taken when conflicting claims are present at one time. Suppose for example that those who have virtue and ability are exceedingly few in number, how is distribution of power to be made? Are we to regard their fewness in the light of the work to be done, asking whether there are enough of them to run the city? Or are we to say that we cannot make a city out of them unless their numbers amount to such and such? The question is a perpetual one and arises in all claims to political power. Thus, those who base their claim on wealth would seem to have no just claim at all, nor those based on birth; for if one man is very much richer than the rest, on this principle strictly observed he will have to be sole ruler over all, and similarly one who is superior in good birth will have to rule over all whose claim is based on free birth. The same thing could well happen where the constitution is an aristocracy, based on goodness; for if one man is better than all the other good men within the citizen body, then on this principle he ought to have authority over them. Again, suppose that the majority ought to be sovereign because they are stronger than the few, and suppose one man, or more than one but still fewer than the many, to be stronger than the rest, then these would have to be sovereign rather than the majority.

All these considerations seem to show that none of these criteria can be right; they all result in one set of men claiming that they themselves should rule and the rest be subject to them. For surely, whether their claim rests on wealth or on virtue, it remains true that against their pretensions the majority will have some justice on their side. It is quite possible on occasion for the many to be better than the few, and richer too, when considered not singly but together. Wherever these conditions occur there is no difficulty in answering a question which people very often put, the question whether a lawgiver, who genuinely seeks to make the laws that are most right, ought to legislate for the good of the majority or for the good of the better sort.

That is because in the given case the majority and the better sort are the same people. But the right principle is the good of the whole community, as Aristotle hastens to add.

By the 'most right' we mean 'fairly and equally right', and that means for the good of the whole state and the common weal of the citizens. A citizen is in general one who has a share both in ruling and in being ruled; this will not be identical in every kind of constitution, but in the best constitution it means one who is able and who chooses to rule and to be ruled with a view to a life that is in accordance with goodness.

Although none of these merits, birth, wealth, virtue, carry an absolute right to power, surely virtue, that is, moral and intellectual ability, is a quality that is always needed for the exercise of power. Where it occurs in the majority, as has just been said, no difficulty arises, but when one man of quite extraordinary powers and ability arises, he must be regarded as outside the normal constitution. He must either be removed (a common practice in Greek states but potentially a waste of a good man) or given the supreme position to which his unique merits entitle him. To speak of an outstanding personality as 'a god among men' would come quite naturally to a Greek; it is little more than a proverbial expression like 'Triton among the minnows'.

But if there is one man so superlatively excellent (or several but not enough to make the whole complement of a city) that the goodness and ability of all the rest are simply not to be compared with his (or theirs), such men we take not to be part of the state but to transcend it. To judge them worthy of mere equality with the rest would be to do them an injustice, so far superior are they in virtue and political capacity. We may reasonably regard such a one as a god among men. In that case clearly legislation, the aim of which we have been discussing, is not relevant, since legislation must refer to equals in birth and capacity; and there is no law that can govern these exceptional men. They are themselves law and anyone who tried to legislate for them would be snubbed for his pains. The great men might well say what the lions in Antisthenes's fable said to the hares who asserted their claim to equality with them – 'show us your claws and your teeth'. It is just this impossibility of controlling them that led to the practice of ostracism in democratically organized cities. These appear to have attached such immense importance to the principle of equality that they ostracized and removed out of the city for certain periods anyone whose power was deemed to be excessive, whether this power was due to wealth or popularity or any of the other ways of gaining political influence.* The tyrant who removes a dangerous rival is simply acting on this principle and those who condemn the advice given by Periander to Thrasybulus – 'lop off the tops' – are not fully justified.† The method is useful not for tyrants only, and tyrants are not alone in practising it; oligarchies and democracies do just the same. For ostracism has very much the same effect as cutting off the tops and exiling the leading men. Nor is the practice of weakening possible rivals confined to internal politics; it is the regular practice of great and powerful states in their dealings with other cities or nations.‡ Indeed this whole question of rival power closely concerns all governments, not merely the crooked ones, in which rulers resort to such methods for their own advantage, but also right forms of constitution.

Thus Aristotle cannot help seeing the outstanding man as more of a problem than an asset. He continues to regard any departure from the normal with dislike and this leads him into some rather ludicrous analogies.

The same refusal to tolerate that which stands out may be seen also in the other arts and sciences. A painter would

* An example from mythology: the Argonauts left Heracles behind because the Argo herself would not have on board one so vastly greater than the rest of the crew.

† To Thrasybulus's messenger Periander returned no answer, but, while walking in a field, reduced all the stalks to one level by lopping off the tallest. The messenger did not know the meaning of this but reported the action to Thrasybulus, who understood that he ought to remove the outstanding men.

‡ Examples: (1) The Athenians, as soon as they were strong enough, reduced Lesbos, Chios, and Samos to submission, contrary to the terms of the confederacy, and (2) the Persian king often humbled the Medes, Babylonians, and others who prided themselves on their earlier supremacy.

not allow the symmetry of his representation of a living creature to be destroyed by making one foot disproportionately large, however magnificent the foot might be. A shipbuilder would not make the stern, or any other part of the ship, out of proportion. A choirmaster would not include among the members a singer whose voice was finer and more powerful than all the others. On this showing there is no reason at all why rulers who forcibly remove rivals should not remain on good terms with their subjects, provided that in taking this action their own rule is beneficial to them. Therefore the theory behind ostracism has some measure of political justice in it in cases of admitted disproportion, excessive wealth or popularity. Of course if the lawgiver can so construct society from the start that there will never be any need of such drastic medicine, so much the better. Otherwise the best we can do, if occasion arises, is put matters right by some such method.*

In the deviation forms of constitution ostracism, like everything else, is exercised for the personal benefit of the rulers and this makes it just in that limited sense only. That is obvious enough, but when it comes to the best type of constitution, there is a real difficulty. We may grant that the use of ostracism is justified in the cases of excessive influence or riches or popularity, but where a man is preeminent in character and ability, what are we to do? No one will say that such a man ought to be banished or deported; yet we ought not to rule over him, for that would be like asking Zeus to share his government with men. It only remains therefore to let nature take its course; he will govern and we will gladly obey him. Thus such men are kings in their cities, permanent kings.

In Chapter 7 above, the six forms of constitution were set out, three right or normal and three deviations from the norm. Since then the

* In fact it did not work out this way; things were not put right, because men, instead of seeking to protect their national life, used ostracism as a weapon in party strife.

discussions about justice and sovereignty in the state have been carried on with the rule of the few or of the many as a constitutional background. There has been no mention of monarchy in this connexion – naturally enough since questions about sovereignty and the just distribution of political power have no relevance, at any rate when the monarchy is an absolute one. But in the first place not all monarchies are absolute; there are varying degrees of monarchical power; and secondly absolute monarchy, if it is of the right type and not a tyranny, must have its place.

We follow Aristotle in using the term 'kingship' to denote any of the right forms of monarchy and 'tyranny' for the wrong. Tyranny is wrong, irrespective of the personality of the tyrant, first for the reason originally stated, that it is rule exercised for the ruler's own benefit; second, that it is power seized by force and not based on law; and third, that it is exercised over unwilling subjects. The kingships are right, because they are aimed at the interests of the whole community, who are willing subjects, and their power is legal both in its exercise and in its acquisition. Even absolute power may be legally acquired, either by heredity or by election.

14

After what has just been said it might be a good thing to turn aside for a moment and consider kingship, since we hold that it is one of the right or straight forms of government. We have to inquire whether or not kingship, rather than some other, is advantageous for the good ordering of life in any country or city, or if it is advantageous for some and not for others. But first we must decide whether there is only one kind of kingship or a number of different kinds. It is easy to see that there are several kinds and that the manner of government is not the same in every case.

The clearest example of constitutional kingship is that found in the Lacedaemonian constitution. Its power is limited; but when a king leads forth an army out of the country, he is supreme in all matters relating to the war; to the two kings is committed also the care of religious matters. Such a kingship is like a perpetual and independent army command; he has no power to put anyone to death except in the course of a military expedition.* This then is one type of kingship – command of the army tenable for life; it may be acquired either by heredity or by election. Alongside this there is another type of sole rule, such as is found in certain non-Greek kingships. These have complete power equal to that of tyrannies but they are legally established and hereditary. Their rule, however, is as of master over slave, and it is because barbarians are by natural character more slavish than Greeks (and Asiatics than Europeans) that they tolerate this despotic rule without resentment. Therefore, while they can be described as tyrannies for these reasons, they derive stability from their legality and their hereditary succession. They can also be distinguished from tyranny by the fact that the ruler has a royal, not a tyrant's, bodyguard; a king's bodyguard is composed of citizens carrying arms, a tyrant's of foreign mercenaries. And the king rules over willing subjects according to law, the tyrant over unwilling subjects; so that the one receives protection from his citizens, the other needs it against them.

These then are two types of monarchy; there is a third, which used to exist among Greeks of old. This type of ruler is called *aesymnētēs*; he was in fact a kind of elected tyrant. This type of rule differs from the barbarian kingship just described only in being non-hereditary; it is equally legal. The rulers held office sometimes for life, sometimes for a stated period or until certain things should be accomplished; for example the people of Mytilene elected Pittacus for the purpose of repelling the exiles who tried to come back led by Antimenides and the poet Alcaeus. We know that Pittacus

* Compare what Homer tells us about the rights of a commander in the field in ancient times. Agamemnon had to put up with being abused in meetings of assemblies, but once an expedition had begun, he had power of life and death. So much is implied in his words 'Anyone whom I shall catch skulking away from the fighting . . . his body shall become the prey of dogs and birds, and no escape, for the power of death is in my hand.'

was chosen from one of the songs of Alcaeus in which he says, 'With mass-adulation they appointed low-born Pittacus to be tyrant of their feckless and unlucky city'. Of this kind of ruler we may say that in so far as their rule was that of a master or despot, they were tyrants; in so far as they were chosen by willing subjects, they were kings.

There was a fourth kind of kingship which existed in heroic times. It was both hereditary and legal and willingly accepted by subjects. These kings started by being bene-factors of the people, making discoveries in the arts of peace or war, or welding the people together, or providing them with land. So they became kings accepted by their subjects, and for their successors in the next generation they were hereditary monarchs. They held control of leadership in war and of sacrificial matters not reserved for priests. They also pronounced judgements at law; they did this some on oath, some without oath, the oath being taken by raising aloft the royal staff or sceptre. In early times these kings had continuous control of all the affairs of the state, both in-ternal and external; but later in some cases they re-linquished some of their duties, in others they were deprived of them by the people. The duty of offering sacrifices to the gods is the only one which everywhere was left in the hands of the kings, still so called; but it is really only where they retained the leadership of armies and expeditionary forces that we can properly use the term kingship.

These then are the four forms of constitutional kingship: (1) monarchy in heroic times; it was acceptable to the people and was based on certain clearly defined duties and privileges, the king being judge, army commander, and religious head, (2) barbarian monarchy, acquired and held legally and by heredity but exercised despotically, (3) *aesym-nēteia* or elective dictatorship, and (4) the Lacedaemonian monarchy, hardly more than a hereditary generalship tenable for life. These are the distinguishing marks of these four kinds. But there is also a fifth, not restricted in any of these ways, in which the king single-handed is in control of everything: he has the same independence as each separate nation or state has in controlling its own affairs, which it manages in the same way as a household is managed. For household management is, as it were, the royal power of the house; so what I call Absolute Kingship is the entire administration of a state or of a nation or nations.

The first four types of monarchy were all in some way restricted; the fifth is unrestricted. Hence there are really only two main classes. Of the four limited monarchies the Lacedaemonian is taken for comparison because it is the most restricted. But for that very reason it is not typical of monarchy; limitation of royal power involves some distribution of power, which takes place also under any other system of government. Hence only absolute monarchy needs to be discussed in this connexion. And this at once raises a problem: so long as we were discussing distribution of power under oligarchy or democracy, we were led to the conclusion (end of Chapter 11) that where possible the laws should be sovereign. But now we have postulated a monarch who makes his own laws and whose superlative excellence appears to entitle him to do so. The answer to the question what is to be done in such an event is not given till the end of the book (Chapters 17 and 18), and what follows now has relevance to any form of state in which personal authority and legal authority could exist side by side.

15

We may say then that there are really only two types of kingship to be considered – the absolute and the Lacedaemonian. The others fall between these two extremes for the most part, as having less power than the absolute but more than the Lacedaemonian. So there are two questions to be asked, first whether or not it is a good thing for states to have a perpetual commander-in-chief, appointed either by birth or by election, and second whether or not it is a good thing that one man should have full powers in all matters. The former question, relating to generalship of the kind mentioned, is concerned with laws rather than constitutions, since it is possible for such an office to exist under any constitution. I am therefore leaving it aside and concentrating on the other, because it relates to kingship as a form of constitution. We must therefore examine it and attack the problems that we find there.

We must begin by asking an old and fundamental question – whether it is better to be ruled by the Best Man or by the Best Laws. It is the view of those who believe that monarchical government is good that the laws enunciate only general principles and cannot therefore give day-to-day instructions on matters as they arise; and so, they argue, in any kind of work that requires skill it is foolish to be guided always by the book or by the letter of the law. Even in Egypt a doctor is allowed to depart from his text-book instructions if the patient is not well after four days; if he does so earlier, he does it at his own risk. For the same reason it is obvious that to rule by the letter of the law or out of a book is not the best method.

On the other hand, rulers cannot do without a general principle to guide them; it provides something which, being without personal feelings, is better than that which by its nature does feel. A human being must have feelings; a law has none. Against that one might say that a man will give sounder counsel than law in individual cases. It seems clear then that there must be a lawgiver – the ruler himself, but also that laws must be laid down, which shall be binding in all cases, except those in which they fail to meet the situation. What happens in such cases? When the law either will not work at all or will only work badly, ought the power to act rest with the one best man or with all the citizens?

In our own day verdicts are given, recommendations are made, decisions are arrived at, by men acting together, and all these decisions refer to separate problems and individual cases. Now any one individual, when compared to the rest, may be inferior. But the state consists of many men and this gives it the same kind of superiority as a communally provided banquet has over one that is offered by a single person. Therefore the many are on numerous occasions also better judges than one man, whoever he may be.

Again, the many are less easily corrupted or 'squared'. As a larger amount of water is less easily polluted, so a larger number of people is less easily corrupted than a few. The judgement of one man is bound to be warped if he is in a bad temper or has very strong feelings about something. But in the other case it would take a lot of doing to arrange for all simultaneously to lose their tempers and warp their judgements.

If we accept this, we must make sure first, that the many are also the free-born and second, that they only depart from the provisions of the law in cases which the law itself cannot be made to cover. This latter may not be at all easy to secure where numbers are large; but if the good, that is good men and good citizens, are in the majority, then when we put the question 'Which is the least liable to be corrupted, the sole ruler or the numerically larger body who are all good?', the answer can only be 'the larger body'. And if it is urged that the many will split into fractions, which the one cannot do, the answer is that they too are good and serious-minded people no less than your 'one man'. If then we may describe this rule of the majority who are all good as rule of the best men, true aristocracy, and the rule of one as a kingship (and therefore good of its kind), then as a form of government for states aristocracy is preferable to kingship.*

Here now a digression. Aristotle speculates as to what may have been the course of early constitutional development. He gives a different reconstruction in the next book (IV, 13). But these speculations and generalizations about the past that occur in Plato and Aristotle are to be regarded as part of their philosophical armoury, not as part of their historical equipment.

Perhaps we have here a clue to the reason why monarchical rule first started, namely the difficulty of finding

* The presence or absence of armed forces is unimportant; the essential is to get a homogeneously good majority.

enough men of outstanding ability and virtue, all the greater since in those days populations were small. An especial function of good men is to confer benefits and it was in recognition of the good that they had done that good men were appointed to be kings. Then, when a larger number of equally good men became available, people no longer tolerated one-man rule but looked for something communal, and set up a constitution. But the good men did not remain good; they began to make a profit out of that which was the common property of all. And to that we may plausibly ascribe the origin of oligarchies, since love of money is a mark of the oligarch. The next change was to tyrannies, and from tyrannies to democracy. For the struggle to get rich at all costs tends to reduce the numbers of the rich and so increase the power of the masses, who rise up and form democracies. And now that there has been an all-round increase in the size of cities, one might say that it is hard to avoid having a democratic constitution.

Some problems connected with kingship.

Those who hold that it is best for states to be ruled by kings will have to consider some further questions, such as those relating to the king's sons. Are his offspring also to be kings? Considering what kind of persons some of these have turned out to be, we would have to say that hereditary succession is harmful. You may modify the principle by giving the king power to depart from it. But it is hard to believe that he will ever *not* hand on his kingdom to his children; that would be to expect too much of human nature. Then there is this question of armed force; is the intending monarch to have about him a bodyguard, with which he will be able to impose his will on those who seek to resist his rule? Or how is he to make his authority effective? For even if his authority is such that he can only act in accordance with the law and do nothing of his own volition that is contrary to law, it will still be necessary for him to have sufficient power to secure the observance of the laws. This question, in so far as it relates to this kind of king whose powers are limited by the constitution, is perhaps not difficult to answer. He must have armed force, and it should be strong enough to overpower one man or a band of men but not the whole population. This is the principle which was followed in earlier times, when guards were assigned to a man who was being named as tyrant or *aesymnētēs*; so too, when Dionysius asked for a bodyguard, somebody advised the Syracusans to limit it to just the number required for that purpose.

Aristotle has wandered away from the question posed at the beginning of the chapter (15). All these discussions about the relations between monarchy and law have been concerned not with absolute but with constitutional monarchy – a subject which he professed to have dropped. He now returns to absolute monarchy, repeats something of what he said at the beginning of Chapter 15, and then once again discusses the authority of the law and the authority of the individual. It looks as if there may have been at one time a double set of Aristotle's notes.

16

We must now turn to consider the other kind of king, whose every act is in accordance with his own personal volition. For the kind of monarchy that is called 'constitutional' does not, as has already been pointed out, belong to any one form of constitution; perpetual generalships may exist in democracy or in aristocracy or in any other constitution; and it is not unusual to put one man in charge of the whole administration, as is done in Epidamnus and to a lesser extent in Opus. But we are now speaking of absolute kingship, meaning by that one whereby the king rules over everything according to his own will and pleasure.

There are some who hold that it is not in accordance with nature that one man should be in authority over all the citizens, when the state is made up of persons who are equal. For, they say, natural equals must have the same natural rights and status; and so, if it is bad for the health of different, and therefore unequal, persons to have the same, and therefore equal, diet or clothing, this is also applicable to honours and offices: and the converse also is true. Justice therefore demands that no one should do more ruling than being ruled, but that all should have their turn. So we are back again with law, for this arrangement for taking turns *is* law. It follows therefore that it is preferable that law should rule rather than any single one of the citizens. And following this line of reasoning further we must add that even if it be shown that certain persons ought to rule, these persons should be designated protectors of the law or its servants. Offices there must be, they say, but it is not right that there should be only one man holding them, at any rate where all are equal.

Again, in reply to the usual objection that there are matters about which the law appears incapable of giving a decision, in such cases a human being would be equally incapable of finding an answer. It is in order to meet such situations that the law first educates men and then empowers them to decide, and to deal with these undetermined matters to the very best of their just judgement. Moreover it allows for improvements to be made, wherever after trial a new proposal is shown to be better than the existing regulations. Therefore he who asks Law to rule is asking God and Intelligence and no others to rule; while he who asks for the rule of a human being is bringing in a wild beast; for human passions are like a wild beast and strong feelings lead astray rulers and the very best of men. In law you have the intellect without the passions.

Another argument used against the supremacy of law is that which uses an analogy with medicine, or other professional skill, and alleges that it is a bad thing to practise the art of healing out of a book, far better to call in those who know how to practise it. But this analogy is false. The doctor does not do anything for friendship's sake that is against his rational judgement; he cures his patient and takes his fee; but people in office of government usually do all manner of things on the basis of their likes and dislikes. Of course if you really suspected that the doctors had been bribed by your enemies to make an end of you, then you would naturally prefer 'medicine out of a book'. Again, doctors when ill call in other doctors to treat them, and trainers other trainers when they themselves go into training – on the principle that it is impossible to give true judgement when one's own interest and one's own feelings are involved.

The link between this sentence and the next one becomes apparent when we remember that it was one of Aristotle's foibles to look for the middle way and see all virtues as the mean between two extremes. The law is not committed beforehand, does not lean to one side or the other, and this is right. Some disconnected observations follow.

So it is clear that the search for what is right is a search for the mean; for *the law is the mean.*

Laws of morality are both more binding and more fundamental than positive law; so that if a man, as ruler, is less fallible than written laws, he is more fallible than laws of morality.

Of course, if a man is the only ruler, there will be much that he cannot easily supervise; he will therefore need to have other officials appointed under him; it makes no difference whether these were there at the beginning of his rule or were appointed subsequently. Besides, if, as has been said before, a good man has a right to rule because he is better, then two good men are better than one. Hence the Homeric expression 'Let two go together' and Agamemnon's prayer 'Would that I had ten such counsellors'.

In our own day there are officials, such as judges, who are empowered to give decisions about matters on which the law is not able to decide. But it is generally agreed that where the law is capable, its decisions should stand as authoritative. But there are things which can and others which cannot be included in laws; and it is this fact that gives rise to difficulties and raises the old question, Which is preferable, the rule of the best man or the rule of the best law? Among the matters which cannot be included in laws are all those which are generally decided by deliberation. The advocates of the rule of law do not deny this, do not suggest that the intervention of a human being in such decisions is unnecessary; they merely say that there should be not one person only but many. An individual ruler, if he has been educated by the law, may be expected to give good decisions, but he has only one pair of eyes and ears, one pair of feet and hands, and cannot possibly be expected to judge and to act better than many men with many pairs. Monarchical rulers, as we see in our own times, knowing this, appoint a number of people to be their eyes and ears, hands and feet; for these same people, being friendly to their rule, they make sharers in it. If they are not friends, they will not act according to the king's will, which is the basis of monarchy. On the other hand if they are friends, both of the king and his rule, monarchy still breaks down, because a friend must be equal and similar. Therefore if the king thinks that these men ought to share in the government, he is thereby declaring that equal and similar persons ought to rule; and this is the contention of the opponents of kingship.

Thus we return to absolute kingship, some objections to which have just been stated.

17

But these objections, though valid in some cases, are perhaps not valid in others. For surely there exist in the natural order of things (1) that which requires to be ruled by a master, (2) that which requires to be ruled by a king, and (3) that for which constitutional rule by citizens is both just and expedient.* But from what has already been said it is clear that among those who are equal and alike, it is neither just nor expedient that one single man should be in authority over all the rest, whether he rule with laws or without, he himself then being law, and whether he is a good man ruling over good men, or not good over not good, nor even if he excel in goodness, except in certain circumstances.

What these circumstances are I must now state, though to some extent they have been stated already [end of Chapter 13]. But first I must define what is meant in this connexion by the terms 'royal', 'aristocratic', and 'citizen' or belonging to a polity.

A people requires royal rule if it is of such a kind as naturally to accept a royal family of outstanding goodness as the leaders in the state. A people should have aristocratic rule if it can be governed by free persons who are in themselves leaders, as having the ability and virtue that are required for political office. For citizen-rule a people must have some military capacity and must be able to rule and be ruled according to a law which distributes offices on a basis of merit to those who are well-off financially.

When therefore either a whole family or a single individual can be found, so outstanding in virtue and ability that his goodness outstrips that of all the rest, then we have those circumstances to which I referred, and it becomes right and just that this family should be royal and sovereign and that this one outstanding man should be king. For, as has been said earlier, this meets the requirements of that justice which *all* are wont to demand in setting up constitutions, whether they are making them aristocratic or oligarchic or democratic. For they all base claims on superiority, though the superiority is not the same in each case but differs in the way already stated [Chapter 8]. When the all-round superiority is quite outstanding, it would be wrong that such

* The rule of the tyrant does not exist in the order of nature; nor do those constitutions which we have described as 'deviations', for they are contrary to nature.

a man should be put to death or exiled or ostracized or required to be ruled over in his turn. For while the part is not naturally greater than the whole, yet that is exactly the position of one so outstandingly excellent as I have described. There is therefore nothing for it but to obey such a man and accept him as sovereign, not in alternation but absolutely and completely.

On kingship then and on its various forms and whether or not it is a good thing for states, and for which states, and in what manner, to all those questions let these be our answers.

It will be noticed that Aristotle has really said very little about absolute kingship, either the kind of man or the circumstances in which absolutism is a good thing. This makes it impossible to say with certainty whether he had Alexander the Great in mind or not; but at least we can say that there is no mention of great conquests as a necessary qualification for monarchy. Next follows a tail-piece which looks back over Book III and forward to discussions which are given in Book VII.

18

But since we say that there are three right constitutions and that of these the best must of necessity be that which is administered by the best men (and that may mean one man alone, or one entire family, or a people outstanding in goodness, some able to rule, others to be ruled, with a view to the most desirable life), and since further it was shown in the earliest chapters [Chapter 4] that in the best state it is bound to happen that the goodness of the good man and of the good citizen should be identical; it follows clearly that the same method and the same means are required to make a good man and a good state, whether monarchically ruled or aristocratically. And so it will be the same education and the same morals that will make a good man that will also make a man fit to perform the duties of a citizen and those of a king. Now that these matters have been settled we must next endeavour to speak about the *best* constitution, what it is like in its nature and how it is to be brought about.

This promise is redeemed in Books VII and VIII. Hence it was for a time customary for editors to print these two books here, and even to renumber them. In the next three books the emphasis is not on the absolute best but on the most serviceable kind of constitution for actual use. To this the name 'polity' is given, as in Book III, Chapter 7. There is a general cohesiveness about Books IV, V, and VI and in the second chapter of Book IV Aristotle gives a partial table of contents. But when it comes down to detail there is much disarray.

BOOK IV

The book opens with one of Aristotle's generalizations (cf. III, 1) whose relevance becomes clear when he gives examples. Applied to the art of politiké *its effect is to show how wide is its scope. Theorists in politics are apt to neglect the practical side, and to ignore local conditions; and apart altogether from particular instances it ought to be possible to frame a constitution which would be generally serviceable; and this Aristotle finds in that 'aristocratic' democracy to which he gave the name 'polity' (III, 9).*

I

In all the arts and sciences whose subject matter is not a part but a whole and is itself wholly concerned with one class of objects, it is the task of one art or science to investigate all that appertains to that class of objects. Thus, if physical training be one such art and the body its object of study, its task is to determine what kind of things are advantageous for what kind of body and what therefore is the best kind of training; for the best must necessarily appertain to the body best endowed and best equipped. It is also the business of gymnastic to seek what is the best single form of training which will serve the greatest number. And further, even if a man has no ambition to acquire either the fitness of condition or the skill needed for athletic contests, but something less [*text uncertain*], it is the business of teacher or trainer to impart that degree of ability too. We see the same comprehensive principle at work in medicine, shipbuilding, clothing, and every other form of professional skill. And it is clearly true also of the science of politics, whose task is to discuss the best constitution, what it is and what it would be like if it could be constructed exactly as one would wish, without any hindrance from outside. But that is only its first task. Another is to consider what constitution is suited to what people. For to attain the best is perhaps impossible; so the good lawgiver and the genuine politician will have regard both to the 'absolute best' and to the 'best in the circumstances'. There is also a third which starts from what is already there; I mean he must be able to discuss also a constitution which is given, both in its original state and how once started it may last longest; I am thinking particularly of a city which falls short of the two mentioned, having neither the best constitution, with ample provision for its needs, nor yet the best possible in the circumstances. Besides these there is a fourth to be recognized – what constitution will suit all or nearly all cities. This is a practical question and the majority of those who give their views on *politeia*, however well they may do it in other respects, fail on the practical side. For we must consider not only the best but also the possible, likewise also that which is easier and more generally available.

But there are of course some today who concentrate on the search for the highest perfection, others too who talk about some general type rather than the absolute best yet neglect entirely the constitutions that are available and simply give their approval to the Lacedaemonian or some other. But what is needed is the introduction of a system of government which the people involved will accept, and feel able to operate, starting with what they have got. For it is a no less difficult task to set an existing constitution on its feet than to create one *de novo*, just as unlearning a lesson is harder than learning it in the first place. Thus it is a duty of an expert in politics, in addition to those stated, to be able to render assistance to actual states, as has just been said. But he cannot do this without knowing how many forms of constitution there are. It is today the practice among some people to say that there are only two: only one democracy, only one oligarchy. But this is not true and ignores the many differences between constitutions and the many different ways of putting them together.

The same understanding which enables our political expert to discern these will also enable him to see what laws are best, what are best fitted for the various constitutions. For one ought to frame laws to fit constitutions (as indeed is always done) not constitutions to fit laws. We may distinguish the two thus: *Constitution* is the arrangement which states adopt for the distribution of offices of power, and for the determination of sovereignty and of the end which the whole social complex in each case aims at realizing. *Laws* are distinguishable from descriptions of constitutions in that they prescribe the rules by which the rulers shall rule and shall restrain those that transgress the laws. This makes it quite clear that for the purpose of making laws it is necessary to start with knowledge of the number of constitutions and their differences one from another; it is impossible for the same laws to be good for all oligarchies and all democracies, since there are more than one form of each, both of oligarchy and of democracy.

The ideally best state should be ruled by the very best men, one or more than one, kingship or aristocracy. 'Polity' does not qualify for that, but it is the best all round for general use. It is also likely to be easily accepted because it extends citizenship to include a fairly large number; but the aristocratic principle is respected by limiting citizenship to men of virtue, of adequate intelligence, and of sufficient property.

2

In our first inquiry into constitutions we analysed them as follows: the *right* constitutions, three in number – kingship, aristocracy, and polity; the deviations from these, likewise three in number – tyranny from kingship, oligarchy from aristocracy, democracy from polity. Aristocracy and kingship* have already been discussed, and the distinctions between them drawn; we have also determined when the

* The inquiry into the best constitution is identical with the inquiry into the meanings of these two words, because both forms of constitution have the same aim, that is a way of life that is based on virtue endowed with material goods.

point is reached when kingship is to be adopted. It therefore remains to discuss polity, which is called by the name
which is common to them all, and then the other three,
oligarchy, democracy, and tyranny. As to which of these
three deviations is the worst and which the second worst –
this is obvious; for the deviation from the first and most
perfect must be the worst. Kingship, unless it is receiving a
name to which it is not entitled, must exist in virtue of the
supreme excellence of him who exercises the kingly office.
Accordingly, tyranny is the worst and is farthest away from
polity; oligarchy comes second, for aristocracy is very
different from this kind of constitution; democracy is the
least objectionable of the deviations. One of my predecessors [Plato, *Politicus* 303A] has expressed his views on
these matters, but he takes a different view from mine. He
thinks that where all are reasonably good, oligarchy and
the rest being quite workable, then democracy is the worst
of them; but when all are bad, democracy is the best. My
view is that these constitutions are entirely bad and
erroneous; and it is therefore improper to speak of one
oligarchy as better than another but only as less bad.

*The programme now outlined has reference first to the greater
part of what follows down to the end of chapter 13, where there is
another pause. The fourth and fifth of the topics here listed appear
to refer to parts of Book VI and Book V respectively.*

But let us leave that question aside and go on to discuss
(1) the differences between constitutions – we take it for
granted that there is more than one form of oligarchy and
democracy, (2) what is the most universal, the most
generally acceptable constitution after the best, and any
which is in fact well-constructed and based on the principle
of getting the best men but is at the same time suitable for
the most states – what constitution will answer to that
description? (3) among other constitutions which is preferable for whom, since probably for some democracy is

essential, for others oligarchy, (4) in what manner one who is setting up these constitutions should go to work in each several case, each particular form of both democracy and oligarchy, and lastly (5) when we have given as good and succinct an account of all these as we can, we must tackle the question what are those things which cause breakdown in constitutions, and those which keep them in going order, both the general causes and those applicable to particular cases, and what gives rise to these.

In this chapter and part of the next there is a good deal of repetition of previous remarks but also digressions from them; for example the dividing of constitutions into two main types instead of three, or, including deviations, four instead of six.

3

The reason for plurality of constitutions lies in the plurality of parts in states. We observe in the first place that all states are composed of a number of households, and then that of the population some must always be wealthy, others poor, others of moderate means; furthermore the rich and the poor are respectively armed and unarmed. We also observe that the common people are divided into three occupational classes, agricultural, commercial, and manual workers. There are also differences among the upper classes, according to their wealth and the extent of their property. We ask, for example, how many horses a man keeps.* In addition to wealth there are other *differentiae* – birth, virtue, and all the other elements to which we referred under aristocracy, when we were analysing the essential parts of any state. Sometimes all these sections of the community have a share in citizenship, sometimes the majority, sometimes less than

* Horse-rearing is always expensive. In ancient times the cities that had cavalry were the wealthy oligarchies and they made use of horses in war against states whose borders were contiguous. We see this in Chalcis and Eretria and, on the Asiatic side, Magnesia on the Maeander, and other horse-rearing areas.

that. It thus becomes clear that there must be various constitutions differing in form from each other even as their parts differ in form. A constitution is the ordering of the offices of authority; and everywhere distribution is made either on an unequal basis, according to the power and influence of the participants, or on an equal basis, that is equality between propertyless and propertied. There must therefore be as many forms of constitution as there are ways of ordering in respect of superior powers and with reference to differences between the parts. But they may all be grouped together under two heads. In the same way as the winds are sometimes classified into northerly and southerly, the rest being deviations from these, so there are two types of constitution – the democratic and the oligarchic. For aristocracy is a kind of oligarchy and polity, as we call it, a kind of democracy, as the west wind goes along with north and the east with the south. The same kind of duality some people find also in music; they lay down two modes, Dorian and Phrygian, and give one or other of these names to all musical compositions. People therefore have formed the habit of looking at constitutions in this way. But our own classification is better, as well as more accurate, keeping the terms oligarchy and democracy for the deviations. The well-constituted states are two (or perhaps only one) and all others are deviations, either from the absolutely best or from a harmonious and well-balanced mixture. These deviations we label oligarchical, if they are too closely-knit and oppressive, democratic if they are too loose and easy-going.

Numbers are not the only criterion for distinguishing oligarchy from democracy. Compare Book III, Chapter 8.

4

It is a mistake, which people habitually make today, to define democracy and oligarchy in terms too simple and absolute, saying that there is a democracy where the mass of the people is sovereign (as if the majority were not also sovereign in oligarchies and everywhere), and an oligarchy where few are sovereign. Suppose a total of one thousand three hundred; one thousand of these are rich, they give no share in government to the three hundred poor, who also are free men and in other respects like them; no one would say that these thirteen hundred lived under a democracy. Or again, suppose the poor to be few, but to hold sway over the well-to-do, who are more numerous than they, no one would call such a constitution oligarchical, unless a share in all rights were given to the others, the rich. Therefore we should say rather that it is a democracy whenever the free are sovereign, oligarchy when the rich are sovereign, but that what actually occurs is that the former are many, the latter few; many are free, few are rich. Supposing that offices of government were distributed on a basis of height, as is said to be done in Ethiopia, or of handsome appearance, then there would be an oligarchy, because the numbers of very tall or very handsome men are small. Nevertheless that does not provide adequate ways of defining these constitutions. Both consist of a number of parts, of groups of people; whenever the free are not numerous, but rule over the majority who are not free, we still cannot say that it is an oligarchy, nor that it is a democracy where the rich rule in virtue of superior numbers. These instances are not entirely imaginary: the former existed in Apollonia and Thrace; for in each of these the free population was much smaller than the rest and office was confined to those persons of distinguished ancestry who had taken part in the original settlements. The other state of affairs existed at one time in Colophon, where before the war with Lydia the majority had amassed great wealth. A democracy exists whenever those who are free and are not well-off, being in the majority, are in control of government, an oligarchy when control lies with the rich and well-born, these being few.

A comparison between the variety of animals and their parts, combined with fixity of species, and the variety of states.

That constitutions are many, and why they are many, has now been shown. Let us now start from that point [Chapter 3, beginning] and show that they are even more numerous than was stated, and say what they are and what causes them to exist. It has been agreed that every state is not a single entity, but all are composed of many parts. Now if our chosen subject were not the forms of constitution but the forms of animal life, we should first have to answer the question 'What is it essential for every animal to have in order to live?' And among those essentials we should have to include such things as organs of sense-perception, organs for the acquisition and assimilation of nourishment, mouth and stomach, and in addition parts of the body which enable the animal to move about. If these were all that we had to consider and there were differences between them, different kinds of mouth, of stomach, of sense-organs, and of locomotion, then the number of ways of combining these will necessarily make a number of different kinds of animals. For it is biologically impossible for one and the same species of animal to have different kinds of mouth or ears. So when you have included them all, all the possible combinations of these will produce forms of living creatures and the number of forms of animal life will be equal to the number of collocations of essential parts. We may apply this to the constitutions mentioned; for states too have many parts, as has often been said. These are (1) the bulk of the people concerned with food-production, tillers of the soil, (2) the part called banausic, by which we mean people who follow those occupations which are indispensable in the work of a city,* (3) the commercial, by which we mean that section which spends its time on buying and selling, wholesale and retail trade, (4) the hired labourer section, (5) the class which will defend in time of war. This last is just as in-

* Further divided into the absolutely essential and those who minister to a higher standard of comfort or of culture.

dispensable as the others, if the people is not to be at the mercy of aggressors. For I think that to give the name 'state' to a naturally subject or servile institution is one of those things that are impossible; a state is self-directing and independent, which is just what a slave is not.

This last sentence is directed against Plato Republic, *II, where a reconstruction of the simplest form of social organization did not include soldiers. Aristotle now develops this.*

For this reason I find the treatment given to this topic in the *Republic* to be more clever than convincing. For Socrates says that a city is compounded of four essential elements, and that these are the weaver, the farmer, the leatherworker, and the builder; then, finding these to be not sufficient, he adds metal-workers and those in charge of indispensable livestock, then the merchant and the retailer. This is the full complement of the first city and it is apparently based on the supposition that every such organization is formed for the sake of minimum existence and not rather for a higher purpose, also that its need for leatherworkers is equal to its need for farmers. To defenders in war he assigns no place until territorial expansion involves them in a clash with neighbours and war breaks out. And surely there also ought to be among the four, or any other number of component elements, one whose duty it will be to decide and pronounce upon matters of justice. If the mind is to be regarded as part of a living creature even more than its body, then too in cities we must regard the corresponding parts as more important than what merely conduces to utility and necessity; I mean such things as fighting-qualities and all that belongs to the administration of justice, and over and above these, that counselling faculty which is political wisdom in action. It is irrelevant to my argument whether these qualities are to be found separately in several people or in the same; it is quite normal for the same persons to be found bearing arms and tilling the soil. If then both these are to be parts of the state, it is clear that the military element is part of the state from the start.

Those who render service by their possessions are a seventh class; we call them the well-to-do. An eighth class is composed of those who are employed by the state or who render service in connexion with offices of government. A state cannot do without administrative officers, and there must be persons capable of holding office and rendering service of this kind to the city either continuously or in turn. There remain those who have just been discussed, the counsellors and those who give decisions where matters of justice are in dispute. Now if all these must exist in cities and must act in accordance with morality and justice, it becomes essential that there should be more possessed of *virtue* among those who take part in the work of the city. All other capacities may very well coexist in the same persons; the same people may be soldiers, farmers, craftsmen; judges and political counsellors may be the same. All these have some claim to virtue also and believe themselves to be capable of most of the offices of government. But the same people cannot be both rich and poor, and that is why the prime division of classes in a state is into the well-to-do and the propertyless. Further, owing to the fact that the one class is for the most part numerically small, the other large, these two appear as antagonistic classes. So constitutions reflect the predominance of one or other of these and two types of constitution emerge – democracy and oligarchy.

It is clear from the next sentence, which repeats what was said a page or two back, and from repetitions and inconsistencies which follow, that the material left by Aristotle has fallen into disarray.

That constitutions are many and why they are many has been said before; let us now show that there are more forms than one both of oligarchy and of democracy. But this too is clear from what has been said. There are on the one hand the general run of people, the demos, on the other the top people, the notables as we call them. In each of these there are numerous kinds or classes. For example among the people one set is engaged on agriculture, another on handicrafts, and yet another in the market, buying and selling. Another set take to the sea, and there engage in different pursuits – they fight or trade or carry passengers or catch fish.* To these we may add the labouring class and those whose possessions are so small that they cannot have any time off, also those who are not of free citizen birth on both sides and any other similar kind of people. The distinguishing marks of the upper class or notables are wealth, birth, virtue, education, and the like.

Classifying democracies, from moderate to extreme. The sharp distinction which Aristotle draws between a decree and a law did not exist at Athens. He is here expressing disapproval of this, rather than stating a fact.

The first, and most truly so called, variety of democracy is that which is based on the principle of equality. In such the law lays down that the poor shall not enjoy any advantage over the rich, that neither class shall dominate the other but both shall be exactly similar. For if, as is generally held, freedom is especially to be found in democracy, and also equality, this condition is best realized when all share in equal measure the whole *politeia*. But since the people are the more numerous class and the decision of the majority prevails, such apparent inequality does not prevent its being a democracy.

Democracies may also be classified according to the presence or absence of a modest property-qualification, and also according to the extent to which the constitution is

* In many places large sections of the population are engaged in occupations connected with the sea; fishermen are numerous at Tarentum and Byzantium, traders at Aegina and Chios; at Athens many are engaged in ships of war, at Tenedos in passenger traffic.

itself subject to law. Thus we have a succession: (1) Access to office dependent on property-assessment, this being kept low, but under review, so that he who possesses the requisite amount is eligible but ceases to be eligible if he loses it; (2) all citizens, unless they fail to pass a scrutiny as to birth, are eligible, but the laws are supreme; (3) everyone, provided only that he is a citizen, is eligible, but again the law is supreme; (4) the same as in the preceding but the people is sovereign and not the law. This occurs when the will of the people, expressed in decrees or resolutions, can overrule the provisions of the law. It is the popular political leaders, the demagogues, that bring about this state of affairs.

When states are democratically governed according to law, there are no demagogues; the best citizens are securely in the saddle; but where the laws are not sovereign, there you find demagogues. The people becomes monarchical, one ruler composed of many persons. What kind of multiple rulership, collective or individual, Homer meant, when he spoke of it as being a bad thing, I do not know. But at all events the monarchical demos now under discussion, not being controlled by laws, aims at absolute power and becomes like a despot, giving promotion and honour to those who curry its favour. Hence such a democracy is the exact counterpart of tyranny among monarchies; its general character is exactly the same. Both lord it over the better class of citizen and the resolutions of the one are the directives of the other; the tyrant's flatterer is the people's demagogue, each exercising influence in his sphere, flatterers on tyrants, demagogues on this type of popular body. They are able to do this primarily because they bring every question before the popular assembly, whose decrees can supersede the written laws. This greatly enhances their personal power because, while the people rule over all, *they* rule over the people's opinion, since the majority follow their lead. Moreover, when people object to the exercise of authority by officials on the ground that the authority belongs to the people, the demagogue seizes this as an excuse for abolishing the office. So if you were to say that such a democracy was not a constitution at all, you would in my opinion be perfectly right. Where laws do not rule, there is no constitution. The law ought to rule over all, and officials make rulings in individual cases; then we can speak of a constitution. So if democracy is one of the recognized constitutions, it is clear that this kind of set-up, where everything is governed by popular decree, is no true democracy; for no decree can have universal validity. So much for the classification of democracy.

A parallel list for oligarchies is now given with a note on revolutions and counter revolutions.

5

Of oligarchy there are four types: (1) access to office restricted by a property-qualification such that the not so well-off, being more numerous, have no part in government, but participation is open to him who acquires property; (2) a very high property-qualification, so high that not all offices are filled and the officials themselves make up the deficiency by a process of co-option;* (3) hereditary, son succeeding father in office; (4) also hereditary, but the officials, not the law, having sovereign power. This type of extreme oligarchy holds among oligarchies a position analogous to that of tyranny among monarchies, and to that extreme democracy of which we have just been speaking. An oligarchy of this type is sometimes called a 'power-group'.

This completes our list of types of oligarchy and democracy; but it should not be forgotten that things often turn out differently in practice. There are plenty of instances of a constitution which according to its law is not democratic, but which owing to custom and way of upbringing is

* If this co-option is made from among all, the practice is considered to be aristocratic, if from a limited group only, oligarchical.

democratic in its workings; there are likewise others which according to law incline towards democracy, but by reason of custom and upbringing operate more like oligarchies. This is especially apt to happen after revolutions involving a change of constitution. The citizens do not at once discard their old ways, but are at first content to gain only moderate advantages from their victory over the opposing side, whichever that may be. The result is that the laws which preceded the revolution continue to be valid, but power is in the hands of those who are engaged in making changes in the constitution.

Further notes on the same subject from a different angle, at times anticipating Chapter 13. Those who are legally qualified to participate fully in a constitution may not be able to afford to take office, legal or administrative. It was a mark of extreme democracy to pay holders of office a salary out of state revenues obtained from outside.

6

The statements already made have shown the various forms of democracy and oligarchy. For if we consider the sections of the population that make up the whole people, we see that either all the sections have a share in the constitution or only some and not others. When the farming element, being in possession of a moderate amount of property, is the predominant section, the work of the constitution goes on in accordance with the laws; because so long as they work they have enough to live on, but they cannot afford to take time off in order to hold office, so they install the law as guiding principle and themselves only attend the necessary meetings of the Assembly of the people. But the rest of the population, as soon as they acquire enough property to qualify them according to the law, also have the right to participate. Thus it becomes true to say that *all* property-owners participate, and this is a democracy. For where all do *not* participate, that is in general a mark of oligarchy. But to be able to take time off for public duties is not possible without support from the revenues of the state. This then is one form of democracy and we have given reasons for so calling it.

Another form of democracy based on the next distinction depends on birth, for, in addition to property, free birth is the other regular criterion. Here office is open to all about whose birth there is no question, all that is, who can afford time off. In such a democracy the laws are sovereign, because there is no revenue. Again, participation may be open to all who are free but they do not in fact participate for the reason already stated; so here too the law is inevitably sovereign. The fourth and extreme form of democracy is also in point of time the last to develop. The reason for this lies in the growth of cities. Not only are they much larger than they originally were but they have much larger revenues. This makes it possible for all citizens to participate; those who have no property of their own are able to play their part in the legal and administrative work of their state because they receive a salary for doing so. This affects the common people most of all; they have no encumbrances, while the wealthy, who have property to look after, are often unable to attend public assembly or courts of law. Thus in this fourth kind of democracy not the laws are sovereign but the bulk of the unpropertied class.

So much for the four kinds of democracy; a similar succession of types can be observed in oligarchies. First, when the property-owners are many but the total amount that they own is not large and no individual has much. Participation in government is open to every property-owner and because of the large numbers who thus become members of the citizen-body the laws and not the men are necessarily supreme. This is because it is farthest removed from the exercise of rule by a single person and because the citizens have neither so much property that they can afford to neglect it and not work at all, nor so little that they need to be subsidized by the state. Hence they are bound to think it best that the laws should rule and not they themselves. Next, when the owners of property are fewer than in the previous case and their property larger, we have the second type of oligarchy. Having more power they expect to make their position more profitable. So they restrict entry into the citizen-body from outside their number to those of their own choosing; but because they are not yet sufficiently powerful to rule without law, they legalize this method by enactments. If this restrictive process is intensified and they become fewer in number and greater in wealth, the third stage of oligarchy is reached. In this they keep offices of power in their own hands, but do so in accordance with a law which provides for sons succeeding their fathers at their death. The final stage is reached when they overtop all the rest in wealth and influence; this kind of power-group rule is near to single rule, its members rule and not the law. This is the fourth and extreme form of oligarchy, corresponding exactly to the extreme form of democracy.

Aristocracy in the strict sense has already been dealt with in Book III, to which reference is made in this chapter. But since the essential thing about an aristocratic constitution is that it is composed of the best men, the word is often loosely applied to any constitution which officially or unofficially attaches importance to choosing the best men, even when it is oligarchical in its pursuit of wealth or democratic in its interest in the common people. Such constitutions show a mixture of aims, but they are not formal mixed constitutions like 'Polity', which also is apt to get the epithet aristocratic. See Chapter 8.

7

There are besides democracy and oligarchy two constitutions, one of which – aristocracy – is generally included in the list of four – monarchy, oligarchy, democracy, aristocracy. The other makes a fifth on that list; it is called by the name which is common to them all, for we call it *politeia*, polity.* Aristocracy, which we dealt with earlier in this work, is aptly named 'rule of the best'; but the name should properly be given only to that which is composed of the absolutely best in virtue, not simply to one composed of those who are good in relation to some hypothetical standard. For it is only when absolute virtue is taken as the standard that good man and good citizen can be one and the same; the good men in other cases are good only in relation to their own form of society. However, the name aristocracy is used to mark a distinction both from oligarchy and what we call polity, that is to say, it describes a constitution in which election to office depends on merit not on wealth. This constitution differs from the other two and is called aristocratic. For even in constitutions which do not publicly associate themselves with the promotion of virtue there are nevertheless citizens of outstanding merit who are regarded as good men. So where, as at Carthage, the constitution has a threefold aim – wealth, virtue, and the good of the people – the epithet aristocratic may be applied to it, also to Sparta, where there is a dual purpose – virtue and the good of the people – and a mixing of the two, democracy and virtue. So we may say that apart from aristocracy properly so called, which is the best, there are these two and also a third which occurs when what we call polity inclines rather towards the rule of the few.

On 'polity' see Book II, Chapter 6, latter part.

8

We have still to discuss what we call polity (and also to discuss tyranny). We have placed it here because it is not a deviation-form and neither are the above-mentioned

* Owing to the fact that it is rarely found in practice it is overlooked by the typologists of constitutions, who therefore, like Plato, include only four in their list.

aristocracies. In strict truth they have all deviated from the most perfect constitution and so are counted among deviations, and these secondary aristocracies are deviations in the sense in which we spoke of them earlier. It is reasonable to defer mention of tyranny till the end because in comparison with the rest it is not really a constitution, and our whole inquiry is about constitution. Having now explained why it occupies this position I proceed to discuss polity; for now that oligarchy and democracy have been defined, the meaning and function of polity become clearer, since, to put it in a word, polity is a mixture of oligarchy and democracy.

Aristotle appears to be in a dilemma. He wants to use the term 'polity' for a mixture which contains many oligarchical elements, education and good birth, so long as these are associated with goodness, that is, so long as they are really aristocratic, but he does not approve of calling these polities aristocracies, because (Chapter 13) they were formerly called democracies. At the same time he wishes to claim for them some of the good qualities associated with the 'rule of the best'.

Those mixtures which lean more towards democracy are generally called 'polities', and those which lean towards oligarchy 'aristocracies', because education and good birth belong more to the well-to-do. Moreover the well-to-do appear to have those things for the sake of which malefactors commit crimes, hence they are called upper-class, well-educated, 'notables'. Since therefore aristocracy aims at distributing the highest positions to the best of the citizens, it is said that oligarchies also are composed on the whole of the educated classes. But one thing I think is quite impossible – that a state which is controlled not by the best but by the worst should be well and lawfully governed, and likewise that a state without good laws should be ruled by the best. It is not good and lawful government where the laws are good but are not obeyed. There are thus two ingredients in Good Order – obedience to the laws laid down and good laws to be obeyed (it is quite possible to be obedient to bad laws). Obedience may be given either to the best laws available in the circumstances or to the absolutely best.

It is the especial mark of aristocracy that distribution of offices and privileges should be made in accordance with the excellence and virtue of the recipients. Virtue is the guiding principle of aristocracy, as wealth of oligarchy, freedom of democracy.* In most cities the constitutional form of polity is made out to be more aristocratic than it really is. The aim of a mixture of oligarchy and democracy is merely to have regard to the interests of both rich and poor, both wealth and individual freedom. But oligarchic readily passes for aristocratic, since almost everywhere the well-to-do and the well-educated upper class are co-extensive. But since there are the *three* grounds for claiming equal rights in a constitution – 'I am a free man', 'I am a man of property', and 'I have character and ability',† – it is clear that the term 'polity' should be applied to the dual mixture, rich and poor, and the term 'aristocracy' kept for the triple mixture, the rich, the free, and men of 'virtue'. This however is only a second grade of aristocracy, not the true and primary.

I have now shown that there are other constitutions besides monarchy, democracy, and oligarchy, and what these are. It is clear too how the one aristocracy differs from the other, and how polity differs from aristocracy; but the two are closely related.

In making a polity by mixing oligarchy and democracy we may either (1) take two relevant features one from each and, if they are

* The majority-principle is not a distinguishing mark; it belongs to all three. In oligarchies and in aristocracies and in democracies whatever has been decided by the larger part of those who participate in the constitution – that is binding.

† A fourth claim, that based on noble birth, really arises out of the two last of these three – property and virtue. For noble birth is wealth plus virtue going back to one's forebears.

*compatible, adopt them both, or (2) take neither of them as they
stand, but effect a compromise, or (3) take half of each.*

9

Our next task is to discuss in the light of what has been
said how what we call polity stands in relation to democracy
and oligarchy, and what has to be done in order to bring it
into being. The characteristic features of democracy and
oligarchy will emerge at the same time; for we must seize
upon the differences between these and then as it were
accept a contribution from each of them and combine
them in one or other of three ways. The first is to take a
characteristic piece of legislation from both. For example,
in oligarchies they impose a fine on the wealthy for non-
attendance as judges in the law-courts and they do not pay
the less wealthy for their attendance; in democracies no
fines for non-attendance are imposed on the wealthy and
the less wealthy receive pay for their services. A combination of these would be compatible with both and mid-way
between them, and would therefore match our idea of
polity as a mixture of the two. That is one way of joining
the two. A second way is to take something intermediate
between the two sets of provisions. Thus for membership
of the national assembly in democracies there is no property-
qualification (or only a very small one), in oligarchies the
level of property-assessment is high. Here neither is compatible with the other but a level can be fixed mid-way
between. The third method is from two sets of regulations
to take one part from the oligarchical system, the other part
from the democratic. For example the filling of offices: to
do this by lot is regarded as democratic, by selection
oligarchic; a property-qualification is oligarchic, its absence
democratic. Take therefore one from each, the oligarchical
selection of officials and the democratic freedom from
property-qualification, and the result is both polity-like and
aristocratic.

So much for the method; as for the quality of the mixture,

the fusion is good whenever it is possible to describe the resulting constitution either as democracy or as oligarchy. It is surely the very excellence of the blending that creates this dual impression in those who speak of it. A middle position creates the same impression; each of the two extremes appears in it. This dual impression is given by the constitution of the Lacedaemonians. Many people try to make out that it is a democracy because it has a number of democratic features: the educational system, under which the sons of the rich are reared in the same way as the sons of the poor and receive an education which could be given also to the sons of the poor; similarly at the next stage of youth, and when they are grown up, there is no outward mark of distinction between rich and poor; and there are the same arrangements for feeding in communal messes, and the rich wear clothing which any poor man could get for himself. There is also the fact that the people choose the members of the council of elders and are eligible for the ephorate, two of the most important bodies in the state. Others call it an oligarchy because of its many oligarchical features: the absence of the use of the lot, all officials being elected; the power of the few to pronounce sentence of death or exile, and many others. A constitution which is a really well-made combination of oligarchy and democracy ought to look like both and like neither. It should also maintain itself by means of itself and not through outside agencies. It is not doing that when the number of those who wish it to continue is greater outside the country than inside it (a condition which can equally arise in a bad constitution), but only when no section of the community would wish to have a different constitution. We have now mentioned the way in which polity ought to be established and likewise the kinds which are called aristocracies.

In the following short chapter on 'tyranny' in relation to other types of monarchy Aristotle refers us to previous discussions (Book III, Chapter 14). That which is technically the rule of a tyrant

need not necessarily be without law and there are obvious resem-
blances to kingship. Mention of tyranny is therefore justified.

10

We undertook also to say something about tyranny, not
because there is much to say but so that it might take
its place in our inquiry; for even to it we assign a place of a
sort in a list of constitutions. We defined kingship in an
earlier part of this work and discussed whether kingship,
in the most usual sense of that word, was or was not a good
thing for states, also who are to be appointed kings, and how
and from what source. When dealing with kingship we also
defined two forms of tyranny, both because the type of
power exercised by a tyrant is almost interchangeable with
that exercised by kings, and because both forms of rule can
be according to law.* But the two forms of tyranny differ
from each other; in one, the more kinglike of the two, rule
is both according to law and over willing subjects, the other
is more 'tyrannical', rule despotically exercised according
to decisions of the tyrants. There is a third type of tyranny,
the most extreme and the exact converse of absolute kingship. Any sole ruler, who is not required to give an account
of himself, who rules over subjects all equal or superior
to himself and rules to suit his own interest and not theirs,
can only be described as a tyrant and his rule a tyranny of
this third kind. No one willingly submits to such a government, if he is a free man. These are the kinds of tyranny
and their respective bases.

In the eleventh chapter Aristotle returns to polity and defends it on
different grounds. The argument rests on one of his best-known
philosophical principles, that virtue is a mean between two extremes.

* For example, among certain non-Greeks, sole rulers with absolute
power are *elected* to that office; and among ancient Greeks of long ago
there were sole rulers of this type called *aesymnetae*, elected tyrants
[Book III, Chapter 14].

This ethical principle leads easily, if not very convincingly, to the doctrine of a constitutional middle way now propounded, but it is hard to reconcile it with absolute kingship. Constitutions of a middle type are extremely rare, such was the violence of Greek political strife, and Aristotle says he knows of only one in Greek history; presumably he means Solon's.

11

What is the best constitution and what is the best life for the majority of states and the majority of men? We have in mind men whose standard of virtue does not rise above that of ordinary people, who do not look for an education that demands either great natural ability or a large private fortune, who seek not an ideally perfect constitution, but, first, a way of living in which as many as possible can join and, second, a constitution within the compass of the greatest number of cities. These requirements are not fulfilled by the aristocracies that we have just been discussing; an aristocratic constitution does not fall within the competence of most cities unless it approximates closely to what we call polity. (The adherence of both to aristocratic principles allows us to use the one name.) Decision on all these points rests on a single set of elementary principles. If we were right when in our *Ethics* we stated that Virtue is a Mean and that the happy life is life free and unhindered and according to virtue, then the best life must be the middle way, consisting in a mean between two extremes which it is open to those at either end to attain. And the same principle must be applicable to the goodness or badness of cities and states. For the constitution of a city is really the way it lives.

In all states there are three sections of the community – the very well-off, the very badly-off, and those in between. Seeing therefore that it is agreed that moderation and a middle position are best, it is clear that in the matter of possessions to own a middling amount is best of all. This condition is most obedient to reason, and following reason is

171

just what is difficult both for the exceedingly rich, handsome, strong, and well-born, and for the opposite, the extremely poor, the weak, and the downtrodden. The former commit deeds of violence on a large scale, the latter are delinquent and wicked in petty ways. The misdeeds of the one class are due to *hubris*, the misdeeds of the other to rascality. Add the fact that it is among the members of the middle section that you find least reluctance to hold office as well as least eagerness to do so; and both these are detrimental to states. There are other drawbacks about the two extremes. Those who have a super-abundance of all that makes for success, strength, riches, friends, and so forth, neither wish to hold office nor understand the work; and this is ingrained in them from childhood on; even at school they are so full of their superiority that they have never learned to do what they are told. Those on the other hand who are greatly deficient in these qualities are too subservient. So they cannot command and can only obey in a servile régime, while the others cannot obey in any régime and can command only in a master-slave relationship. The result is a state not of free men but of slaves and masters, the one full of envy, the other of contempt. Nothing could be farther removed from friendship or from the whole idea of a shared partnership in a state. Sharing is a token of friendship; one does not share even a journey with people one does not like. The state aims to consist as far as possible of those who are like and equal, a condition found chiefly among the middle section. And so the best government is certain to be found in this kind of city, whose composition is, we maintain, a natural one. The middle class is also the steadiest element, the least eager for change. They neither covet, like the poor, the possessions of others, nor do others covet theirs, as the poor covet those of the rich. So they live less risky lives, not scheming and not being schemed against. Phocylides's wish was therefore justified when he wrote 'Those in the middle have many advantages; that is where I wish to be in society.'

It is clear then both that the political partnership which

operates through the middle class is best, and also that those cities have every chance of being well-governed in which the middle class is large, stronger if possible than the other two together, or at any rate stronger than one of them. For the addition of its weight to either side will turn the balance and prevent the extravagances of the opposition. For this reason it is a happy state of affairs when those who take part in the life of the state have a moderate but adequate amount of property; for where one set of people possesses a great deal and the other nothing, the result is either extreme democracy or unmixed oligarchy or a tyranny due to the excesses of the other two. Tyranny often emerges from an over-enthusiastic democracy or from an oligarchy, but much more rarely from middle-class constitutions or from those very near to them. The reason for this we will speak of later when we deal with changes in constitutions.

The superiority of the middle type of constitution is clear also from the fact that it alone is free from fighting among factions. Where the middle element is large, there least of all arise faction and counter-faction among citizens. And for the same reason the larger states are free from danger of splitting; they are strong in the middle. In small states it is easy for the whole body of citizens to become divided into two, leaving no middle at all, and they are nearly all either rich or poor. Democracies too are safer than oligarchies in this respect and longer lasting thanks to their middle class, which is always more numerous and more politically important in democracies than in oligarchies. For when the unpropertied class without the support of a middle class gets on top by weight of numbers, things go badly and they soon come to grief.

An indication of the truth of what we have been saying is to be found in the fact that the best lawgivers have come from the middle class of citizens – Solon, for example, whose middle position is revealed in his poems, and Lycurgus, who was not a king at Sparta, and Charondas and most of the rest. The facts also show why most states have been either democratic or oligarchic; for the middle class being frequently small, whichever of the two extremes, the property-owners or the people, is on top ignores the middle section and conducts the government according to its own notions, and so the result is either democracy or oligarchy. Then again, owing to constant strife and civil war between the people and the wealthier class, neither side, whichever of the two succeeds in gaining the mastery, ever sets up a constitution fair and acceptable all round. Taking political supremacy as a prize of victory they proceed to make a democratic or an oligarchic régime as the case may be. Also, the great cities, when they come to exercise ascendancy over other Greek states, installed democracies or oligarchies in them according to the constitution which each had at home, looking entirely to their own advantage, not to that of the cities themselves. So for these reasons a really 'middle' kind of constitution is seldom or never encountered anywhere. Only one of a long succession of statesmen succeeded with the consent of his fellow citizens in introducing a social order of this kind. And to this day into whatever city you go, you will find that they do not even want a fair settlement; the aim is to get on top, failing which they accept a condition of defeat.

Which constitution is best for the majority, and the reasons for deeming it the best, will be clear from the above. As for all the rest, the different kinds of oligarchy and democracy which we say there are, it is not difficult to arrange them in order of merit, this one better, that one worse; for now that the best is decided upon, proximity to it denotes better, and the farther away one moves from middle-polity, the worse; unless of course one postulates a different standard, for it is possible to discard the preferable in favour of the more expedient.

12

It is most proper to follow what has been said by a discussion of the question what constitution is advantageous for what states, what kind of society for what kind of people.

First we must grasp a principle which is universally applicable to them all: it is essential that that part of the population which desires the maintenance of the constitution should be larger than that which does not. Now every state can be measured either qualitatively or quantitatively, I mean by such qualities as freedom, wealth, education, and good birth, or by quantity, that is by numerical superiority. Look at the parts which make up a state; it is possible that quality may be present in one, quantity in another. The non-noble may be numerically greater than the noble, the poor than the rich; but the quantitative superiority is not enough to outweigh the qualitative inferiority. These must be weighed one against the other. Where the number of the poor is sufficiently large to outweigh any qualitative defeat, there democracy is natural; and the type of democracy will depend on the type of people which has the numerical superiority in each case. Thus, if those who cultivate the soil make up the superior numbers, the democracy will be at the top of the scale; if those engaged in menial work and receiving pay for it predominate, then it will be at the bottom, and the rest in-between. Where, on the other hand, the rich and important people have a greater qualitative superiority than quantitative inferiority, there is oligarchy; and once again its type will depend on the degree of qualitative superiority in those who form the oligarchy.

But at all times a legislator ought to endeavour to attach the middle section of the population firmly to the constitution. If he is framing laws oligarchical in character, he should have the middle class always in view; if democratic, he should again make them attractive to the middle class. Wherever the number of the middle class is larger than a combination of the two extremes, or even than one only, then there is a good chance of permanence for the constitution. There is no danger of rich and poor making common cause against *them*; for neither will want to be subservient to the other, and if they are looking for a compromise, they will not find any better than the middle-class polity which they have already. Their mistrust of each other would make it impossible for them to accept the system of alternation in office. But on all occasions the mediator is well trusted by parties, and the one in the middle is mediator. The better mixed a constitution is, the longer it will last. It is a mistake made by many, even by those seeking to make an aristocratic constitution, not only to give too great preponderance to the rich, but to cheat the people. In the long run mistaken good gives rise to unmistakable evil; for the successful power-grabbing of the rich does more harm to society than lust for power in the people.

Mention has twice been made of the need to convince the majority in a state that it is in their interests that the constitution should be maintained. Some of the less straightforward ways which are employed for this purpose are now mentioned. Oligarchy can be made to appear less objectionable to the people in five ways, and these may even strengthen its position. It is less easy for democracies to delude oligarchs, and the question becomes merged in the general question of mixing the two into a moderate polity. But it is by no means clear when Aristotle is using politeia *in the general sense of constitution and when he means his middle-class 'polity'.*

13

There are various devices which may be employed in order to give a constitution a more attractive appearance. An oligarchy has five lines of approach to the people – the Assembly, the offices of power, the law-courts, the carrying of arms, and the institutions of physical training. Thus first, membership of the Assembly may be open to all, fines for non-attendance imposed only on the rich (or much larger fines on them than on others). Next the offices: those above a certain property-qualification are not allowed to decline office on the grounds of its expense, but the poor are. Thirdly the law courts: fines are imposed on the rich if they do not serve but the poor are exempt (or else, as in Charondas's laws, small fines in the one case, large in the other). Sometimes membership both of Assembly and jury-court is thrown open to any persons who ask to have their names put on the roll; but if, being thus enrolled, they fail to appear in the Assembly or the court, they incur large fines. It is the deliberate intention that the threat of a fine should cause people to avoid enrolment; and non-enrolment means that they attend neither law-court nor Assembly. Similar regulations are made about carrying arms and gymnastic training. It is lawful for the poor not to possess arms; the rich are fined if they do not have them. And if they fail to attend gymnasia, there is a penalty for the rich but none for the poor. Thus the possibility of a penalty causes the rich to attend; the poor, having no penalty to fear, absent themselves.

These are oligarchical devices in the framing of regulations; in democracies they are made in the opposite sense. They provide pay for the poor who attend Assembly or law-court and impose no fine on the rich for non-attendance. That is why, if it is desired to make a fair mixture of oligarchy and democracy, the right thing to do is to draw upon both sides and include both the payment and the fine. In this way all have a share; otherwise the resultant constitution will be in the hands of one set or the other. In principle citizenship ought to be reserved for those who can afford to carry arms. This means imposing a property-qualification, which cannot be done absolutely and once and for all. The amount must be fixed no lower than is absolutely necessary to ensure that the number of those who qualify is larger than those who do not. For the poor are generally content not to be eligible for the highest offices, provided only that they are not liable to be ill-treated or deprived of what is their own. That, however, is far from easy to get; those who hold political power do not always behave like gentlemen. In time of war those who have no resources of their own are reluctant to serve as soldiers unless they are fed, but are quite ready to fight if rations are provided. In some states the citizen-body includes those who have served as hoplites as well as those now in service; this was the case in Malis, but only those actually serving were elected to hold office. The earliest constitution (after kingship) among the Greeks was in fact composed of warriors, of the cavalry in the first place,* then, when cities became larger and the infantry stronger, these too were included and the number of citizens became much larger. For this reason what we nowadays call 'polities' were formerly called democracies. But the polities of those early times strike us very naturally as being oligarchical or royal; for owing to the smallness of the population their middle class was not large, and so, being neither numerous nor well-organized, they were more content to allow others to rule.

We have now stated why constitutions are of various kinds, why there are others besides those commonly mentioned (not one kind only of democracy, and the rest similarly) and further what are the differences and the causes of them, and in addition which, speaking generally, is the best of the constitutions and which of the others suits what kind of people.

The above summary only partly corresponds to the first three items in the 'table of contents' given in Chapter 2. The remainder of this book deals chiefly with the processes involved in government in different constitutions, a topic which follows naturally enough, since there is practical value in it and the book began with a reminder of the need to be practical as well as theoretical. Whatever be the form of government, it must provide for three things (1) discussion and decision about what is to be done, (2) officers of state of all grades to carry out the policy, and (3) a judicial system. On the investigation (euthuna) referred to in this chapter see below, Chapter 16.

14

In dealing with our next topic, how government works, we must speak again about the constitutions, both in general

* Because they were the first to be organized in fighting units, which gave them preponderant strength. The ancients had no experience and no organization, without which infantry is useless, so that the strength rested with the cavalry.

terms applicable to all and also severally, using in each case the appropriate starting point. There are three elements in all constitutions, and every serious lawgiver must look for the best set-up for each of the three; if these are well done, the constitution will be well made, and the differences in constitutions correspond to the different set-up in each case. The three elements are, first, the deliberative, discussion about everything of national importance, second, the executive, the whole complex of officials and authorities, their number and nature, the limits of their powers, and the methods by which they are selected, and third, the judicial system.

The powers of the deliberative or policy-making element cover decisions as to war and peace, the making and dissolving of alliances, legislation, the penalties of death, exile and confiscation of goods, the election of officials, and the investigation into their conduct during tenure. The right to decide on all these matters must either be given to all the citizens or all to some (e.g. to one or more official body) or some to certain persons, others to others, or some to all, others to some. To give all the citizens sovereign power in all matters is democratic; such complete equality is the aim of the demos everywhere.

There are various ways in which the 'all to all' principle may be applied: First, all perform the work but they do so by sections,* and only come together for legislation and for constitutional matters and to hear pronouncements from the officials. A second method also involves collective responsibility of all, but they come together only for the purposes of electing officials, making laws, deciding on war and peace, and holding investigations; the remaining matters being dealt with on the recommendations of officials appointed for the purpose in each case, these officials being appointed either by lot or by selection. A third method is for all the

* As in the constitution of Telecles at Miletus. In others too there is an arrangement whereby only the officials for the time being deliberate, but all the citizens enter upon office in turn, from the tribes and the smallest parts until the whole process is complete.

citizens to meet together over offices and investigations, to deliberate on wars and alliances, but for the rest, the officials, chosen as far as possible for the purpose, manage everything; expert knowledge is an essential prerequisite for such officials. Under the fourth method all come together to deliberate about everything, and the officials take no final decisions but only provisional. This is the way a modern extreme democracy works and it corresponds to an oligarchy that is run by a power-group and to a monarchy that is a tyranny.

All these four methods are in principle democratic; where only some decide about all matters, the principle is oligarchic. This principle likewise can be applied in different ways: first, when those eligible to participate in deliberation are selected on the basis of a property-qualification that is not too high, and are on that account fairly numerous, when they obey the law and do not attempt what it forbids, when the attainment of the required property level confers the right to participate, then, though an oligarchy, such a constitution by reason of its moderation deserves the name 'politic'. Next, when not all these participate in deliberation but only a pre-selected few, then, even though they rule according to law no less than the previous set, it should be called 'oligarchic'. When again those who make up the deliberating authority themselves co-opt their own new members, and further son succeeds father, and they have power over the laws, that arrangement is essentially and in the fullest sense oligarchical. Finally, when all have control of certain matters, such as war and peace and investigations, and the rest are left to the officials who are appointed by selection, the constitution is an aristocracy. Also, some matters may be under the control of selected persons, others of those chosen by lot, and these latter may be taken either from all or from a pre-selected few, or the selected and the lot-chosen may function together. Some of these features are characteristic of aristocracy, others of polity itself.

We have now analysed the deliberative element in relation to the constitutions. And the administration of each constitution corresponds to a different point in our analysis. But for a democracy in the fullest sense (I mean one in which the people is sovereign even over the laws) it will be found advantageous to adopt for the deliberative element a procedure used by oligarchies for the judicial. I am referring to their practice of using fines for non-attendance as a means of making sure that those whom they want to serve as judges really do appear in court.* To do this in relation to the citizen-assembly would, as I say, be beneficial, as it will ensure the presence of the upper class as well as the common people, and they will deliberate the better when they do so together. It is a good thing also that the membership of the deliberative element should be determined either by selection or by lot, and, if by lot, then an equal number from all sections of the population; and whenever the popular party is numerically much superior to the rest of the members of the *polis*, it is a good thing not to provide pay for them all for their attendance, but to pay only a number equal to the number of upper-class members. The remainder will then either be unpaid or excluded altogether.

In oligarchies on the other hand it will be found expedient to pick a few extra members from the people or else, as is frequently done, to set up a committee (Pre-councillors, Law-guardians, are names sometimes given), and then to deal only with such business as has already been through their hands. In this way the demos will participate in deliberation without being able to set aside the provisions of the constitution; it will moreover pass resolutions that are identical or at any rate not inconsistent with the recommendations of the committee. Another alternative is to bestow only advisory powers on the whole body, reserving full deliberative powers for the officials of the committee. To do this one is obliged to do just the opposite of what is done in polities and make the people sovereign when it rejects, not sovereign when it comes to any other decision; for then there must be a further reference to the committee for

* Democratic governments, wishing to secure the attendance of the poor, provide pay for them.

ratification. In the constitutions which are truly polities they act in the reverse manner; the smaller body has an absolute right of veto, but not of giving a final decision in any other sense; the matter is then always referred to the larger body. This then is the way in which an account should be given of the deliberative and sovereign element in the constitution.

Not all executive offices are offices of authority involving ruling: but after some inconclusive remarks the search for a definition is dropped as being one of academic interest only.

15

Next, great variety is also to be found in the working of the executive element, the officials and their offices; questions arise about their number and their powers, about length of tenure of office (six months in some cases, in some even less, a year very often, but also longer periods). Should tenure be for life or for a very long period? And if neither of these, then the question arises whether a man should hold office for one period only or be eligible for a second term. Then there is the setting up of the executive authorities – of whom are they to be composed, by whom appointed, and in what manner? We ought to be able in all these matters to determine how many different ways there are and then apply them, looking to see what manner of offices and officials are best for what types of constitution.

Another question, and one not easy to answer, is how to define 'office of authority'; what kind of officers can be regarded as ruling? The association which we call the political, the state, needs a great many people to take charge of various things, so many that we cannot designate them all as rulers, neither those appointed by lot nor those elected. I am thinking in the first instance of the priests, whose office is quite different from the political offices. Then there are the heralds and the trainers of choruses; envoys to be sent abroad are also appointed by selection. Some of the matters to be taken charge of are political in themselves but others are, rather, economic. Of the political some may affect all the citizens (e.g. the office of general while they are under arms), or affect a section only (e.g. controller of women or children). A common type of economic officer (who is also frequently elected) is food-controller. There are also menial jobs which, when resources permit, will be performed by slaves. Roughly speaking we may say that offices of authority are those empowered to deliberate and make decisions on certain matters and to issue orders, particularly this last, since command is the essence of rule and authority. All this makes hardly any difference in practice; disputes about the terms have not resulted in any decision. But it is a question which has further philosophical implications.

Turning to more practical questions we ask what and how many are the essential offices, essential, that is, if there is to be a state at all; we ask also which offices without being essential are yet useful for a good constitution. Such questions need to be discussed in relation to every constitution and in particular to small states. For in the larger states it is both possible and necessary to assign separate tasks to separate officials, one to each man,* whereas in the smaller a number of offices have to be concentrated in a few hands.† But sometimes the small cities require the same offices and laws as the large, but the small need the same persons to serve frequently, in the others this need arises only at long intervals. Thus there is really no reason why a number of different responsibilities should not be assigned to a single body; they can be kept separate in practice, and as a way of counteracting lack of manpower it is essential to make committees serve more than one purpose. A hook will hang a roast as well as a lamp. If therefore we can say how many

---

* Possible because of the larger population; it is open to many to take office and one man never takes the same office twice, or only after a long interval: necessary because every assignment gets better attention when it is the business of one official not of many.

† On account of the small population. It is not easy for many to hold office; for who will there be to succeed those in office?

offices are essential for any city at all, and how many are non-essential but still ought to be there – knowing all this it will be easier to deduce what offices are fit to be amalgamated into one.

Another point not to be overlooked is fittingly mentioned here: What matters ought to be dealt with by setting up separate authorities in different places, and which others by a single authority, whose writ is valid everywhere? I am thinking of such matters as keeping order in the busy city-centres. Should there be a separate market-controller in every place or one for everywhere? Should work be distributed in assignments according to the kind of work or according to the persons holding office? Is all regulation of good order a task for one man or is it different in relation to women and children? Similar questions arise when we consider offices in relation to constitutions. Does the constitution make any qualitative difference in the office? Thus, are the same officials equally competent at law in democracy, in oligarchy, in aristocracy, and in monarchy, though differing of course in the persons composing them, in aristocracies the well-educated, in oligarchies the rich, in democracies the free born? Or are some really different in respect of differences in the offices, and in some places do the same offices serve best, in others different offices? For it may happen that here a powerful, there a minor, office fits the situation best.

There are however offices peculiar to certain places and not found everywhere. For example the 'pre-council' committee already mentioned. This is not a democratic institution but the *Boulē* or Council itself is; for a body of this kind whose duty it is to go through the business beforehand and arrange it is necessary so that the demos shall get through its work. If this council consists of only a few men, the whole set-up is oligarchical. A pre-arranging committee must necessarily be few in number; therefore this is always an oligarchical feature. Where both council and committee exist, there the members of the committee have greater power than the ordinary members of the council; for the office of councillor is democratic, that of 'pre-councillor' oligarchic.

The power of the council may be weakened at the other end also, as in those democracies in which the people itself takes a hand in everything. This is apt to happen wherever members of the people's Assembly are well paid for their attendance, because this gives them time off to come to meetings regularly and decide everything themselves. Controller of children, controller of women, and officers with duties similar to these are aristocratic not democratic; for who could prevent the women of the lower classes from going out when they want to? It is not oligarchic either, for the wives of oligarchic rulers are rich and pampered.

The remainder of this chapter does not show Aristotle at his best or most lucid. Yet it is typical of his method; only that here he carries mechanical analysis and schematization beyond the point where they serve any useful purpose.

So much for the present on these matters; I must next try to describe the setting up of offices from the beginning. The different ways in which this can be done fall into three main groups, the combination and permutation of which will necessarily be found to include all the ways. First we ask who are those who make the appointments, second, from among whom do they make them, third in what manner is it done. To each of these three questions there are three pairs of alternative answers: either all citizens appoint or only some do; appointments are made either from all citizens or from a class set apart (the qualification for which may be a property-amount or good birth or merit or even some quite other thing) * and the method may be either the lot or selection. Again, each of these pairs may be combined thus: some appoint to some offices, all appoint to others; some offices filled from all, others from some; some filled by lot, others by selection. Of each of these there are four different alternatives: all from all by selection or all from all by lot (either from all at once or by sections one at a time – tribe, deme, or

* As at Megara, where only those qualified who had been among the returning exiles who had fought against the people.

brotherhood, and so on through all the citizens, or else from all on every occasion) or there may be alternation of the two. Again, if the appointers are only some not all, the appointments may be made either by selection from among all or by lot from among all, or by selection from a class or by lot from a class, or partly one way and partly the other, I mean partly by lot, partly by selection. This gives twelve methods in addition to the two combinations. Of these the two 'all from all' methods are democratic – all from all either by lot or by selection or by both, that is, appoint to some offices by lot, to others by selection. But that not all should appoint but only some, doing so at one time and either from among all or from a class, by lot or selection or both (that is, some by lot, some by selection) – *that* is 'politic', characteristic of polity. To appoint some from all, either by lot or by selection or both, is also politic but aristocratically so; it is more oligarchic when some offices are filled from all, others from a class only. Thoroughly oligarchic is it when a class appoints from a class, both a class from a class by lot (it makes no difference that this is not in fact done) and a class from a class by both methods. When some only select from among all, and all then select from those thus selected, that is aristocratic.

Such then are the number, nature, and distribution in relation to the different constitutions of the ways of setting up offices. Which way is best for what people and how they should be brought into operation are questions which can only be decided in conjunction with decisions about what offices there shall be and what shall be their spheres of authority. By 'spheres of authority' I mean such things as control of revenue and control of security; the latter, which falls under the authority of a *stratēgos* or general, is very different from the central commercial transactions and contracts.

Next the judicial system is summarily treated. It is assumed that there will be a separate court for each of the eight main types of suit. The first of these to be mentioned is the 'euthuna', *a scrutiny or investigation made before an outgoing official can obtain a 'clearance', and not necessarily a proceeding against him. It is strange that there is no mention of suits about legacies and about property generally, which we know to have been of frequent occurrence. But the whole chapter is only a series of scraps and unfulfilled intentions.*

16

Of the three elements, only the judiciary now remains to be discussed. Its various forms may be analysed on the same basis as the other two elements. There are three *differentiae* of courts of law: we may classify them according (1) to the persons composing them, (2) to the matters coming under their jurisdiction, (3) to the manner of appointment. In regard to the first we ask whether members are drawn from all or from a class; in regard to the second we ask how many types of court-cases there are; in regard to the third we ask whether appointment is by lot or by selection. I begin with the second of these, the types of court. There are eight of these (1) investigations, (2) offences against the public weal, (3) offences against the constitution, (4) disputes between officials and others about imposition of fines, (5) cases relating to private contractual obligations of some magnitude, (6) slayings,* (7) foreigners,† (8) relating to minor transactions involving sums between one drachma and five, or a little more; for even these require a legal decision though not a large court. I will say no more about these cases or about cases of murder or about those involving foreigners, but will speak of those relating to the body-politic; for if these are mismanaged, serious cleavages and even revolutionary changes in constitutions are likely to follow.

---

* These trials will be of four kinds (whether before the same or a different set of judges) – (1) deliberate slaying, (2) unintentional slaying, (3) where the offence is admitted but justification is claimed, (4) where the charge is brought against persons exiled for murder and now returned. A reputed example of this is the court in Phreatto at Athens, but such courts are rare at all times and only to be found in the larger cities.

† Two kinds, one for foreigners disputing with foreigners, the other for foreigners disputing with citizens.

All will act as judges in all the cases classified, being appointed inevitably either by lot or by selection, or partly one way and partly the other, or else, dealing with certain types of identical cases, some by lot others by selection. Thus there are four types; and four others where the appointments to the jury-courts are made on a sectional, not on a universal basis. For once again, those who judge on all matters may be chosen from a section only (or partly by choice and partly by lot) or some courts dealing with some matters may consist of both elected members and members appointed by lot. These then are the types. But in appointments to the judiciary too we may have a combination of methods, part of a court appointed from among all, part from a section or class; or both together, as happens if members of the same court are appointed some from all, others from some, and either by selection or by lot or by both. The possible ways of constituting courts of law have now been stated; of these the first (all from all) is democratic, the second (some from all) is oligarchic, the third (partly from all and partly from some) is aristocratic and politic.

The fifth book fulfils one of the promises made in the second chapter of Book IV – to discuss both the preservation and the dissolution of constitutions and the causes which lead to these. Minor changes not amounting to dissolution are briefly mentioned; but Aristotle is thinking chiefly of revolutions, carried through violently and resulting in a new constitution. This was the type of change most familiar and most feared; hence the anxiety to avoid all change and to cultivate stability: discontent is a constant threat to stability; and inequality, being a kind of injustice, is a potent cause of discontent. There is reference to Book III, Chapter 12, where the 'just' and the 'equal' and the two kinds of equality have been discussed. As there is more equality in democracy than in oligarchy, the former is generally the more stable. The Greek word statis, which bulks largely in this book, is not exactly 'revolution', but the state of affairs that comes about when tension has become so great that an outbreak of violence is inevitable. It will be noticed that 'inequality' is generally 'superiority'.

1

We have now dealt with nearly all the matters that we promised, but we have still to discuss what are the causes of change in constitutions, their nature and number, what are the destructive agencies that affect each constitution, and from what kinds into what kinds they generally change. We must likewise consider what factors make for the preservation of constitutions, both in general and of each kind separately, also by what means each of the types of constitution could best be preserved.

We should begin by referring to the fundamental basis of any state – the kind of justice and equality which is aimed at. There are, as has been said before, many constitutions which are supposed, though wrongly, by all their members to embody justice and proportionate equality. Democracy is based on the idea that those who are equal in any respect are equal absolutely. All they say, are alike free, therefore all are absolutely equal. Oligarchy is based on the supposition that those who are unequal in one respect are unequal absolutely; being unequal in wealth they suppose themselves to be unequal absolutely. Again, democrats, because all equal, claim equal participation in everything; oligarchs, being unequal, claim a larger share, because 'more' is unequal. Now all these have a sort of justice in them but it is a mistake to think of it as absolute justice. And this is why, whenever the members of a state cease to regulate their sharing in it according to its fundamental principle in each case, they find themselves in a situation of potential revolution. Those members who are of outstanding merit would have by far the greatest justification for rebelling, but they least often do so; they are the only people to whom the term 'absolutely unequal' can be properly applied. Then there are those who being superior in birth claim that they are too good for mere equality, just because of this inequality of birth; for those who have inherited from their forebears both excellence and wealth are called nobly-born. These are generally speaking the origins of revolutions, the sources from which they spring.

Hence the changes which take place may be of two kinds according to whether they involve a complete change from one constitution to another, or only a modification of an existing one. Examples of the former are from democracy to oligarchy, from oligarchy to democracy, from these to polity and aristocracy, or the reverse. In the other case those who seek change wish the existing constitution to continue but want it to function through themselves, whether it be oligarchy or monarchy. Or again it may be a matter of degree; they may wish an oligarchy to be more broadly or less broadly based, a democracy to be more democratic or less, and similarly with the other constitutions, either a relaxation or a tightening up. There are also changes affecting only a part of the constitution – the establishment or abolition of a particular office, for example the alleged attempt by Lysander to abolish the Lacedaemonian monarchy, or of King Pausanias to abolish the ephorate. In Epidamnus too

there was a partial change in the constitution; they instituted a council in place of the tribe leaders, an oligarchical
change, but it is still the rule that whenever any officer is
being elected, existing officers must be present at the gathering of members of the citizen-body. The sole archon too was
an oligarchical feature of this constitution.

As I was saying, inequality is generally at the bottom of
internal warfare in states, for it is in their striving for what is
fair and equal that men become divided.* There are two
kinds of equality, the one dependent on numerical equivalence, the other on equivalence in value. I use 'numerically
equal' to cover that which is equal and the same in respect
of either size or quantity, and 'proportionately equal' for
that which is equal in value. Thus numerically the difference between three and two is the same as the difference between two and one, so that the amounts of difference are
numerically equal. But the relationship of four to two is proportionately equal to the relationship of two to one; two is
exactly the same fraction of four as one is of two, namely a
half. But while men agree that absolute justice is proportionate justice based on value, they differ, as has been said
before, about the value. One group believes that if men are
equal in any respect, they are equal all round; the others
claim that if they are not equal but superior in any respect,
they have a right to preferential treatment in all matters.
It is for this reason that there are, broadly speaking, two
kinds of constitution, 'that of the people' and 'that of the
few', democracy and oligarchy. The number of people in
whom noble birth and virtue are found is very small, but
other marks of inequality are present in a larger number, so
that while you could not find anywhere a hundred men of
good birth and high standards, you could in many places
find that number of rich.

To lay it down that the equality shall be exclusively of
one kind or the other is a bad thing, as is shown by what

* I am speaking of states where there is no proportionate compensa-
tion for unequals. A perpetual monarchy ruling over equals is always
unequal.

happens in practice; no constitution lasts long that is constructed on such a basis. The reason for this is that to start from an initial and fundamental error makes it impossible not to run into disaster at the end. Therefore we must make use of both numerical equality and proportionate equality. Nevertheless democracy is steadier and less liable to revolution than oligarchy. In oligarchies there are two possible cleavages, one between the oligarchs and the rest and one of the oligarchs among themselves. In democracies on the other hand the only possible direction of revolution is towards oligarchy, there is virtually no such thing as an internal *stasis* within a democracy. Also, a constitution of the middle classes is nearer to 'that of the people' than to 'that of the few', and is of all such constitutions the most reliable.

Antecedent causes of revolution Chapters 2–4.

2

When we are considering whence arise revolutions and changes affecting the constitution, we must begin with the fundamental causes. These fall into three groups, and we must classify them accordingly: first, the conditions that lead to revolution, second, the objects aimed at, and thirdly all the various origins of political unrest and of violent cleavages among the citizens.

That which causes conditions leading to change is chiefly and generally what we have just been speaking of – inequality. For those who are bent on equality start a revolution if they believe that they, having less, are yet the equals of those who have more. And so too do those who aim at inequality and superiority, if they think that they, being unequal, are not getting more, but equal or less.* The lesser rebel in order to be equal, the equal in order to be greater. These then are conditions predisposing to revolution. Now as to motives: we find these to be profit and dignity, also their opposites;

* The aims are sometimes justifiable, sometimes not.

for in striving to avoid loss of money and loss of status, whether for their friends' sake or for their own, men often bring about revolutions in their states. Thirdly, the origins and causes of the disorders which make men act in the way described and strive for the objects mentioned – there are perhaps seven of these but the number might well be larger. Two of these are the same as already stated – profit and dignity, but in a different way. They play a part now, not as stimulating men to fight against each other in order to acquire them, as in the former statement, but because men see others getting a larger share of these, some rightly, some wrongly. The five other causes in this group are cruelty, fear, excessive power, contemptuous attitudes, disproportionate aggrandizement. To these we may add, in rather a different way, lobbying and intrigue, sheer inattention, imperceptible changes, dissimilarity.

3

What effect cruelty and the profit-motive have and how they operate as causes hardly needs to be pointed out. When those in power are cruel and oppressive and out to make a profit for themselves, they fight both against each other and against the constitution to which they owe their power to act; excessive profit can be made at the expense of individuals as well as at the expense of the nation. Obvious also is the importance of dignity, and how it can be a source of disaffection; those who see others honoured and themselves degraded soon become revolution-minded; the situation is certainly unjust whenever either the honour or the dishonour is contrary to deserts, but it is just, whenever it is in accordance with deserts. Next, excessive power: this is to be seen in any case where one or more men exercise power out of all proportion to the state or to the power of the citizen-body. Monarchy and the domination of a power-group commonly emerge, one or other of them, from these conditions.*

* It is to put an end to excessive concentration of power that the practice of ostracism is followed in some places, Argos and Athens, for

Fear operates in two ways: those who have committed a crime look for overthrow of government, because they fear punishment; those who have reason to fear wrong from others hope thus to forestall it, like the upper class at Rhodes who conspired against the people on account of the lawsuits that were being brought against them.

Contemptuous attitudes too lead to revolution and civil war. In oligarchies, when those who have no share in the constitution are the largest class, they deem themselves greater than the oligarchs and look down upon them. This attitude is also found in democracies, when the upper classes show their contempt of the disorder and inefficiency.*

How disproportionate aggrandizement *vis-à-vis* the rest of the community may become a cause of revolutionary change may be illustrated by a comparison with our bodies. The body consists of parts, and all growth must be in proportion, lest the proper balance of the whole be upset, since otherwise the body becomes useless; as it would if feet a yard long grew on a body a foot high, or when a part of the body grows its bone or tissue like those of some other animal; for just as much depends on the kind of growth as on the amount. So too a state consists of parts, any one of which may start growing bigger without being noticed. For example, in democracies and polities there is apt to be an increase in the number of citizens who are not well-off. Sometimes a disproportionate increase is due simply to a chain of events. Thus at Tarentum many of the prominent citizens were defeated and slain by the Iapygians, then soon after the Persian wars a democracy took the place of a polity. An increase in the number of poorer people also took place at Argos as a result of the slaying by Cleomenes the Spartan of the so-

example. But it is much better to look ahead and prevent the rise of such outstandingly powerful men than to let things slide and look for a remedy afterwards.

* At Thebes things were so badly managed after the battle of Oenophyta that the democracy was overthrown; so too that of Megara, whose fall was due to its own chaos and anarchy, and that of Syracuse before the tyranny of Gelon, and the people's government at Rhodes before the upheaval which brought it to an end.

called 'seventh-day class'; thus they were obliged to bring in some of the outlying dwellers. At Athens losses in battle reduced the numbers in the upper class and the list of their names steadily diminished as the war against Sparta went on. This kind of thing may also occur, though more rarely, in democracies, the change being in the reverse direction. For when the number of the rich increases, or their wealth becomes greater, their power also becomes greater and oligarchy or power-groups result.

This completes the list of seven causes. To these, as he has said, at least four can be added, not quite parallel since they operate differently, three of them leading to revolution without violence.

Changes of constitution can also take place without violence. Lobbying and intrigue, lack of vigilance, and change so gradual as to be imperceptible – these are three ways in which this may come about. At Heraea they changed from holding elections to drawing lots, simply because they found that the successful candidates were those who did most canvassing. It is owing to lack of vigilance that those who are not friendly to the constitution are sometimes allowed to get into key-positions. This is what happened at Oreus, where a certain Heracleodorus got into the government and set up a polity or a democracy in place of an oligarchy. Then there is extreme gradualness; it very often happens that a considerable change in a country's laws and customs takes place imperceptibly, each little change slipping by unnoticed. Thus in Ambracia there was a property-qualification, a small one, required for citizenship; this was gradually reduced and became so low that it might as well have been abolished altogether.

Fourthly there is a group of minor and more external causes.

Then there is difference of race or nation, which remains a source of dissension until such time as the two groups learn to live together. This may be a long process; for just as a state cannot be made out of any and every collection of people, so neither can it be made at any time at will. Hence civil strife is exceedingly common when the population includes an extraneous element, whether these have joined in the founding or have been taken on later. Thus Achaeans were associated with Troezenians in the founding of Sybaris, then becoming more numerous they cast out the Troezenians. (This was the origin of the guilt of the Sybarites.) In Thurii too Sybarites quarrelled with the rest of the founders; they made the unwarranted claim that the land belonged to them, and they were expelled. At Byzantium a number of fresh colonists hatched a plot, but were found out and expelled after a fight. The people of Antissa after receiving Chian exiles fought with them and threw them out. The people of Zancle accepted a number of Samians but they themselves were forced to leave. The people of Apollonia on the Black Sea brought in additional settlers and quarrelled with them. At Syracuse after the period of tyranny they made citizens of the tyrant's foreign mercenary soldiers, then fell out with them and it came to fighting. Most of the Amphipolitans were expelled by the Chalcidians whom they had brought in.*

Sometimes there are geographical reasons for internal strife; the lie of the land may not be conducive to the unity of the state. Thus at Clazomenae those on the Mole were at variance with those on the Island, likewise the Colophonians and Notians. At Athens there is tension between the dwellers in the city itself and those in Piraeus; the latter are more emphatically democratic in outlook. We know how in warfare crossings of rivers and other watercourses, even quite small ones, tends to cause troops to split up. So it seems to be in politics too; every distinction leads to division. Of course these geographical divisions are not the most impor-

* In oligarchies the many rebel on the ground of not being justly dealt with; being equal they are not getting equal treatment, as I said earlier. In democracies it is the notables who rebel, because, though more than equal, they get merely equal treatment. [A misplaced note.]

tant. I should put first the distinction between good men and bad, then the distinction between rich and poor, and the rest after that in varying degrees.

Some further causes, or rather occasions, of change; incidents and situations which are likely to lead to revolution.

4

Now revolutions, though concerned with large matters, may spring from small causes. Very great differences are involved and even the smallest disputes are important when they occur at the centres of power. This happened at Syracuse in early times. The constitution was changed as a consequence of a dispute between two young men, both members of the ruling class, about a love-affair. When one of the two was away from home, the other seduced the boy-lover of his friend. He in turn showed his indignation by inducing the other's wife to come and live with him. As a result all members of the citizen-body found themselves obliged to take sides with one or the other and split into two factions. It is therefore essential to guard against this kind of thing at the very start and resolve all disputes among leaders and those in power. One false step at the beginning may be fatal, but well begun is half done, as the proverb says, so that a small error at the start is equivalent to one twice the size in the later stages.

Disputes among leading citizens generally have an effect on the whole city, as happened in Hestiaea after the Persian wars, when two brothers quarrelled over the distribution of their father's estate. One of them was poor; and when his brother did not openly declare the amount of the property or reveal the cache which the father had discovered, he got the support of the democrats. The other, who had much property, was supported by the wealthier class.

At Delphi a quarrel among the relatives about a marriage was at the bottom of the political disputes which followed.

The intended bridegroom, forecasting bad luck by an omen which he saw when he came to fetch his bride, went away without her. Her family considered that they had been insulted, and when the young man was sacrificing, they planted some temple-property in his possession, and subsequently had him put to death for sacrilege.

At Mytilene too a dispute over inheritance was at the root of many troubles for the city, including that war with the Athenians in which Paches captured their city: Timophanes, a member of the wealthy class, died and left two marriageable daughters. A certain Dexandros wanted them for his two sons, but was rejected and came away empty-handed. Then, being local commissioner for Athenian affairs, he spurred Athens into action. At Phocis a dispute over inheritance took place between Mnaseas father of Mnason and Euthycrates father of Onomarchus; and the resulting feud became the origin for the Phocians of the Sacred War. At Epidamnus also a change of constitution arose out of matrimonial affairs. One of the citizens had promised his daughter in marriage; the father of the intended bridegroom became a magistrate and imposed a fine on this citizen who, feeling himself to be unfairly treated, led a rebellion of those who were not sharers in the constitution.

Another set of causes which may lead to change in any direction, into democracy, into oligarchy, or into polity, is to be seen when a government or a part of it becomes more powerful or more popular. Thus at Athens the Council of the Areopagus gained greatly in esteem during the Persian wars: it was considered to have increased the efficiency of the constitution. Then again the Athenian democracy was greatly strengthened, both because of the large numbers who served in the navy and had been responsible for the victory at Salamis, and because the Athenian ascendancy thus gained rested on sea-power. At Argos the aristocrats gained much credit for the victory over the Spartans at Mantinea and tried to use the occasion to put down the democracy. On the other hand at Syracuse credit for the victory in the war against the Athenians belonged to the people, who changed the constitution from a polity into a democracy. At Chalcis the people joined with the upper classes in removing the tyrant Phoxus and then promptly seized power; and in Ambracia the people joined with the invaders to cast out the tyrant Periander and got the constitution into their own hands.

The important thing to remember is that those who are responsible for the exercise of power, whether they be individuals or organs of government or tribes or what you will, great or small, it is they who cause the disturbance that leads to revolution. They may do so indirectly, as when the rest, jealous of their power, begin a revolution, but also directly, when they themselves are so superior that they are no longer content to remain on terms of equality with the rest.

Constitutional changes also occur when opposing sections of the population are evenly balanced, such as the richer class and the people, when there is no middle class or only a very small one. For when one section of the population, whichever it may be, is very much superior, the other is not likely to risk opposing those who are obviously stronger. It is for this reason that those who are superior in goodness hardly ever start a revolution; they are few against many.

Generally then in all types of constitution the causes and beginnings of revolution are as I have described. As to method, violence and trickery are both used, violence sometimes not at the beginning but subsequently and of necessity. The use of trickery is also dual. In the one case the revolutionaries are successful in their deceit and their rule is at first readily accepted, but subsequently they have to use force to keep their position.* In the other case they use persuasion from the start and then go on using it in such a way that their rule is willingly accepted.

What has been said above applies generally to any occurrence of constitutional change in any state; but we must also

* An example of this is seen in the rule of the Four Hundred who deluded the Athenians into thinking that the king of Persia was going to supply money for the war against Sparta. This was not true, but they went on trying to maintain their oligarchy.

take each type of constitution separately and observe how
revolutions occur in each.

How different constitutions fall.

5

In democracies the most potent cause of revolution is the
unprincipled character of popular leaders. Sometimes they
bring malicious prosecutions against the property-owners
one by one, and so cause them to join forces; common fear
makes the bitterest of foes cooperate. At other times they
openly egg on the multitude against them. There are many
instances of the kind of thing I mean. At Cos the democracy
fell when the popular leaders deteriorated, the more notable
citizens combining against them. Similarly at Rhodes, when
the democratic politicians provided pay for naval ratings
and tried to stop refunding to naval commanders the expenses which they had incurred. These, therefore, weary of
incessant law-suits, were obliged to form an association and
put down the democracy. At Heraclea too the democratic
party was brought low just after the foundation of the
colony – and all because of their own leaders, whose unjust
treatment of the upper-class citizens caused these to leave
the city one after another; finally the exiles gathered forces,
returned, and put down the democracy. The democracy at
Megara was dissolved in a similar way: here the popular
politicians, in order to have money for doling out to the
people, banished many of the notable citizens; this went on
until the number of those thus exiled became so large that
they returned, won a battle against the people, and set up
the oligarchy. The same thing happened also at Cyme in the
time of the democracy, whose fall was brought about by
Thrasymachus, and in the other cases also you can see
changes taking place after the same manner.

Sometimes, in order to win the favour of the multitude,
they oppress the leading citizens and cause them to unite;
methods of oppression include forced capital-levy, as well as

a levy on income for public services; another method is to bring slanderous accusations against the rich with a view to getting their money transferred to the public purse.

In earlier times a change from democracy to tyranny took place whenever popular leader and military leader were one person; indeed most of the early tyrants started by being demagogues. The reason why this does not occur nowadays is that in the old days popular leaders were drawn from those who had led troops, not from the skilled speakers, for there were none. Today with the spread of skill in oratory the able speakers become popular leaders, but owing to their ignorance of warfare are not appointed to commands, except in a few insignificant instances. One reason why tyrannies were more frequent in the past than they are today is that offices of great power were entrusted to certain people; at Miletus tyranny arose out of the office of presidency, for the president had many and great powers. Another reason is that cities were smaller in those days and the people lived all over the countryside, busy with their labours there; so their leaders, if they wanted to be warlike, used to aim at tyranny. They could all do this because they had the confidence of the people, a confidence based on hostility to the rich. At Athens for example Peisistratus became tyrant by leading a revolt against the rich landowners of the plain. At Megara Theagenes, finding the cattle of the rich straying over the grazing lands by the river, slaughtered them; and Dionysius, who spoke out strongly against Daphnaeus and the rich, was judged to be deserving of his office of tyrant; he was a man of the people and his hostility to the rich won him the people's confidence. Change also takes place in another direction – from old or ancestral democracy to the modern or extreme type. For when officers are chosen by election not based on property and the people are the electors, those who are eager to secure election lead the demos on and on, until they bring it about that the people become sovereign even over the laws. A way of preventing or minimizing this is to make the tribes electors to the offices and not the whole people.

Such are, generally speaking, the causes of changes away from democracy. Turning now to changes in oligarchies, we find two types most conspicuous, one due to opposition to the oligarchy, the other to dissension within it. Thus there is always likelihood of revolution, if the oligarchs oppress the people; almost anyone would adequately fill the role of popular leader in such circumstances. But he is particularly effective when he comes from the oligarchy itself, like Lygdamis at Naxos who afterwards ruled as tyrant there. There are various ways in which opposition from without may cause an oligarchy to fall. Sometimes the danger actually comes from the rich, from those of the rich who are not included in the government. For sometimes the number of those in office may be very small. This has been known to occur in Massilia, in Istrus, in Heraclea, and in other cities. Those who had no share in the government kept on agitating until first elder sons and then younger were admitted to a share. For in some places it is not permitted for father and son to hold office simultaneously, in others not elder and younger brothers. At Massilia the oligarchy changed into something rather like a polity, but at Istrus it ended by becoming a democracy, and at Heraclea the number of oligarchs was increased to six hundred. At Cnidus too revolution was due to strife among the upper classes themselves, owing to the fact that the numbers participating in government were small, and, as has been mentioned, if a father was a member, a son might not be, and of a number of brothers only the eldest. The people stepped in, chose a leader from among the upper classes, whose dissension made them an easy prey, and carried out a successful coup. At Erythrae too in early times under the oligarchy of the Basilidae, in spite of the excellent way in which they were governing, the people, not liking being ruled by a few men, changed the constitution.

The other type of revolution arises directly out of the

oligarchy itself and the rivalry over leadership within it. Their leaders are like demagogues; there are two kinds of demagogy, one which functions within the ranks of the few, on occasion very few indeed, the other when members of an oligarchy act as demagogues to the people. Examples of the first are the demagogy of Charicles and his men within the oligarchy of the Thirty at Athens, likewise that of Phrynichus and his associates in the oligarchy of the Four Hundred. Of the second, a good example was Larissa, where the oligarchs, called Citizen-Guardians, played the demagogue to the mob because they were elected by them. And it is apt to occur in any oligarchy the members of which are not elected by the class of persons eligible for office, but offices are dependent on a high property-qualification or on membership of a political club, and the electors are the hoplites or the demos, as happened at Abydos, and where the jury-courts are not manned by the whole citizen-population,* and further whenever one set tries to reduce the size of the oligarchy still more, for then the excluded persons, looking for the equality which is theirs, are forced to summon the people to their aid.

Then too there are oligarchies whose fall is due to the extravagant living of their members. For persons of this type seek to make innovations, either aiming at tyranny themselves or putting up some other person. Thus at Syracuse it was Hipparinus who made Dionysius tyrant, and at Amphipolis the additional Chalcidian settlers were brought by a man called Cleotimus, who on their arrival set them against the well-to-do; at Aegina the person who had carried through the negotiations with Chares tried to change the constitution because he had no money left. Sometimes they do not wait for the money to run out but begin by making changes. Sometimes they secretly help themselves to public funds; and then, either they themselves stir up strife in order to conceal their embezzlement, or else others do so in order to call attention to it, as happened at Apollonia on the Black Sea.

* Demagogy in connexion with law-suits may well lead to change in constitution, as happened at Heraclea on the Black Sea.

An oligarchy which is of one mind with itself is not easily destroyed from within; a good example is the constitution at Pharsalus, where a few men continue to have authority over many simply because they know how to treat each other properly. But if an attempt is made to set up one oligarchy within another, its dissolution follows. This occurs whenever, with a total citizen-body that is not large, not all the few are eligible for the highest offices. It happened in Elis, where the constitution was oligarchical but very few persons were ever even added to the governing body or council of elders, because the existing members held office for life and the total was fixed at ninety; moreover the method of election favoured the group in power, like that of the Spartan Council of Elders.

Changes away from oligarchies may take place either in war or in peace. In war oligarchies are obliged, owing to their mistrust of the people, to employ mercenary soldiers, and this may lead to their downfall; for the man to whom they have committed the command of these troops often becomes tyrant, as Timophanes did at Corinth, and if there are several of them, they set up a ruling clique of themselves. Sometimes, just for fear of these results, they are obliged to employ the people in defence and give them a share in the constitution. In peace, on the other hand, owing to their mutual mistrust they commit the country's defence to mercenary soldiers with a neutral commander, who sometimes has the whip hand over both parties; as did Simus at Larissa under the rule of the Aleuadae, and Iphades at Abydos, when he led one of the clubs.

Revolutions also take place because one set of oligarchs is thrown out by another, and because feuds arise out of law-suits or dealings connected with a marriage. Some disputes of matrimonial origin have been mentioned already; to these may be added the Knights' Oligarchy at Eretria, which was brought low by Diagoras, who had suffered an injustice connected with a marriage. The revolutions at Heraclea and at Thebes were due to a law-court verdict;

on a charge of adultery the court at Heraclea inflicted punishment on Euction, rightly but in a manner which led to feud, and at Thebes the court found against Archias, and their enemies were so set on revenge that the men were tied to a pillory in the market place.

Many oligarchies have fallen owing to their excessively despotic rule, brought low by some of their own members who disapproved; the oligarchy at Cnidus, for example, and that at Chios. A combination of circumstances sometimes leads to changes both in what we call polities and in those oligarchies in which membership of the council, the law-courts, and other offices is open only to those of a certain property-qualification. For very often the property-amount, when it is first fixed, is well-suited to its purpose at the time; that is to say on its basis few in the oligarchy participate in the constitution, in the polity all the middle class. But prosperity ensues, thanks to a period of peace or some other good fortune, and it comes about that the same amounts of property are worth many times as much as before in the scale of assessment, and so everyone becomes eligible for everything, either quickly or over a period of changing values.

These then are the causes of change and revolution in oligarchies. We may add this general remark: both oligarchies and democracies are sometimes replaced not by their opposites but by constitutions still of the same class. For example a democracy or an oligarchy that is bound by its laws may change into a democracy or an oligarchy with power over its laws, or vice versa.

Revolutions in aristocracies are next discussed, in a rather different way because aristocracy is based not on numbers, but on quality (ἀρετή). Yet it is clearly a form of oligarchy since the excellent are always few. But Aristotle's favoured 'polity' (p. 165–9 above) is also based on excellence and therefore a kind of aristocracy, yet at the same time it is more democratic than oligarchy. So aristocracy and polity are here treated together, not without some confusion. The changes at Thurii described in this chapter are obscure.

7

One reason for revolutions in aristocracies is the fact that only a few people are eligible for office. This, as we have noted, applies equally to oligarchies; for aristocracy is a kind of oligarchy; the rulers in both are limited to a few, but the basis of limitation is not the same. But in respect of numbers certainly aristocracy is the rule of the few. Objection to this monopolizing of full citizen rights by one group is bound to be made (1) whenever there is a section of the people who have convinced themselves that they are the equals of the rulers in excellence. For example at Sparta those known as Partheniae (equal in birth but illegitimate) started a plot, but were found out and shipped off to Sicily as colonists who founded Tarentum. Again (2) when great men, in no whit inferior in ability, are kept down by the more highly-placed, as was Lysander by the Spartan kings. And (3) when a man of courage and vigour gets no share in honour and office, like Cinadon who conspired against the Spartiatae in the time of Agesilaus. And (4) when there is a wide disparity in property amounts owned by members. This condition is likely to come about in time of war; it occurred at Sparta as a result of the Messenian war, as can be seen from the poem of Tyrtaeus called 'Eunomia'; some were so hard pressed by the war that they demanded a redistribution of land. And (5) when one man is powerful and is capable of becoming more so; he aims at becoming sole ruler, as was said of Pausanias, who had led the Lacedaemonian forces in the Persian war, and Hanno the Carthaginian.

But the chief cause of collapse, both in polity and in aristocracy, is a deviation from the principles of the constitution itself. Thus in polity it is the failure to secure a proper mixture of oligarchy and democracy, in aristocracy failure to mix these and virtue, but especially the pair, democracy and oligarchy. For most of those that are called aristocracies, as well as those that are called polities, aim at mixing these two, and the differences between them lie in this sphere, that is, in how the mixing is done. It is success or failure in making a good mixture that makes some more and others less permanent. Those that lean rather towards oligarchy are called aristocracies, those that lean towards democracy are called polities; and the effect is to make polities less liable to fail than aristocracies. This is due to the fact that size is an element of strength; where a larger number have equal shares, they are more content, but those who have the advantages of riches and a constitutionally privileged position as well are apt to abuse their power and enhance their fortunes.

As a general rule, if a constitution has a tendency in one direction, those who wish under it to augment their power will look for changes in the same direction, polity tending towards democracy, aristocracy towards oligarchy. But the opposite is also possible; aristocracy may shift towards democracy, when the poor are oppressed and exercise a pull in that direction; and polity may change to oligarchy, once it loses the qualities which make it last, namely its equality according to deserts and its freedom of individual possessions. This occurred at Thurii. On the one hand, because the property-qualification for holding office was too high, it was reduced and the number of offices increased. On the other, the upper classes illegally got possession of all the land, being enabled to do so as the constitution became more oligarchic. Then the people, trained in arms during the war, became stronger than the garrison troops. So in the end the possessors of more than their share had to give it up.

A further consequence of the fact that all aristocratic constitutions are controlled by a few is that the leading citizens make greater profits; for example at Sparta, where the large estates keep coming into the hands of a few. In both also the leading citizens have greater freedom to do as they please and marry as they please. It was just this that ruined the city of Locri: a connexion by marriage was formed with the tyrant Dionysius, a thing which would never have happened in a democracy, or even in an aristocracy in which the elements had been properly mixed.

Changes in aristocracies generally take place unobserved, because the dissolution is a gradual process. We have already remarked that this is a general principle applicable to all constitutions, because even the smallest thing may lead to changes. If for example the citizens abandon some small feature of their constitution, next time they will with an easier mind alter some other and rather more important feature, until in the end they change the whole set-up. Thurii again affords an example. There the important political office of general could legally be held only every fifth year by the same man. Some of the younger men were skilled in fighting and the rank and file of the troops esteemed them highly. This group had no use for the politicians of the day and believed that they could easily dispose of them. They first set about annulling this law, so as to make it possible for the same men to hold office as general continuously. They knew that the people would willingly vote them into office. These officials who were charged with looking into the matter, Councillors as they were called, while at first inclined to oppose, were eventually won over with the rest; they supposed that in changing this law they would be leaving the rest of the constitution intact. But later, when other changes were proposed which they wanted to stop, they found that now they were powerless to do anything. So the whole set-up of the constitution was altered and it passed into the hands of the powerful group that had started the process of revolution.

Constitutions may be changed from the outside as well as from within; for example, if a neighbouring constitution is of the opposite kind and is not far away, or, if far away, especially powerful. Both the Athenians and the Lacedaemonians illustrate this in their history; the Athenians everywhere brought low the oligarchies, the Lacedaemonians the popular governments.

So much then for the origins of constitutional change and revolution.

How to ensure stability and avoid revolutionary change (Chapters 8 and 9). The reference is to 'constitutional sophistries' seems to be to Book IV, Chapter 13.

8

Our next topic is the preservation of constitutions, both in general and in particular cases. The first and obvious point to make is that if we have properly grasped the causes that destroy constitutions (and I think we have), then we know what things will preserve them. For opposites are productive of opposites, and destruction is the opposite of preservation.

Now in constitutions that are well-blended it is essential to take precautions against anything being done contrary to the laws of that constitution, and in particular to guard against the insignificant breach. Illegality creeps in unobserved; it is like small items of expenditure which when oft-repeated make away with a man's fortune. The spending goes unnoticed because the money is not spent all at once and this is just what leads the mind astray. It is like the sophistic argument which says 'If each is small, all is small', which may or may not be true; the whole or the all may be made up of small amounts without being small. Against such an initial mistake we must be on guard; and equally we must not trust those arguments of political sophistry that are designed to delude the multitude. (What I mean by sophistries in relation to constitutions has already been explained.)

We must next observe that many aristocracies (and oligarchies too) remain in being, not because their constitutions are secure, but because those who hold office of government give proper treatment both to the members of the citizen-body and to those outside it; that is to say, they do not treat the latter unfairly but allow their leaders to participate in the constitution, and do not suppress or degrade those who are eager to rise or deprive the many of their gains; and among themselves and the rest of those who share in the constitution they treat each other in a democratic spirit, that is to say, equally, since equality over the whole number of citizens is the democrats' aim, and equality among equals is not only just but advantageous. Hence if the number of citizens is large, there is great advantage in having a system which includes democratic features, such as tenure of office for only six months, so as to give all, being equal, an equal chance to share in it; their equality makes them, as it were, into a demos, and so, as we have observed, very often popular leaders arise from among these. Also, these oligarchies and aristocracies are less likely to fall into the hands of power-groups, for it is not so easy to do wrong in a short as in a long tenure of office, which means that tyrannies are likely to occur in oligarchies as well as in democracies; for the greatest men in each case aim at sole rule for themselves, popular leaders in the one, power-group leaders in the other, or else those who hold the highest office, if they hold it for a long period.

Constitutions last longer not only when any possible destroyers are at a distance, but sometimes just because they are close by; for through fear of them men keep a firm hold on their own constitution. So it becomes the duty of those who have the interests of the constitution at heart to create fear on its behalf, so that all may be on the lookout and not allow their watch on the constitution to disperse like sentries at night; the distant fear must be brought home. They must also take the further precaution of checking by means of legislation the rivalries and ambitions of the leading men, and restrain those not involved before they too become drawn in; it is not every man but only a real statesman who can discern in its early stages harm that is being done.

We have seen that changes in oligarchies and polities may be due to the property-qualifications required for citizenship, these remaining fixed while the money in circulation is greatly increased. To meet this situation the best thing to do is to assess the total rateable valuation in the light of this increase, the new total thus contrasted with the old. In some cities this is done every year, in the larger every third or every fifth year. And if the value is then found to be much greater or much smaller than it was when the qualifications for citizenship were first laid down, it should be lawful to increase the assessments or lower them; if the value has gone up, they are increased in proportion to the rise, if the value has fallen, they are decreased in proportion to the fall. If the situation is not met in this way and no adjustments are made in oligarchies and polities, then, if the value has fallen, change is liable to take place from polity to oligarchy and from oligarchy to power-group domination; if it has risen, the changes will be from polity to democracy and from oligarchy to polity or democracy.

The stability of a constitution may also be endangered by the behaviour of individuals – the over-ambitious and those who want to make money. Aristotle must have been well aware (cf. Book IV, Chapter 6) of the difference between receiving a salary from public funds and simply helping oneself, but here they are confused.

It is a practice common to democracy and oligarchy and every constitution not to augment the power of any one man out of proportion, but to try and bestow on him minor promotions at long intervals, not great advancement all at once; for that is bad for him, not every man can master the intoxication of success. Or if that is not possible, at any rate avoid heaping honours on a man all in a bunch and then removing them in a bunch; the process should be gradual. And they try to exercise restraint by laws in such a way that no citizen becomes excessively influential by reason either of his wealth or his family connexions; or if that cannot be done, to require such men to remove themselves, and out of the country too. But since men start revolutionary changes for reasons connected with their private lives, an authority ought to be set up to exercise supervision over those whose activities are not in keeping with the interests of the community; and this applies equally to the interests of oligarchy and of democracy and of all the rest. For the same reasons exceptional prosperity in one section of the community is to be guarded against. The danger can be met by not entrusting assignments and responsibilities to one section alone but to different and opposing sections. (I am opposing the educated class to the generality and the wealth to the more indigent.) An endeavour should be made either to merge the poorer with the richer or to augment the number of those of medium wealth; this dissolves the unrest that is due to the inequality.

It is most important in every kind of constitution that the legal, and especially the financial, arrangements should be such that holding office is not a source of financial gain. This needs to be particularly watched in constitutions that are oligarchically framed. For the majority do not so much resent being debarred from office, indeed they are glad to be allowed time to attend to their own affairs, but they do not like to think that officials are helping themselves to public money. Their resentment then becomes two-fold; they are deprived of both office and profit. Also, it is only by observing this principle that it ever becomes possible to combine democracy and aristocracy in a single state. It would then be possible for both the upper class and the demos to get what they really want; for it is democratic that holding offices should be open to all, aristocratic that only the upper class should fill them, and this is exactly what will happen when there is no profit to be made out of the offices. For those who are not well-off will not want office unless there is money in it, preferring to look after their own affairs, while the rich will be able to accept office, as they need no subsidy from public funds. The effect of this will be that the poor will be satisfied, because they will become better-off through spending their time at their work; and so too will the rich because they are not ruled by the Common Man. In order to prevent peculation from public funds, the handing over of state-property to a successor should take place in the presence of all the citizens; lists should be made and copies made available to brotherhoods, companies, and tribes. And in order to ensure that profitless offices do not go unfilled they should be rendered more attractive by attaching to them honours and privileges for those who give distinguished service.

In democracies the rich ought to be treated with con-

sideration; there should be no levy on capital with redistribution of property, nor any redistribution of income, such
as goes on unnoticed in some cities. It is better, even if they
want to, not to let the rich undertake those costly services
which are not of public utility – financing a torch-race or a
training of a chorus, or other like services. In an oligarchy,
on the other hand, special attention must be paid to the welfare of those who are not well-off; to them should be assigned
those offices which carry a salary; a tort committed against
them by one of the rich should carry a severer penalty than
one committed among the rich themselves; there should be
no right of free testamentary disposition, only kin should
inherit, and the same person should not be permitted to
inherit more than one estate. In this way disparity of wealth
will be less and a greater number of the poor will join the
ranks of the well-to-do. It always pays, whether in a democracy or an oligarchy, to give equality or even preference in
other matters to those whose participation in the constitution is minimal, to the rich in a democracy, to the poor in an
oligarchy. This does not mean that they should be given
offices of power; these should be reserved exclusively, or at
any rate generally, for members of the constitutional body.

*The character of those in power and their relations with the ruled
are important factors in maintaining stability.*

9

There are three essentials for the holders of the reins of
government – loyalty to the established constitution, capacity for the work involved, and the kind of goodness and
honesty that belong to the particular way of life in question.
(The moral standards are not the same in every constitution,
so that differences in the notion of rightness are inevitable.)
But there is a question here: when all these are not to be
found in the same person, how is the choice to be made? If
one man has military skill but is a low fellow and not well-
disposed to the régime, while another is honest and loyal,

how is one to choose between them? It seems to me that we must look at two things – the qualities that are general among all men and those that are less common. Generalship depends more on experience than on goodness, as military skill is less common than honesty. It is the other way round in the case of an office which involves oversight of other men and safe custody of goods; this requires honesty above the average but no knowledge that is not to be found among all men. Another question might be asked: if both loyalty and capability are present, what need is there of virtue? Will not these two of themselves bring about all that is needful? As against that it may be said that men may possess these two qualities and still be morally incapable; and if they are incapable of doing what is best, what is right, for themselves, whom they know and love, will they not also be on occasion incapable of doing what is best for their country? In sum, all those principles of a city's laws which we regard as advantageous to the constitution in each case, all these are constitutional safeguards, including that oft-mentioned and most important principle – to ensure that the number of those who wish the constitution to be maintained is greater than of those who do not.

Extremists and doctrinaire theorists are a threat to stability.

Alongside these there is one thing that must not be overlooked, though it often is in constitutions that deviate from the norm – the principle of the middle way. Many steps, apparently democratic, may be taken that lead to the fall of a democracy and the same may happen in oligarchies. Some people, believing that their own view of goodness is the only right one, push that view to extremes. They fail to realize that a nose which deviates from perfection by being either hooked or snub is still an excellent nose and looks like one as well; but if the process is carried to excess, first it will lose the proportion which belongs to this part of the body and finally it will not look like a nose at all, because of the extreme to which either the hook or the snub has been pushed. And as this is true of other parts of the body also, so it is with constitutions. Both oligarchy and democracy may be tolerably good, though they deviate from the standard of perfection; but if one carries either of them to excess, first the constitution will become worse and finally hardly even a constitution at all. Therefore both the lawgivers and the practising politician must learn to distinguish between those democratic measures which preserve and those which undermine democracy, and oligarchical measures in the same way. For it is not possible for either oligarchy or democracy to exist and continue to exist without the existence also of both the wealthy and the people. If the distinction between them is abolished by the equalization of property, the resulting constitution will of necessity differ from both, that is to say, constitutions have been destroyed by means of legislation carried to excess. These mistakes are made both in democracy and in oligarchy. In democracies they are made by the popular leaders whenever the people have power even over the laws; they make one city into two by their constant attacks on the rich. Yet they ought, for the sake of stability, to behave in just the opposite way, always appear to be speaking on behalf of the rich. So too in oligarchies its members should always appear to speak on behalf of the people; and the oath which they take should be the very reverse of that which is in fact taken by some today: 'I will make the people my enemy and do all I can against them.' Both the intention and the language here are wrong; they ought to make this declaration on oath 'I will do no wrong to the people.'

If education is to help stability, it must be directed according to the kind of society which it is desired to maintain. Aristotle deplores the decay of this doctrine.

But of all the safeguards that we hear spoken of as helping to maintain constitutional continuity the most important, but most neglected today, is education, that is educating citizens for the way of living that belongs to the constitution in each case. It is useless to have the most beneficial rules of society fully agreed upon by all who are members of the *politeia*, if individuals are not going to be trained and have their habits formed for that *politeia*, that is to live democratically if the laws of society are democratic, oligarchically if they are oligarchic; for as one individual may get out of hand for want of training, so may a whole city. Now by education for a constitution I do not mean simply teaching the young to do the things that oligarchically-minded or democratically-minded people enjoy doing, but that their teaching should enable them to live as an oligarch in an oligarchy, as a democrat in a democracy. Unfortunately what actually happens is that in oligarchies the sons of the rulers are brought up to enjoy ease and comfort, and the sons of the poor, being trained and inured to toil, are both more willing and better able to start a revolution. And what happens in democracies too is the very reverse of beneficial, in those, that is, which are regarded as most democratically-minded. The reason for this lies in the failure properly to define liberty. For there are two marks by which democracy may be known – 'sovereignty of the majority' and 'liberty'. The right is equated with what is equal and the decision of the majority as to what is equal is regarded as final and valid; liberty is defined as doing what one wants. So in such a democracy each lives as he likes and for his fancy of the moment, as Euripides says. This is bad. It ought not to be regarded as a denial of liberty to have to live according to the constitution but rather as self-preservation.

The causes of change and decay in constitutions, as well as the means of preserving and maintaining them, are for the most part as I have described.

Actually these have been discussed only in relation to oligarchy and democracy. In the tenth and eleventh chapters they are treated in rela-

tion to monarchy, both legitimate kingship and illegitimate tyranny. Intrigue and scandal, vice and hatred, play a large part.

10

It remains to deal with monarchy or the rule of one man, both the causes of its collapse and the means of its preservation. What we find happening in both kingship and tyranny follows closely what has been said about the others; for kingship has the same basis as aristocracy – superior excellence, and tyranny is a compound of extreme oligarchy and democracy. This makes tyranny most hurtful to the ruled; it is made up of two bad types and contains the deviations and errors that derive from both. As for origins, kingship and tyranny arise directly out of that which contrasts with them, each form of monarchy being opposed to the other. Kingship aims at enlisting the support of the people for the good men; a king is made king by the good men on account of his superiority in virtue or deeds of valour, or the superiority of his virtuous family. The tyrant springs from the people, from the mob, and directs his efforts against the upper classes, to the end that the people may not be oppressed by them. This is clear from the facts; it is fairly generally true to say that tyrants have mostly begun as popular leaders, being trusted by the people because they disliked the upper class.*

* Certainly in cities that have grown to considerable size this is the way tyrannies originate. But there have been other ways: some early tyrannies arose out of kingships that had been false to ancestral traditions and had aimed at making their rule more despotic; others were elected into the highest offices (in very early times people were elected to various offices, civil and religious, for long periods of tenure). Tyrannies have also come into being when oligarchies have chosen one man and invested him with the greatest powers. For all these ways the opportunity lay ready to hand, provided only that the will was there, for the power existed either in the royal rule or in the high office. Some examples of tyrannies of different origins are (1) from an established kingship – Pheidon of Argos and others; (2) from high offices – Phalaris and the tyrants of Ionia; (3) from the position of popular leader – Panaetius of Leontini, Cypselus of Corinth, Peisistratus of Athens, Dionysius of Syracuse, and others.

Some differences between kingship and tyranny.

Kingship, as we have remarked, depends on the same principle as aristocracy; it is based on merit – either individual virtue, or good birth, or distinguished service, or all these together with a capacity for doing things. For it is just those who have done good service or have the capacity to do it, either for cities or for nations, that have been honoured with the title of king. Some, like Codrus, saved their people from subjection by war; others, like Cyrus, have set them free or have acquired territory and founded cities, like the kings of the Lacedaemonians, of the Molossians, of the Macedonians.

A king aims to be a protector – of the owners of property against unfair losses, of the people against oppression. But a tyrant, as has often been said, does not look to the public wish, unless it happens to coincide with his personal interest. The tyrant's aim is his pleasure, the king's his duty. Hence they differ even in their appetites and ambitions; the tyrant grasps at money, the king at honour. A king's bodyguard is made up of citizens, a tyrant's of foreign mercenaries.

That tyranny has the disadvantages of both democracy and oligarchy is clear. From oligarchy it derives two things: (1) the notion of wealth as the end to be pursued – and certainly wealth is essential to him, as it provides the only way of keeping up a bodyguard and a luxurious way of living – and (2) mistrust of the people; hence they deprive them of arms, ill-treat the lower classes, and keep them from residing in the capital. These are common to oligarchy and tyranny. From democracy is derived hostility to the upper classes, whom they bring low by open methods or secret and send into exile as being potential rivals and persons who cause hindrance to the government. Of course then these are the people among whom originate plots for the tyrant's overthrow; they are resolved either to rule themselves or at least not submit like slaves. We are reminded of the advice given by Periander to Thrasybulus, to lop off the tallest stalks, implying that he should always remove the outstanding of the citizens.

Men rise up to destroy a tyrant either because they have been ill-treated by him or because they fear him or because they have a low opinion of him and regard him as easy prey.

Now it has been said, or at any rate implied in what we have said, that the same causes operate towards revolutionary change in monarchies as in the other constitutions. For a sense of injustice, fear of, and contempt for, a ruler – these often cause men to rebel against monarchies; and ill-treatment frequently includes physical violence as well as seizure of goods. And as the motives are the same, so also are the aims. Great wealth and privilege are characteristic of the sole ruler, king or tyrant, and these are things which all men want for themselves. Attacks on rulers may be directed against their persons or against their office. If men have been personally ill-treated, their attack will be on the tyrant's life; for a tyrant's cruelty may take many forms and each will provoke anger and resentment. And the angry are keener on vengeance than on high office.

Here are some examples of revolutions which had their origin in personal resentment. The fall of the Peisistratidae, whose ill-treatment of Harmodius's sister and of Aristogeiton caused much indignation, Harmodius on account of his sister and Aristogeiton on account of Harmodius. The occasion for the attack on Periander of Ambracia was that when he was drinking in company with his boy-lover he asked him whether he was yet with child by him. Pausanias's attack on Philip was due to the fact that he allowed him to be tortured by Attalus's men. Amyntas the Little was attacked by Derdas for boasting about a youthful seduction. Evagoras of Cyprus was murdered by a eunuch, whose wife had been seduced by the king's son. Many attacks on rulers have arisen out of resentment caused by a monarch's sexual offences against his subjects, such as Crataeus's attack on

Archelaus. Crataeus was always resentful of the enforced liaison and the slightest excuse was enough to turn him against him; but there was also the fact that the king had broken faith; he had promised one of his two daughters to him but gave him neither.* But at the bottom of the coolness between them there was always the ill-feeling that had an erotic origin. For a similar reason Hellenocrates of Larissa joined in the attack. Archelaus had made sexual use of his young body but did not, as he had promised, let him return home. Hellenocrates concluded that the intercourse had been due to wanton cruelty and not to passionate love. At Aenus Python and Heracleides made away with Cotys because of what he had done to their father, and Adamas rebelled against Cotys because he had as a boy suffered castration at his hands. There are many cases also of anger being aroused not by sexual offences but by physical violence, the victims of which have killed or tried to kill the perpetrators, who include both members of a tyrant's circle and a royal house. In Mytilene, for example, when the sons of Penthilus went about in gangs, carrying clubs and beating up people, Megacles with the help of friends put them down. Later Smerdes killed Penthilus, by whom he had been dragged out of bed beside his wife and beaten. Then there was the attack on Archelaus instigated and led by Decamnichus. The reason for his anger was that he had given him to the poet Euripides to be scourged; and Euripides was angry because he had made some remark about the poet's foul-smelling breath. There were many other plots and assassinations arising out of causes of this kind. Similarly when fear is at bottom; for this too has been one of the causes of rebellion, both in the constitutions and under the rule of one man. For example, Artabanus murdered Xerxes because he feared him, feared the accusations made against himself – that he had hanged Darius not on Xerxes's orders, but thinking that

---

* Involved in a war against Sirra and Arribaeus he gave the elder to the king of Elimea and the younger to Amyntas his son, thinking that this was the best way to avoid discord between him and his son by Cleopatra.

Xerxes would acquiesce, being too drunk to remember what had taken place.

Thirdly, contempt. Sardanapallus rendered himself contemptible by being seen carding wool with the women, and was murdered by one who saw him.* Dion's attack on the younger Dionysius was due to the contempt in which he held him; the tyrant was never sober and the citizens shared Dion's contempt for him. Sometimes even a monarch's friends think him of so little account that they attack him. His reliance on them allows them to disregard him and makes them confident that he will never notice anything. And those whose aim is to seize power for themselves are also up to a point actuated by contempt; they feel they are strong enough and contemn the risk, and their strength causes them to undertake the attack lightly, as do commanders of armies opposed to tyrants. A case in point is Cyrus, who despised Astyages, both his power and his manner of life; the power had become impotent, the life a continuous round of self-indulgence. Similar was the attack of Seuthes the Thracian on Amadocus under whom he was a general. Some attack their masters for a mixture of reasons; Mithradates attacked Ariobarzanes both because he despised him and because he wanted his money.

Attacks that are inspired by contempt for the tyrant are generally carried out by men who are by nature bold, and also hold high military office in his service. For natural courage combined with physical power makes men ready for anything and for this double reason they are confident of easy success before they make their attack. But when the motive is ambition, a different set of causes operates from those already mentioned. It is not true to say that, as some men attack tyrants because they have an eye on the immense profits and honours which accrue to them, so too every ambitious man is ready to take the risk. The fact is that, while the former act for the reason given, the latter look upon the matter as they would look upon any other

* At least, that is the story told; and if it is not true of him, it is pretty sure to be true of someone else.

exceptional occasion that offered a chance of making themselves famous and notable; they attack a monarch in order to bring glory to themselves, not because they want his monarchy. Still, there are not very many who go ahead with only this in mind; there must in addition be disregard of personal safety, should the venture miscarry. They should not lose sight of Dion's principle, difficult though it is to abide by. Dion took only a few men with him against Dionysius, saying that he did this because, whenever he could advance with success, he was satisfied to have completed that much of the enterprise; thus, if it should happen that after taking but a few steps in the direction he should be slain, he would have died a noble death.

A tyranny, like any of the constitutions, may be destroyed from within or from without. From without, if there is a more powerful state that is opposed to tyranny; the desire to destroy it will certainly exist because of the fundamental opposition, and when the power is added to the desire men always act. Democracy is fundamentally opposed to tyranny on Hesiod's principle that 'two of a trade never agree', for democracy is the extreme of tyranny. Kingship and aristocracy are also fundamentally opposed to tyranny, and for this reason the Lacedaemonians brought low many tyrannies, as did also the Syracusans during the time when they had a good constitution. From within, when there is a rift among those closely connected with the tyrant's court, for example the tyranny of Gelon and, more recently, that of Dionysius. In the former Thrasybulus brother of Hieron established an influence over Gelon's son and led him into a life of sensual pleasure. His purpose was to secure the succession for himself. The family got together, stirred up the citizens, and aimed to bring about the fall of Thrasybulus, not of the tyranny as such. But their supporters, seizing their chance, got rid of the whole lot of them. In the other case Dion led a force against Dionysius, to whom he was related by marriage, and had popular support; he overthrew Dionysius but was afterwards slain himself.

*Mention of revolution from within seems to bring Aristotle back
again to personal animosities. Before going on to speak briefly of the
possibility of revolution in a good monarchy, he sums up on tyranny
by recalling that oligarchies and democracies of the wrong type could
also be destroyed either from without or within, and if from within,
the causes there too are generally moral and psychological.*

The two chief reasons for attacks on a tyranny are hatred
and contempt. Hatred of tyrants must always be present but
their fall mostly comes when they come to be despised as
well as hated. This can be seen from the fact that men who
have themselves won the position have generally maintained
their rule, but those who have acquired it from a predeces-
sor have nearly all lost it. Living only to enjoy themselves,
they soon cease to count for much and give the would-be
attackers plenty of chances. Perhaps we ought to include
anger as part of hatred, since to a large extent it leads to the
same actions. But anger is often more effective than hatred.
Angry men go into the attack with greater intensity just because this passion does not involve their reasoning powers,*
as hatred may well do. Anger is accompanied by pain,
which makes it difficult to exercise reason: hostility is not
painful. In short then the same causes, which we found
operating in unmixed and extreme oligarchies and extreme
democracies, are just those which operate in tyrannies; for
these extreme forms are really multiple or distributed
tyrannies.

Kingship is the least liable to suffer destruction from without; it is therefore durable. Most of the occasions of a fall are
due to causes arising from within. Of these there are two
kinds: one, when those who participate in the royal rule
quarrel among themselves, the other when kings try to rule
more dictatorially, claiming control of more than they are
legally entitled to. But nowadays there are not many kingdoms, and such as there are are more like a tyranny or a

---

* To be ill-treated makes men follow their passions rather than their
reason, and this is just what brought about the fall of the Peisistratidae
and many of the others.

one-man despotism. For kingship implies government with consent as well as sovereignty over the greater part of affairs; the number of persons who are all on the same level is large and none of them stands out or comes near to attaining the high standard required for ruling. Men do not readily consent to be ruled by such ordinary people, and if by force or by fraud one of them attains that position, that is no longer kingship but tyranny.

We must add a further cause of downfall to those stated, one that is characteristic of hereditary kingdoms. Those who inherit may be persons of no account, whom it is hard to respect; and though the power they possess is royal, not tyrannical, they may abuse their position. The end of kingship is then imminent; for when subjects cease to consent, a king is no more a king; but a tyrant is still a tyrant, though his subjects do not want him.

For these reasons and others like them monarchies suffer destruction.

Dealing next with ways of preventing revolution in monarchies, Aristotle again has much more to say about tyranny than about kingship, which being based on consent is much more stable. Tyranny is based on force and, traditionally, maintained by force. The other way for a tyrant to maintain his position is to cultivate certain features of kingship.

11

As to the preservation of monarchies, the general principle of opposing or counter measures still holds good, but a special principle applicable to kingdoms is that they should always tend towards greater moderation in the use of power. The fewer those spheres of activity where power is absolute, the longer will the régime surely last. The monarchs themselves become less despotic; they are more like their subjects in habits and character and they therefore arouse less envy among them. That is the secret of the long life of the Molossian kingdom; and as for the Lacedaemonian, we can point first to the fact that from the very start the ruling was divided between two kings and second, that Theopompus in addition to many other measures of moderation instituted the office of the ephors. This diminution of the royal power had in the long run the effect of strengthening it. In a sense Theopompus did not reduce it but increased it, as he himself is reported to have said in reply to his wife, when she asked if he was not ashamed to be passing the kingdom on to his sons in a lesser state than he had inherited it from his father: 'Certainly not,' he replied, 'the kingdom that I pass on to my successors is much more durable.'

There are two quite different methods, or rather principles of method, by which tyrannies can be made to last. I deal first with what may be called the traditional method, since it has been the administrative principle followed by most tyrants. Periander of Corinth is credited with having introduced many of the ways of applying it, but the Persian government offers many parallels. Here belong all the old hints for the preservation (save the mark!) of tyranny, such as 'Cut off the tops and get rid of men of independent views,' and 'Don't allow getting together in clubs for social and cultural activities or anything of that kind; these are the breeding grounds of independence and self-confidence, two things which a tyrant must guard against,' and 'Do not allow schools or other institutions where men pursue learning together, and generally ensure that people do not get to know each other well, for that establishes mutual confidence.' Another piece of traditional advice to a tyrant tells him to keep the dwellers in the city always within his view and require them to spend much time at his palace gates; their activities then will not be kept secret and by constantly performing servile obligations they will become used to having no minds of their own. There are other precepts of the same kind and having the same purpose among the Persians and other foreign monarchies. Similarly a tyrant should endeavour to keep himself aware of everything that is said or done among his subjects; he should have spies like the

Tittle-tattle women, as they were called at Syracuse, or the Eavesdroppers whom Hiero used to send to any place where there was a meeting or gathering of people. It is true that men speak less freely for fear of such men, but if they do open their mouths, they are more likely to be overheard.

Another traditional way is to stir up strife among all possible opponents of the tyranny, by slander setting friends against friends, class against class, and one monied set against another. It is also in the interests of a tyrant to keep his subjects poor, so that they may not be able to afford the cost of protecting themselves by arms and be so occupied with their daily tasks that they have no time for rebellion. As examples of works instituted in order to keep subjects perpetually at work and in poverty we may mention the pyramids of Egypt, the numerous offerings made by the Cypselids, the building of the temple of Zeus Olympius by the Peisistratidae, and public works under Polycrates of Samos. Subjects are also kept poor by taxation, as at Syracuse under Dionysius, where in five years the value of the entire private property was paid in. The tyrant is also very ready to make war; for this keeps his subjects occupied and in continued need of a leader. Friends are a source of protection to a king but not to a tyrant; it is part of his policy to mistrust them as being potentially more dangerous to him than the rest.

Certain features of extreme democracy are also conducive to maintaining a tyrant's position – the dominance of women in the home and slack control of slaves. Tyrants expect in this way to hear about the activities of the men, for women and slaves do not plot against tyrants; keep them satisfied and they will always be supporters of tyrannies and democracies. Demos, too, likes to be sole ruler. So too the flatterer; he is valued by both. In democracies the popular leader is the flatterer of the mob, at a tyrant's court fawning obsequiousness is the flatterer's function. This makes tyranny favour the baser sort; a tyrant likes those who grovel before him; a man of independent and free spirit will refuse to do this. Men of worth give friendship not flattery, and bad men are useful for bad deeds, as the saying goes.

The typical tyrant dislikes serious and liberal-minded people. He regards himself as the only authority; if anyone sets himself up in rivalry and claims the right to speak his mind, he is felt to be detracting from the supremacy and absolute mastery of the tyrant. Thus his dislike of intellectual pretensions is based on fear; such people are potential destroyers of his rule. A tyrant is also inclined to cultivate the company of foreigners and eat with them rather than with members of his own city; for the latter are potential enemies, the former not actively opposed.

All these are marks of tyranny and ways of maintaining it; there are others, all equally reprehensible. They might all be grouped under three heads, corresponding to tyranny's three aims in relation to its subjects, namely that they shall (a) have no minds of their own, (b) have no trust in each other, and (c) have no means of carrying out anything. Of the three points the first is obvious; resistance is not planned by puny minds. On the second, no tyranny is ever brought low until a certain degree of self-confidence is established; hence tyrants are always hostile to the men of merit as being dangerous to them, not only because of their resistance to tyrannical rule but because they command confidence, both among themselves and others, and abstain from making accusations of each other or anybody. The third group is also clear; no one attempts what is quite beyond his powers, so nobody attempts to destroy a tyranny if the power to do so is not there. These then are the three heads under which we group the tyrant's intentions towards his subjects, and all his acts might be referred to the three principles; he wants his subjects to have no confidence, no power, no minds.

'*The two ways of preserving a tyranny differ in this: in the first it is taken for granted that the subjects of a tyrant are necessarily hostile to him and the aim is to make them* unable *to conspire against him*

. . . whereas in the second the aim is to make the subjects of the tyrant indisposed *to conspire against him'* (*W. L. Newman*).

So much for the traditional method of maintaining tyrannies; the other method really works in the opposite direction. We take our cue from the corruption of kingship. Just as one way of setting a kingdom on the road to destruction is to make its rule more tyrannical, so conversely it protects a tyranny to make it more kingly, always preserving one thing – the power of the ruler, power enabling him to govern not only those who consent but also those who do not. For if he abandons that, he abandons his whole position as tyrant. This is a fundamental principle which must be adhered to; for the rest he may act like a king, or rather like one cleverly acting the part of a king.

Thus in the first place he will think of the general good; he will not spend large sums on giving bounties such as arouse the people's indignation, as when the gifts are the product of *their* toil and labour, while *he* gives lavishly to his mistresses, to foreigners, and to his skilled craftsmen. And in this connexion he will render an account of his revenue and expenditure – a practice adopted by some tyrants in the past. This helps him to pose as an administrator of property and not a tyrant. And he does not have to fear shortage of money, being master of all the resources of the state. Indeed, if a ruler goes abroad much, it is actually safer for him to publish accounts than to collect and hoard a vast sum. There will be less likelihood that those in charge of his finances will try to get the money into their own hands; and when tyrants are away at war they are more nervous about the safety of their property than about the citizens; the citizens go on service with him, financial officers remain behind. Again, when he collects revenue or demands services, it should appear that he is doing these things for the economic welfare of the country, for her military needs at a particular juncture, and generally he should make himself look like a protector and husbander not of his own resources but of the nation's.

In his dealings he should always give the impression of dignity not of cruelty, of being the kind of person who inspires not fear but respect in those who come to see him. This is not easy; a tyrant normally inspires loathing and contempt. Hence if he cannot manage to practise any of the other virtues, he should aim at least at skill in warfare, and try to establish for himself a military reputation. Neither he nor any of his entourage should ever be seen to rape any of the youth, male or female; and this applies equally to the women of his court in their behaviour towards other women. Female sexual excesses have often caused tyrannies to fall. His behaviour must also be unlike that of the typical tyrant in regard to indulgence in eating and drinking. Some tyrants, we know, start the day and continue for days on end in a state of inebriation, and even do so for the express purpose of letting others see how supremely happy and fortunate they are. In such matters moderation is best, or at least to avoid getting drunk in public. It is not the sober but the tipsy man who is easily got at and easily brushed aside, not the wide-awake but the somnolent. So he must in general do the opposite of the things already mentioned as typical of the tyrant; thus in the building and decoration of the city he should be a trustee rather than a tyrant. In religion he should always appear to be more in earnest than anyone else but not so as to give an impression of brainlessness. Men believe that they are less likely to be oppressed by a ruler who is, so they think, a religious man and one conscious of the gods; and they are less likely to plot against him if they believe that he has the gods on his side. Again, when any of his subjects show a marked capacity for anything, he should honour them so much that they come to believe that even in a society of free men they could not have been better treated. Such honours the ruler should bestow in person, leaving punishments to be imposed by officials or tribunals. But there is here a protective principle which applies equally to all kinds of monarchy – not to make any one man great; if need be, let there be several, they will watch each other. If it be found necessary so to single out one man, let him not be one of great boldness of character. Such a one is always ready for the attack, whatever the business in hand. And if it is decided to reduce his power, this should be done gradually; do not remove his whole competence at one blow.

He should abstain from wanton usage in all its forms and two in particular – offences against the person and against youth. This precaution must especially be taken in regard to ambitious men; for while the money-loving chiefly resent ill-usage which affects their property, the ambitious and respectable resent attacks on their status and honour. Hence a tyrant must either not do anything at all to such men or, if he inflicts punishment, it should appear to be fatherly and not as a deliberate degradation. His liaisons with young persons should be based on love, not on power; and generally any apparent diminution of status should be compensated by greater honours bestowed. Of all those from whom attacks on a tyrant's life may be expected they are most to be watched and feared who reck nothing of their own life provided they can take his. Therefore he should avoid giving such men cause to think that they are ill-used, themselves or those in whom they are interested. When anger is the springs of their action men are unsparing of themselves. As Heracleitus once said 'Anger is a difficult enemy; he buys with his life.'

Since cities are made up of two sections, those who have property and those who have not, both, if possible, ought to be convinced that they owe their safety to the régime, and so neither ought wrongfully to use the other. But if one or other of the two is the more powerful, its members ought to be associated in government, so that, should the occasion arise, the tyrant may be able to avoid such measures as the liberation of slaves and the confiscation of arms. For it is sufficient for the purpose of putting down a rising if one or other of the sections be added to the power at the centre.

It would be superfluous to go into any further details about these matters; the general purpose is clear: a tyrant should not appear like a tyrant in the eyes of his subjects, but like a king and a guardian of the house, not a person who is out for his own gain but one entrusted with the affairs of others, aiming not at excess in all that pertains to living but at moderation, one who moreover makes friends with the leading citizens but is also the people's leader. If he acts thus, his rule will most certainly be not only better and more enviable but also more lasting; it will not be hated and feared and it will be exercised over better men, not men reduced to impotent submission; and the tyrant himself will have the right attitude or at least a half-right attitude towards goodness, a man not wicked but only half-wicked.

In practice, however, tyrannies (and oligarchies) rarely last long. Aristotle gives some examples of the more durable.

12

Still oligarchy and tyranny are shorter-lived than any other constitution. The longest tyranny was the Sicyonian, that of Orthagoras and his sons: it lasted a hundred years. These monarchs owed their long innings to the fact that they treated their subjects with moderation and in many matters subjected themselves to the rule of law. Also Cleisthenes was a warlike person and therefore not one to be trifled with. In general they drew the people towards them by repeated acts of care for them. It is even said that Cleisthenes set a wreath upon the head of an adjudicator who refused to declare him the winner; and some say that the seated statue to be seen in the square at Sicyon is of the man who gave that decision. It is said of Peisistratus too that he was once summoned to appear before the court of the Areopagus and submitted. Second place goes to the tyranny of the Cypselids at Corinth, which lasted seventy-three and a half years; Cypselus reigned for thirty years, Periander for forty and a half, and Psammetichus son of Gorgos for three. The reasons for their success are similar. Cypselus was a leader of the people and all through his reign continued without an armed guard. Periander was more of the typical tyrant but he was warlike. Third is the tyranny of the Peisistratidae at Athens. This was not continuous, for twice while reigning Peisistratus was exiled. Thus he was tyrant for seventeen years out of thirty-three; his sons reigned for eighteen years, making thirty-five years in all. Of the rest only the Syracusan (Hieron and Gelon) is worth mentioning, but it did not last long either. Gelon reigned for seven years and died in the eighth, Hieron for ten; Thrasybulus was driven out in the eleventh month. But all round, tyrannies have not lasted long.

In conclusion Aristotle refers to the Republic *of Plato (Books 8 and 9) where an imaginary account is given of changes from one form of constitution into another. Plato's intention was quite different from Aristotle's. His was a psychological study of progressive deterioration from the finest aristocracy to the worst tyranny; it was not a factual record or a piece of political advice. Aristotle seems not to be aware of this and even to attribute to Plato a theory of constitutional cycles which is not in our* Republic. *And if Aristotle really understood Plato's mathematical basis of constitutional change, it is a pity that he did not explain it. The reference to extreme liberty near the end of the chapter shows that something referring to democracy has been lost.*

I have now said all I have to say on these topics both in relation to monarchies and to the constitutions, the causes of their corruption and the ways by which they can be preserved. But I have still to refer to the *Republic* in which Socrates discourses, though in an unsatisfactory way, on the changes in constitution. He starts from the ideally best constitution, but the change which he discerns in it is not peculiar to it but just a general statement. For he says that change is due to the fact that nothing stays the same but changes within a certain period of time; and that this periodicity has its origin in those units of mensuration 'in which a basic proportion of four to three taken in conjunction with the number five produces two harmonies', meaning by that when the unit of mensuration on the diagram is cubed. This implies that Nature may at a certain moment produce bad men, too stubborn for education. This is in itself unexceptionable; people can certainly be found who are incapable of being educated and turned into good men. But why should this be the particular change affecting what he calls the best constitution any more than any other constitution or any people at any time? And throughout that period of time, which he speaks of as changing all things, do things which come into being at different times change at the same time? I mean, if something came into being the day before the turning point, does it then change along with the rest?

My second criticism is this: why should this constitution change into the Lacedaemonian particularly? All constitutions are more likely to change into their opposites than into those like them. The same argument also applies to the subsequent changes which he gives – from the Laconian to oligarchy and from that to democracy and from democracy to tyranny. Surely there are also changes in the reverse direction, as from democracy to oligarchy even more than to one-man rule. Moreover he stops at tyranny and does not say whether or not it will suffer change, or if it does, what will cause the change and into what constitution it will change. The reason is that he would have found it difficult to say; tyranny is indeterminate, there is no knowing how it will change. According to Socrates's theory it ought to change into the ideal constitution, the first and best; the process would then have been continuous and circular. But tyranny can also change into tyranny, as at Sicyon from that of Myron to that of Cleisthenes, or to oligarchy, like the tyranny of Antileon at Chalcis, or to democracy, as did that of Gelon's family at Syracuse, or into aristocracy, as that of Charilaus at Lacedaemon, or at Carthage. Change may also take place from oligarchy to tyranny; which is what happened to most of the older Sicilian oligarchies, in Leontini to the tyranny of Panaetius, in Gela to that of Cleandros, in Rhegium to that of Anaxilas, and in many other cities likewise.

I cannot accept his notion that change into oligarchy is due to the fact that those who hold office are fond of money and fond of making money, and not rather to the fact that the extremely wealthy do not think it right that those who are not possessed of any property should participate in the state on equal terms with those who are. In many oligarchies it is not possible to make money; there are laws to prevent it. But in democratic Carthage they make money and have not yet changed their constitution. Equally unacceptable is his statement that the oligarchical state is two states, one of the rich and one of the poor. The fact is that the oligarchy of which he speaks is no different in this respect from the Laconian, or any other in which not all are equally possessed of property and not all are equally good men. Without any person becoming poorer than he was, men may yet change from oligarchy to democracy, if the poor become more numerous; and from democracy to oligarchy when the wealthy are stronger than the people, so long as the one party is fully intent and the other not alive to the situation. Though there are many causes that give rise to these revolutions, he mentions but one, namely that by their extravagant living men of the oligarchy get heavily into debt and become poor, implying that all or most of them were rich at the start. But this is not true. Certainly whenever some of the leading men lose all their wealth, they try to make extensive changes, but when it is the wealth of lesser persons that is squandered, that is nothing to worry about. And if revolution does take place on such an occasion, it need not tend towards a democratic any more than towards any other form of constitution. What counts in creating a revolutionary situation is not whether the all is spent, but whether honours and privileges are fully shared, and whether people are unfairly treated or ill-used. The possibility of doing exactly what one likes is, he says, furnished by an excess of liberty. There are many different oligarchies and democracies, but Socrates speaks of their revolutions as if there were only one of each.

BOOK VI

*The sixth book contains frequent references to previous discussion in
the fourth and fifth books. It deals with the question how best can
democracies (Chapters 1–5) and oligarchies (Chapters 6–7) be
made to work; but it has the appearance of breaking off unfinished.*

I

So far we have dealt with the number and nature of the
differences in a constitution in respect both of its deliberative and its executive element, the appointments to offices,
the legal system, and what kinds are suitable for what constitutions; we have also discussed the destruction of constitutions as well as their preservation, and the causes and
occasions of these. But since there are in fact different kinds
of democracy, as of the others, it might not come amiss to
pick up the remaining threads of that inquiry and to state
what particular way of constitutional construction is apt and
expedient in each case. We have also to consider possible
combinations of all the ways that have been mentioned; for
a combination of two ways makes a different total result:
an aristocracy may become oligarchic, a polity more democratic. These combinations of different features have never
been investigated, but they ought to be: combinations such
as the following: when there is an oligarchical bias in the
set-up of the deliberative body or in the choice of officials,
but an aristocratic bias in the legal system; or if the legal
and deliberative functions are assigned on oligarchic principles, the electoral on aristocratic; or any other way in
which all the elements in the constitution are not of one
kind. Again, while we have already spoken of the kinds of
democracy most suitable for a specific kind of city, and what
kind of oligarchy for what kind of people, and, of the other
constitutional types, which is advantageous to whom, there
is still much that needs to be said. It ought to be shown not

only which of the constitutions is best for the different cities, but also how these and the others ought to be made to work. Let us now deal briefly with this latter question, beginning with democracy; this will at the same time throw light on its opposite, the constitution which is called by some oligarchy.

To do this we must take all the features of popular rule, all that are considered to be typical of democracy. For out of combinations of these result the forms of democracy, more numerous than and differing from any one democracy. There are two reasons why there are several different democracies; first, the one already mentioned, that peoples differ; one may be agricultural, another engaged in menial tasks, another in work for hire, and when the first of these is added to the second, or the third to both, not only is the quality of the democracy altered every time but also its kind. The other is the one under discussion. For all these features which are inseparable from democracy and are regarded as typical of this form of constitution make different democracies in different combinations according to the number of these features included. It is useful to be able to distinguish each one, for the purpose both of setting up whichever of these constitutions one prefers, and of making improvements. Those who set up constitutions try to bring to the foundation all the associated features without distinction, but they are wrong in so doing, as has been stated earlier when the dissolution and preservation of constitutions was under discussion. Let us now discuss the claims, the ethical standards, and the aims of those who set up democracies.

These three are not treated separately; nor could they be, as liberty and equality are parts of all three.

2

The foundation of the democratic constitution is liberty. People constantly make this statement implying that only in this constitution is there any share in liberty at all; every democracy, they say, has liberty for its aim. 'Ruling and being ruled in turn' is one element in liberty. Then there is the democratic idea of justice as numerical equality, not equality based on merit; and when this idea of what is right prevails, the people must be sovereign, and whatever the majority decides that is final and that is justice. For, they say, there must be equality among the citizens. The result is that in democracies the poor have more sovereign power than the men of property; for they are more numerous and the decisions of the majority prevail. That is one aspect of liberty, one which all democrats regard as part of the definition of their constitution. Another is the 'live as you like' principle. For this too is the mark of a free man, just as its opposite, living not as you like, is the mark of one enslaved. This is the second defining feature of democracy and from it has come the principle of 'not being ruled', not by anyone at all if possible, or at least only in alternation. This is an element in liberty that is based on equality.

From these fundamental principles, and in particular from the principles of ruling and being ruled, are derived the following features of democracy: (1) Elections: all citizens eligible for all offices; (2) rule: all over each and each in turn over all; (3) offices filled by lot, either all or at any rate those not calling for experience or training; (4) no tenure of office dependent on the possession of a property qualification or only on a very low one; (5) the same man not to hold the same office twice or only very rarely – a few permitted exceptions, notably offices connected with warfare; (6) short term of office for all offices or as many as possible; (7) jury-courts all chosen from all the citizens and adjudicating on all or most matters and always on the most important and far-reaching, such as those affecting the constitution, investigations, contracts between individuals; (8) the Ecclesia or Assembly is the sovereign authority in everything, officials having no sovereign power over anything except quite minor matters, or else the Council is sovereign in matters of greatest importance.* Next (9), payment for

* The Council is of all offices the most democratic so long as all the citizens do not receive lavish pay; for lavish pay all round has the effect

services, in the assembly, in the law-courts, and in the offices, is regular for all (or at any rate the offices, the law-courts, council, and the sovereign assemblies, or offices, where it is obligatory to have meals together). Again (10), as good birth, wealth, and culture are the marks of the rule of the few, so their opposites, low birth, low incomes, and low tastes are regarded as typical of the rule of the people. (11) Perpetual tenure of office is not favoured by democracy; and if any perpetual office remains in being after an early revolution, we note that it has been shorn of its power and its holders selected by lot from among picked candidates.

These are the general characteristics of democracies. And from the idea of justice that is by common consent democratic, that based on numerical equality, springs the most thoroughly democratic democracy of the demos; equality such that rich and poor exercise exactly the same influence in government, no individuals having sovereign power but all together on an equal and numerical basis. In this way, so they think, they can create equality and freedom in the constitution.

The following chapter reads like something which Aristotle had written down at some time without being quite sure what use he would make of it. It contains a reference to Book III, Chapter 10. Proportionate equality, dealt with in Books III and V, is badly illustrated here by an example which does not in fact show how weighting the scales in favour of property can alter the balance.

3

The next question is, How will they maintain equality? Ought the property of five hundred persons to be distributed over a thousand, and the thousand have the same

---

of removing its power from this body also; for the demos, when well-paid for its services, insists on handling all disputed issues itself, as has been explained in the discussions preceding this.

power as the five hundred? Or, rejecting equality on these lines, make the distribution as before but then from the five hundred take the same number of persons as from the thousand and give to these control of elections and law-courts? Will this constitution then be most just in accordance with the democratic conception of justice? I should say rather in accordance with the majority-conception of justice; for the champions of democracy say that that is right which the majority decide, while the oligarchs say that it is whatever is decided upon by that part which is represented by the larger property, asserting that amount of wealth is a proper criterion to use. But both these views involve a measure of inequality and of injustice. If we take the view that justice is what the few decide, we have a tyranny; for if one man has property greater than all the other wealthy persons, according to oligarchic justice he alone has a right to rule. If we take justice to be what is decided by a numerical majority, they will act unjustly, confiscating the property of the rich and less numerous, as has been said before. In order to ascertain what an equality might be upon which all parties will agree, we must start by examining the ideas of justice from which they severally begin. Thus it is said that whatever seems right to the majority of the citizens ought to be valid and authoritative. Perhaps so, but not universally or in every case. When a state is made up of two parts, as it usually is, the rich and the poor, we grant that whatever seems good to both groups, or to a majority in each, shall be valid. But if they disagree, the answer is whatever is decided by the majority, reckoned with those of the higher property-qualification. Suppose for example that there are ten of one group and twenty of the other, and a resolution has been supported by six of the rich and five of the poor and opposed by the four remaining rich and the fifteen remaining poor, then whichever has the highest property count, reckoning the property of both rich and poor in each set, their view is final and valid. If they turn out to be equal, that need not be regarded as a difficulty any more serious than an equality of votes in an assembly or law-court; the matter must be decided by lot or in some other recognized manner. And however difficult it may be to find out the truth about equality and justice, yet it is easier than to get men's agreement when you are trying to persuade them to forgo some profit that lies within their grasp. It is always the weaker who go in search of justice and equality, the strong reck nothing of them.

Chapter 4 refers to a fourfold classification of democracies. In the fourth book two such were given, one in Chapter 4 and one in Chapter 6. Neither is here followed exactly, but there is a resemblance to another passage in Book IV, Chapter 4 where five classes of population (one subdivided) were spoken of. Aristotle strongly favours a demos consisting largely of country-dwellers not town-dwellers, chiefly on the ground that its members will be unable to exercise the democratic right of attendance at the meetings of the Assembly. An agrarian democracy requires that the amount of landed property necessary to qualify for citizenship shall be kept very low, so that even the poor may be citizens. Large estates are a hindrance to this, hence the restrictions recommended in what follows.

4

Of the four kinds of democracy the best is that which is first in order, as was said in the preceding parts of our work. It is also the oldest. I am referring to classification by kinds of *people*. An agricultural population makes the best demos; so that it is in fact possible to make a democracy anywhere where the population subsists on agriculture or stock-raising and pastures. For having no great abundance of wealth they are kept busy and rarely attend the Assembly; on the other hand being constantly at work in the fields they do not lack the necessities. So they do not covet others' possessions. They find more satisfaction in working on the land than in the duties of government and citizenship, so long as there is no great profit to be made out of holding office; the many are more interested in making a profit than in winning public esteem. An indication of this is to be found in the fact that they put up with tyrannies in the old days and oligarchies in the present time, so long as work and livelihood are not denied them or their goods taken from them. Some of them quickly acquire wealth; the rest are at any rate not destitute. Moreover to have the power to vote at elections and to call to account outgoing officials makes up any deficiency which those who have political ambitions may feel. For in certain democracies, where the many are entitled to deliberate in council but not to participate in elections to office (electors being selected from all citizens by turns as at Mantinea), * even then, I say, they are content enough.

Hence for this a grarian type of democracy to which we give pride of place it is advantageous as well as customary that *all* the citizens elect to offices, call to scrutiny, and sit in court, but that persons to fill the most important offices be selected from among those possessing a certain amount of property, the greater the office, the higher the property-qualification; or alternatively to use not property but ability as the criterion for holding office. In this way the governing of the country will certainly be well done; the work of ruling will be done by the best men and in accordance with the wishes of the people and without any jealousy of the good men on their part. Moreover this form of administration satisfies the men of culture and distinction; they will not find themselves ruled by their inferiors, and their own government will be just, because others will have the right to call them to account. For this inter-dependence, and not allowing any set of people to please only themselves, is a good thing. Freedom to do exactly what one likes cannot do anything to keep in check that element of badness which exists in each and all of us. Hence it is most important to ensure that in constitutions this most valuable of principles shall be observed – government by good men free from error without detriment to the people at large.

It is clear then that this is the best of the democracies and

* This arrangement is rightly regarded, as it was at Mantinea, as a democratic one.

the reason is also clear, namely its dependence on the quality of the people. In considering next the means whereby a people may be made an agrarian people we find that some of the laws and customs which the ancients often adopted are exceedingly useful, such as absolutely to prohibit the acquisition of land beyond a certain amount, or within certain areas and at a certain distance from the central seat of government. And in many cities in early times it was laid down by law that original parcels of land might not be sold. A somewhat similar effect is produced by the so-called law of Oxylus which prohibits raising money on mortgage on individually owned land beyond a certain amount. In present-day conditions also matters can be kept right by means of the law of the Aphytaeans, which is very useful for the purpose which we have in mind. For the Aphytaeans, though their numbers are large and their land small, are all tillers of the soil: assessments are not based on whole properties but on portions of these so small that even the poor exceed the minimum property-qualification. Next to an agricultural population the best is a pastoral, people who earn a livelihood by herding and rearing livestock. There are many points of resemblance to agriculture proper; indeed when it comes to the operations of war these have the advantage; they are trained to fight, physically fit, and capable of living in the open.

All the other types of population, we may say, that make up the other types of democracy, are greatly inferior to these two. Their lives are inferior, and the work they do has not the quality of goodness; they are mere labourers, hirelings, the most ordinary specimens of humanity. Also this class of person, being constantly in and around the city and the market-place, can all too easily attend the Assembly. An agrarian populace on the other hand is dispersed over the countryside; its members neither appear at meetings nor feel the need of such gatherings to the same extent as a city mob. And where the land-forms of a country are such that the agricultural land is far removed from the city, it is easy to make a good democracy or polity; the populace are then

compelled to make their homes in the country, and so, even
if there is a city-mob, it should not be allowed to get control
of democratic assemblies in the absence of the country-
dwellers. So much then for the first and best kind of democracy and how it should be composed. What we have said
will throw light also on the composition of the others; they
will be inferior to just that extent to which their populations
are inferior.

The most extreme democracy, in which all share equally
in everything, is something which not every state can tolerate; and it is not likely to last, unless it is well held together
by its laws and its moral standards. (I need hardly add more
to what I have said earlier about the way this and the other
constitutions may break up.) As to the composition of this
democracy and the augmenting of the power of the people,
the leaders habitually attach as many men as possible to
themselves and they make them all citizens, both the illegitimate and those born in wedlock, and those also who are of
citizen stock on only one side, the mother's or the father's.
This practice is characteristic of extreme democracy. Popular leaders regularly augment the number of their supporters
in this way but it is not right; the addition of new citizens
ought only to continue until the people just outnumber the
upper and middle classes and not any further. To go beyond
this point makes for disorganization in the constitution and
irritates the notables to such an extent that they barely
tolerate the existence of the democracy.* A small admixture
of the lower classes is not noticed, but a large is all too obvious. There are other steps also which may be usefully
taken in promoting this kind of democracy, as those used by
Cleisthenes when he wanted to strengthen the democracy at
Athens, and by the promoters of democracy at Cyrene. I
mean the establishment of a larger number of tribes and
brotherhoods, the reduction in number of private religious
cults and priesthoods to a few public or national cults, and
generally fixing things so that there is as much social intercourse as possible and a breakdown of the former associations.

* At Cyrene this was actually the cause of a rebellion.

Moreover there is something characteristic of democracy in all the typical features of tyranny – lack of control over slaves (which may be expedient up to a point), lack of control over women and children, and allowing everyone to live as he pleases. These are the backbone of this kind of constitution; most people prefer to live undisciplined lives, they find that more enjoyable than obedience to authority.

Hints on securing stability for a constitution may be drawn from observing and avoiding all that makes for instability. Already (Book V, Chapter 11) it has been suggested that the best way to preserve a tyranny is to make it as little like a tyranny as possible. Here, in Chapters 5 and 6, the same is said of democracy and oligarchy: whatever is untypical is a source of strength, too strict adherence to doctrine is likely to undermine the régime. (We might try and see whether this is applicable to universal franchise, to rural squirearchy in its day, and to nationalization of industries.) These two chapters present another aspect of Aristotle's desire for a mixed rather than a 'pure' constitution, that which sometimes he calls 'polity'. See Book II Chapter 6 at end and Book IV, Chapter 9, and Kurt von Fritz: The Theory of the Mixed Constitution in Antiquity *(New York, 1954), pp. 81–2.*

5

The task confronting the lawgiver, and all who seek to set up a constitution of a particular kind, is not only, or even mainly, to set it up, but rather to keep it going. (Any kind of system can be made to work for a day or two.) We should therefore turn back to our previous discussions about the factors which make for the continued safety of a constitution and those which make for its dissolution. Out of these we shall try to construct a theory of preservation; we shall be on our guard against those features which we found to be destructive, and we shall incorporate those laws, written and unwritten, which shall embrace the greatest number of state-preserving elements. We shall know not to regard as a good democratic (or oligarchic) measure any measure which will make the whole as democratic (or oligarchic) as it is possible to be, but only those measures which will make the democracy (or oligarchy) last as long as possible.

Popular leaders, in their endeavour to win the favour of the masses, make great use of the law-courts; by legal confiscations they augment the people's funds. Those who have the interests of the constitution at heart ought to resist these attempts; it should be laid down by law that money accruing out of fines and confiscations should be used for sacred purposes and not go to swell the people's funds or national exchequer. This will not make potential wrongdoers any less careful, the fines will be exacted just the same; but the masses will be less prone to condemn those on trial, if they know that they are not going to make anything out of it. Besides, the number of cases tried before the people's courts ought to be reduced to a minimum and ill-considered litigation restrained by high costs. For it is not their fellow democrats that they bring into court but men of wealth and distinction. This constitution like any other ought, if possible, to command the support of citizens of all classes. At least those who exercise government should not be regarded as enemies.

In these thorough-going democracies populations are large and attendance at meetings of the Assembly is difficult for people unless they are paid. And unless money for this is forthcoming from the revenues, there is hostility among the upper classes; for the money has then to be raised by taxation and confiscation and the improper use of law-suits – things which before now have caused democracies to fall. Whenever therefore the necessary revenue is not to be had, the number of meetings of the Assembly must be reduced, and the courts, though consisting of many persons, should meet on few days. This helps to make the rich less afraid of the expenses which they have to meet, even if the property-owners themselves receive no fee for attendance at court but only the non-propertied class. It also helps to improve the conduct of suits at law, this through the presence of the wealthy, who are willing to spend a short time in court, but not to spend long periods away from their own affairs. On the other hand if revenues are available, do not do what popular leaders today do – make a free distribution of the whole surplus.* For the duty of the truly democratic politician is just to see that people are not destitute; for destitution is a cause of deterioration of democracy. Every effort therefore must be made to perpetuate prosperity. And, since this is to the advantage of the rich as well as the poor, all that can be got from the revenues should be collected into a single fund and distributed to those in need, if possible enough for the purchase of a piece of land, but if not, enough to start a business or work on the land. And if that cannot be done for all individually, the distribution might be by tribes or some other division each in turn. The rich meanwhile will contribute funds sufficient to provide pay for the necessary minimum of meetings, being themselves relieved of all unnecessary public duties. It has been by running their administration on these lines that the Carthaginians have secured the good-will of their demos. From time to time they send some of them to live in the outlying districts and turn them into men of property. When the upper classes are wise and charitable, they also split up the poor into groups and make it their business to provide them with work and give them a start in life. What is done in Tarentum is also well worth copying; there they have not communal ownership but communal use of property by those who have none of their own. This keeps the masses content. They also divide all the offices into two groups, filling one by selection, the other by lot; the latter allows the people to participate in filling the offices, the former means that they are more efficiently administered. It is also possible to apply this to one and the same office, dividing it in two, so that some holders are appointed by lot, others by selection. So much for the organization of a democracy.

* And when people get it, they want the same again. This sort of welfare assistance is like the proverbial jug with a hole in it.

6

How oligarchy should be handled is fairly clear from the principles already stated. Over against the list of democracies we draw up a list of oligarchies, each corresponding to the democracy opposite to it. We begin with the first and best, which is also the best mixed and is very near to what we call polity. In it differential assessments are necessary, that is, a dual scale, whereby the qualification for holding the lesser but essential offices is low, much higher for the greater offices. Anyone who reaches the required amount of property is entitled to some share in the constitution; by this means enough members of the demos are added to the citizen-body to ensure that they outnumber the non-sharers. But these new members must always be drawn from among the better sort of the people. Similarly with the next type of oligarchy, save that the oligarchical reins are drawn a little tighter. Finally, there is that which corresponds to the extreme democracy. This is the strictest of the oligarchies and most like a tyranny: it is also the worst, and the worse it is, the greater the need to watch it, if it is to survive. But just as our bodies, if they are in a healthy condition, or boats if they are in proper trim for their owners to sail them, can tolerate errors without allowing these to destroy them (whereas bodies in a sickly condition or boats in poor trim and incompetently handled are seriously affected by even minor mistakes), so it is with state-constitutions; the worst of them need most care.

Generally speaking then, in democracies a large population is a safeguard, just because weight of numbers favours the democratic principle of justice and is opposed to the principle of allowing weight to individual merit. But an oligarchy can expect to secure its safety only by enforcing good order.

Hence the need for military force; and the narrower the oligarchy, the greater the need. But just as the quality of a democracy was

*related above to the kind of population and to geographical and eco-
nomic conditions, so now these factors are shown to be important in
determining the military forces.*

7

Population consists of four main elements – the farmers,
the menially-occupied, the traders, and those employed
by others. Armed forces are likewise four – cavalry,
armoured infantry or hoplites, light-armed infantry, naval
forces. In any state therefore whose territory is suitable for
horse-breeding the conditions are favourable for making the
oligarchy secure. This is because the safety of the inhabitants
of such territory depends on the strength of the cavalry, and
horse-breeding is an occupation confined to those who have
large estates. The next form of oligarchy will flourish where
the territory is suitable for hoplites; armour is more within the
means of the well-to-do than the poor. But the light-armed
infantry and service in ships are democratic. And so in
practice, wherever these form a large proportion of the
population, the oligarchs, if there is a struggle, fight at a
disadvantage.* To meet this, one must secure the aid of the
commanders of the armed forces and get them to combine in
one force cavalry, hoplites, and light-armed troops suitably
groomed. Now to incorporate thus a body of light-armed
men of the people divides the armed forces against themselves. But since there is already a difference of two age-
groups, one older, the other younger, the oligarchs' own sons
while still young should be trained in light-infantry work
and then, separated from the boys, become fit for service in
the field. As to giving the masses a share in government –
this may be done (1) as previously stated, in favour of those
who possess a certain amount of property, (2) as at Thebes,
after the lapse of a period of time spent away from menial
occupations, (3) as at Massilia, by making a selection of the

---

* It is by the use of light infantry in civil wars that the masses get the
better of the rich; their mobility and light equipment give them an
advantage over cavalry and the heavy-armed.

most deserving from both those within the citizen-body and those without. Again, the very highest offices, which must be held by those who are fully members of the constitution, should be imposed as burdens, the holder in each case bearing the full cost. This will reconcile the people to having no share in government and make them think more kindly of rulers who pay heavily for the privilege of ruling. It is appropriate, too, that newcomers to office should offer magnificent sacrificial banquets and start some piece of public building at their own expense. The object is that the people, when they share in the banquets and see their city adorned with memorial monuments and splendid buildings, may be satisfied to see this form of government continue. There is the further advantage that these will remain as memorials to the generosity of the notable men. But nowadays those who are connected with oligarchy do not show such generosity, rather the reverse, for it is the profits they are after, not the honour. Such oligarchies are well named 'democracies in miniature'.

These then are the ways in which we think the various democracies and oligarchies ought to be organized.

Like so much else in this book, the eighth chapter looks back to Book IV. It adds to, but does not illustrate, what was there said in Chapters 15 and 16 about offices of government and the administration of the law.

8

Following upon what has been said comes the topic of the proper differentiation of offices of government – what offices and how many and in what spheres each is to operate. This has been mentioned already. Without the essential minimum of offices there can be no state at all; without those concerned with good order and good conduct there can be no well-governed one. And in smaller states the organs of government will need to be smaller, larger in the large, as

has indeed been stated earlier. We must therefore not neglect to consider which of them can appropriately be merged
into one and which ought to be kept separate.

Among the first essentials is control of market places;
there must be some authority charged with the duty of seeing that honest dealing and good order prevail. For we may
say that one of the essential activities of states is the buying
and selling of goods to meet their varying needs; this is the
quickest way to that economic independence which is probably the thing that moves men to come together in one form
of society. Closely connected with this are all matters relating to public and private building within the town, the aim
being to secure orderly planning; streets and buildings have
to be constructed, maintained, and, if need be, rebuilt,
boundaries between properties fixed beyond dispute, and
other matters of the kind connected with what is called town-
government. This includes a number of branches. Where the
number of inhabitants is very large, the branches are separately administered – walls, harbour, water-supply, and the
like. These all have reference to the town. In the country
there is another set of officials charged with similar duties,
called by some Agronomers, by others Foresters. That makes
three assignments so far – agora, astynomy, agronomy.
Next, that office which receives the revenues of the state,
safeguards them and distributes them to the various
branches of the administration; names such as Receivers or
Treasurers are given to these. Fifthly there is the office
which keeps records of legal documents, of contracts made
between private persons as well as law-court decisions; the
same ought also to be the depository of all prosecutions and
suits pending. Sometimes this also is divided, sometimes one
single office covers them all. The officials are called Keeper
of Sacred Records, Registrar, Recorder, and other such
names.

Next, also connected with the law, are the executives.
Their task is both necessary and hard. They have to carry
out the sentences of the courts, to collect monies publicly
declared to be due to the state, and to keep prisoners in

custody. This work is unpleasant; it gives rise to much resentment. So, unless it is very well-paid, people either refuse to undertake it or will only do so if they are given a free hand and can disregard the laws. Yet it is most essential: it is no good having legal decisions on matters of right and justice if these are to have no effect. If it is impossible for men to live in a society in which there are no legal decisions, it is also impossible where they are not carried out. It is therefore better that this work should not be assigned to a single authority, but to various persons from the various courts, and an attempt should be made to distribute the work of publicly declaring the fines to be paid. So too in the collection of fines, the officials should do this only in some cases, in particular, new officials should collect the fines imposed in their predecessors' time, and while they are in office the fines should be collected by a different office from that which imposed them, the fines of market-officers being collected by the town-buildings officers and theirs in turn by others. For the less ill-feeling there is against the collectors, the better the chances of the fines being paid in full. It doubles the ill-feeling to have the same persons impose the fines and collect them; when everything is done by the same people, they are everyone's enemies.

Very often the custody of prisoners is combined with the exacting of punishments, as at Athens in the work of those called The Eleven. It is better here too to separate the two, and to look for the best way of doing this job. For the custody of prisoners is just as important as that which we have been speaking of. But good men especially try to avoid it and it is dangerous to commit it into the hands of the bad, who are themselves more in need of watching than capable of watching others. Therefore there ought not to be one single and perpetual authority charged with the care of prisoners, but use should be made, where the system exists, of the young men doing military service and garrison duty in a particular year. And different sets of officials also can be employed on this work.

The above mentioned offices are the first and most

needed; equally essential and of greater ceremonial dignity and calling for much experience and great trustworthiness are all those connected with the defence of the state, and organized with a view to its needs in time of war. In war and peace alike there must be men charged with the maintenance and protection of walls and gates and with the call-up and military organization of the citizens. In some states many separate offices look after these matters, in others much fewer; in very small states one office covers them all. Names given to the holders of such offices are commander-in-chief and war-leader. Where there are cavalry, light-armed troops, bowmen, sailors, for these too sometimes there are separate officials – nauarch, hipparch, taxiarch, and junior ranks in each case – captains, colonels, squadron-leaders, and so on down to the smaller units. But they all belong to a single class performing the task of defence.

There we leave that topic and observe next that since some, if not all, the offices handle great quantities of publicly-owned property, it is essential to have yet another office, the Treasury. It will receive accounts of expenditure and audit them; it will have no function other than financial. Various names are given to these officials – auditors, accountants, assessors, procurators. As well as all the offices which we have mentioned there is the supreme governmental authority. This has the last word as well as the first; or else, where the demos is sovereign, it convenes and presides over meetings of the people. The convening authority is bound to be the sovereign authority. This office is sometimes called the Pre-Council because it deliberates beforehand, but in democracies it is usually just called Council.

This pretty well covers the political offices but there is religion also to be looked after. Its officials are priests and trustees of sacred property; their task is the protection of existing buildings and the repair of those damaged, and to take charge of whatever else is connected with the worship of the gods. Sometimes all this can be looked after by a single official, in small cities for example. But sometimes we find kept separate from the priesthood a number of officials –

sacrificers, temple-guardians, treasurers of sacred funds. Connected with this there is the superintendence of public sacrifices, that is those which by law are not entrusted to priests, national cults which derive their prestige from the altar of the whole nation. Various names are given to the officials concerned with these – kings, archons, prytaneis.

These then are the most necessary services which a government must maintain. We may recapitulate them as follows: religion, defence, income and expenditure, trade, the town and its harbours, the countryside, legal administration, registration of contracts, prisons and the execution of judgement, auditing and review of accounts, examination of holders of office, and finally discussion and decision on the affairs of the nation. Some assignments are peculiar to cities where culture and refinement are above the average and where great attention is paid to orderly behaviour. Such are control of women, control of children, seeing that the laws are kept, management of gymnasia; and to these we should add the contests, both athletic and dramatic, and any other public spectacles that there may be. Some of these offices are obviously not at all democratic, for example the control of women and children: for the poor, not having any slaves, are obliged to use their women and children as servants. Of the three offices which some use as a basis for the distribution of sovereign power, law-observance officers, pre-council, and council, the law-officers are aristocratic, pre-councillors oligarchic, and Council democratic. We have now sketched in outline pretty well all the offices.

BOOK VII

The seventh and eighth books belong closely to each other and stand somewhat apart from the preceding six. They make an unfinished essay on a favourite theme of Greek thinkers, 'What is the ideal form of polity?' It is introduced by a discussion of the best life, since it must be the aim of the best constitution to secure the best kind of life for the citizens. This is a well-worn but inexhaustible subject; both the Ethics *and the* Politics *are full of it and also Aristotle's more popular essays and public lectures – if indeed either of these is what he means by his 'outside discourses', here referred to (and in Book III, Chapter 6). Although in these books Aristotle is seeking to define the conditions of an ideal or perfect state, he still wants it to be within the bounds of possibility (Chapter 4, beginning). His method and approach are far removed from those of Plato's* Republic, *much more like those of the* Laws. *The first three chapters form an introduction.*

The phrases used in Chapter 1 about happiness of an individual or a city are impossible to translate effectively; the argument largely depends on verbal similarities, not to say ambiguities. 'When Aristotle sought to show . . . that the chief ingredient in happiness is virtue, his work was half done for him by the ordinary use of the Greek language.' * *But let the reader also ponder such English expressions as 'doing well, well-doing, faring well, doing good'.*

I

If we wish to discuss the Best State really adequately, we must first decide what is the most desirable life; for if we do not know that, the best constitution, which we seek, will also elude us. Those who live in a well-ordered society on the basis of their own resources may be expected, barring accidents, to be those whose lives proceed best. We must therefore first come to some agreement as to what is the most desirable life for all men, or nearly all, and then decide

* W. L. Newman, *The Politics of Aristotle* (1892), Vol. III, p. 310.

whether the same kind of life or some other is best for men, both in the mass and taken individually.

I have written a good deal elsewhere, including my outside writings, on the subject of the best life and I propose to make use of these now. Certainly no one will dispute one thing: that there are three ingredients which must all be present to make a happy life – our bodily existence, our intellectual and moral qualities, and all that is external to these. No one would deem happy a man who is entirely without courage or self-control or honesty or intelligence, who is scared of flies buzzing past, who will stop at nothing to gratify his desire for eating or drinking, who will ruin his closest friends for a paltry profit, and whose mind also is either as witless as a child's or as deluded as a lunatic's. But while there is general agreement about these three, there is much difference of opinion about their relative importance, the extent to which each ought to be present and whether there is a point beyond which any of them becomes excessive. Thus people suppose that it is sufficient to have a certain amount of goodness, ability, character, but that there is no limit set in the pursuit of wealth, power, property, reputation, and the like.

Our answer to such people will be twofold. First, it is easy to arrive at a firm conclusion on these matters by simply observing the facts; it is not by means of external goods that men acquire and keep the virtues but the other way round; and to live happily, whether men suppose it to consist in enjoyment or in qualities of character or in both, does in fact accrue more easily to those who are outstandingly well-equipped in character and intellect, and only moderately so in the possession of material goods, more easily, that is, than to those who have more goods than they need but are deficient in the other qualities. Second, the matter can be viewed theoretically as well as empirically and the same general view will be obtained. External goods, being like a collection of tools each useful for some purpose, have a limit; one can have too many of them, and that is of no benefit or even a positive nuisance to their possessors. It is quite otherwise with the goods of the mind; every single one of the mind's good qualities is needed and the more there is of each the more useful it will be. (I apply to these the term 'useful' as well as the more usual 'admirable'.) So, putting it in general terms, we shall say that the best condition of anything in relation to any other condition of a thing is commensurate with the relations between the things themselves. Hence as the mind is superior (both absolutely and relatively to ourselves) both to possessions and to the body, its best condition will necessarily show a proportionate superiority over each of the others. Moreover it is for the sake of our minds that these qualities are to be desired and all right-minded persons ought to desire them; it would be wrong to reverse this priority.

Let this then be agreed upon at the start: to each man there comes just so much happiness as he has of moral and intellectual goodness and of performance of actions dependent thereon. God himself is an indication of the truth of this. He is blessed and happy not on account of any of the external goods but because of himself and what he is by his own nature. And for the same reason good fortune must be something different from happiness; for the acquisition of goods external to the mind is due either to the cause of events or to fortune, but no man is righteous or moral as a result of fortune or a lucky coincidence. These same arguments apply with equal force to the state: the best and best-faring city is the happy city; it is impossible for those who do not do good actions to do well. And there is no such thing as a man's or a city's good action without virtue and intelligence. The courage of a nation, or its justice, or its wisdom, have exactly the same effect and are manifested in the same way as in the case of an individual, who by virtue of his share in these is called just, wise, intelligent.

These remarks must suffice to introduce the subject; it was impossible to start without saying something, equally impossible to try and say everything relevant, for that would be a task for another occasion. For the present let this be our fundamental basis: that life is best, both for individuals and for cities, which has virtue sufficiently supported by material wealth to enable it to perform the actions that virtue calls for. As for objectors, if there is anyone who does not believe what has been said, we must pass them by for the purposes of our present inquiry and deal with them on some future occasion.

The question raised at the beginning, Which is the most desirable kind of life? has not yet been answered in detail: the preliminaries just referred to are still in progress and continue to the end of Chapter 3. But the second question, whether the same life is desirable for both cities and individuals, has been answered in the affirmative. Happiness has been shown to be inseparable from virtue and therefore from the good life. Happiness was the main topic of Ethics *Book I and was there defined as ' an activity of the mind according to perfect virtue' (I, 13). Is the happy life busy and active or is it contemplative? There are some who praise a life of unlimited power, if not for individuals at any rate for the state.*

2

It remains to ask whether or not we are to say that happiness is the same for the individual human being and for the city. The answer again is obvious: all would agree that it is the same. For those who as individuals hold the view that the good life depends on wealth will likewise, if the whole city be wealthy, count it happy; and those who prize most highly the life of a tyrant will deem most happy that city which rules over the most extensive dominions. So too one who accepts or rejects the single individual on the basis of his virtue will also judge the more virtuous city to be the happier. But there are still these two questions needing consideration: (1) which life is one to choose, the life of a citizen, fully participating in the work of the city, or that of a foreign resident, cutting oneself adrift from the political nexus? and (2) what constitution are we to lay down as desirable, and what is the best internal arrangement of the affairs of the state (whether we assume that full participation in these is desirable for all or only for the majority)? This is the important question: the first question was a matter of an individual's choice, this one belongs to political theory and principles and we have chosen to deal with it now. The other question was merely incidental, this one is the core of our inquiry.

Obviously the best constitution must be one which is so ordered that any person whatsoever may act and live happily; but it is disputed, even by those who admit that the life of virtue is the most desirable, whether the life of an active citizen is preferable to one which is free of all commitments, the contemplative life, which some say is the only philosophical life. Both in ancient and in modern times men striving for virtue seem generally to have picked out these two kinds of life, the political and the philosophical, as the only possible. It makes considerable difference which of the two is right, because we must, if we are right-minded people, direct ourselves to the better of the two aims, whichever it may be; and this equally as individuals and as a community of citizens. Some hold that to dominate other states despotically involves the greatest injustice but to do so in a statesman-like way involves none, though it does mean making inroads on the leisure and comfort of the ruler. Others hold that this is no drawback, since the busy life of active statesmanship is the only one worthy of a man, and virtuous activity springing from any of the virtues is just as much open to those who take part in the affairs of the city as to individual private citizens. That is one view, but there is also a set of people who go so far as to say that the only happy life is one of absolute and despotic domination. And in some cities the avowed purpose of the laws and constitution is to enable that city to dominate neighbouring states.

Aggressiveness as a national way of life exists but is not to be commended. External relations need not be hostile.

Hence, even though in most states their legal provisions have for the most part been established on no fixed principle, yet in so far as laws may be said to have a single purpose they all aim at domination. Thus in Sparta and Crete the educational system and most of the laws are directed towards the establishment of military power for the purposes of war; and outside the Greek peoples such nations as are strong enough to enrich themselves, like the Scythians, Persians, Thracians, and Kelts, have always set great store by military power. In some places there are laws designed to foster military courage, as at Carthage where men wear armlets showing the number of campaigns in which they have served. There used to be a rule in Macedonia that a man had to wear a halter until he had slain his first enemy, and at a certain Scythian feast when the cup was passed round only those were allowed to drink from it who had killed an enemy. Among the Iberians, a very warlike race, the tombs of their warriors have iron spikes stuck in them showing the number of enemy slain. There are many other such laws and customs established among different peoples.

Yet surely, if we will but examine carefully, we shall see how completely unreasonable it would be if the work of a statesman were to be reduced to seeing how he could rule and dominate others with or without their consent. How could that be regarded as part of statecraft or lawgiving which is not even lawful in itself? To rule at all costs, not only justly but unjustly, that is simply non-legal, and merely to have the power is not to have the right. One does not find this insistence on power in any of the other professions; it is not the job of a doctor or a ship's captain to persuade or to force patients or passengers. Certainly most people seem to think that domination and government are one and the same thing; they have no compunction about inflicting upon others what as individuals they regard as neither just nor beneficial to themselves. For themselves and among themselves they ask for just government but in the treatment of others they do not worry about what things are just. Of course we may be sure that nature has made some creatures to be treated despotically and others not, and if this is so, we must try to exercise despotic rule not over all creatures but only over those made for such treatment. We do not pursue human beings to hurt or slay them for food, but only such animals as are wild and edible and suitable to be hunted. Surely too a single city could be happy on its own, assuming of course that its internal government is good. It is possible for a city to exist in isolation following its own good laws; the administration of its constitution will not be directed to war or the defeat of enemies, for the non-existence of these is postulated. The conclusion is obvious: we regard every provision made for war as admirable, not as a supreme end but only as serving the needs of defence. It is the task of a good legislator to survey the city, the clan, and every other human association and to see how they can be brought to share in the good life and in whatever degree of happiness is possible for them. There will of course be different rules in different places; if there are neighbouring peoples, it will be part of the legislative function to decide what attitude is to be adopted to this one and that one, and how to use towards each the proper method for dealing with each. But this question 'With what end in view should the Best Constitution be designed?' will be properly dealt with at a later stage in our inquiry.

Leaving this topic to be resumed in the latter part of Chapter 14, Aristotle returns to the general theme of these preliminary chapters – the good life. The reference to 'an earlier passage' is to Book I, Chapter 7.

3

We must now deal with those who, while agreeing that the life which is conjoined with virtue is the most desirable, differ as to how it is to be pursued. Some reject altogether any life of public responsibility, regarding the life of a free man as inconsistent with the work of a statesman and as the most desirable of all lives. Others say that an active public life is best, on the grounds that a man who does nothing cannot be doing well, and happiness and faring well are the same thing. To both parties we may say in reply, 'You are both of you partly right and partly wrong.' Certainly the life of a free man is better than the life of a despotic ruler; there is no worth or dignity in treating a slave as a slave, and issuing instructions to do this or that is no part of virtuous or noble activity. But not all giving of commands is despotic and those who think it is are mistaken. The differences between ruling over free men and ruling over slaves is as great as the natural differences between freedom and slavery, a distinction which has been sufficiently emphasized in an earlier passage. But we cannot agree that it is right to value inaction more than action, doing nothing more than doing something. For happiness is doing something and the actions of good and wise men have as their aim the production of a variety of excellent results.

Unlimited power to do good is rarely used to do only good. It must be conjoined with moral superiority.

But perhaps someone will object that if we define things in this way, it means that absolute sovereignty is best, because it is in a position to perform the noblest actions; and so anyone who is in a position to rule ought not to yield that position to another, but take and keep it for himself without any regard for the claims of friendship or even parenthood or anything else; the best is most to be desired and nothing could be better than to do well. Perhaps there is some truth in this, but only if we suppose that this most desirable condition is going to belong to those who use robbery and violence. But this is most improbable and the supposition is false. For a man who shows no more superiority over his fellows than husband over wife or father over children or master over slave – how can his actions be always good actions? So he that departs from the path of goodness will never be able to do good sufficient to make up entirely for his previous errors. For equals, the right and just thing is to share and take turns, as is fair and equal. Non-equality, superiority, given to equals, unlike positions given to like persons – these are contrary to nature and nothing that is contrary to nature is right. It is only when one man is superior in virtue and in the ability to perform the finest actions that it becomes right to serve him and just to obey him. But it should be remembered that goodness in itself is not enough; there must also be the power to translate it into action.

If all this is true and if happiness is to be equated with doing well, then the active life will be the best both for any state as a whole community and for the individual. But the active life need not, as some suppose, be always concerned with our relations with other people, nor is thinking only effective when it concentrates on the possible outcome of action. On the contrary, thinking and speculation that are their own end and are done for the sake of thinking and speculation – these are more effective because they are themselves the doing well which is their aim, and they are therefore action. Indeed those who build with their thoughts are quite properly spoken of as the creators of external actions also. As for their counterpart among states, cities that are set up away from others and have chosen to live thus in isolation, there is nothing in that to oblige them to lead a life of inaction. Activity may be internal: the parts of a city provide numerous groups or associations that enter into relations with each other. The same is true of any individual person; otherwise God himself and the whole universe would be in a sorry plight, for they have no external activities, only what they can provide for themselves. It is therefore clear that the same life must inevitably be the best for individuals, for states, and for mankind.

The preliminary remarks are now complete. It remains to discuss and describe the Ideal State. Aristotle begins by referring to Book II where others' descriptions were criticized. Plato's Laws *had been much less severely handled than his* Republic. *What now follows (Chapters 4 to 12) is similar in method but not in detail to the* Laws. *First the materials and the conditions, population, size, situation,*

climate (4–7). Next its institutions, social, political, and religious,
especially as concerns citizenship, ownership of land, and division
into classes (8–10). Then the layout of the ideal city itself. All this
is somewhat external; the account of politeia *only begins at Chapter*
13 and it begins with education, which is the main subject of the rest
of Book VII and all that remains of Book VIII. Nowhere in what
here survives is there an account of a constitutional framework such as
Plato in his Laws *described in detail.*

4

Now that our introduction to these matters is finished and
since we have earlier discussed the other constitutions, the
first part of what remains to be discussed will deal with the
question, 'What are the fundamental postulates for a state
which is to be constructed exactly as one would wish, one
provided with all the appropriate material equipment,
without which it would not be the best state?' We must
therefore postulate everything as we would wish it to be, remembering however that nothing must be outside the
bounds of possibility. I am thinking for example of population and territory; these are part of the essential material. A
weaver or a boatmaker must have a supply of the materials
necessary for the exercise of his craft, and the better the provision for these, the finer will be the result which his skill will
produce. So too a statesman or lawgiver must have the
proper material in sufficient quantities.

For the making of a state the first essential is a supply of
men and we must consider both how many they shall be and
of what kind. The second is territory; we shall need to
determine both its extent and its quality. Most people think
that if a city is to be happy it must needs be great. This may
be true, but they do not know how to judge greatness and
smallness in a city. They judge greatness by the number of
people living in it; but one ought to look not at numbers
merely but at power and effectiveness. A city has a function
to perform and the city which is most capable of discharging
that function must be regarded as greatest, rather in the

264

same way that one might say that Hippocrates was 'a bigger man', not as a man but as a physician, than one of great bodily size. However, even granting that we must have regard to size of population, we must not do so without discrimination; we must allow for the presence in the states of many slaves and many foreigners, residents or visitors. Our concern is only with those who form part of the state, with those sections of population of which a state properly consists. Great numbers of these is a mark of a great city, but a city cannot possibly be great which can put into the field only a handful of citizen-soldiers along with a large rabble of inferior persons. A great city and a populous one are not the same. Moreover, experience has shown that it is difficult, if not impossible, for an over-large population to be well and lawfully governed; at any rate I know of no well-constituted city that does not restrict its numbers. The language itself makes this certain. For law is itself a kind of order and to live under good laws is to live in good order. But an excessively large number cannot be orderly; that would require the power of the divine force which holds the universe together, where to be sure we do find order and beauty conjoined with size and multiplicity. Therefore that city will be finest which though large conforms to the limitations just mentioned. But there must also be a proper norm for the size of a city, as there is a normal size for everything else – animals, plants, instruments, and so on. Each of these can only perform its proper function if it is neither too large nor too small; otherwise its true *raison d'être* will be either entirely lost or seriously impaired. Thus a boat a few inches long will not really be a boat at all, nor one half a mile long. If it reaches a certain size, it may be long enough (or small enough) to be called a boat, but still be too small (or too large) to be navigated. It is just the same with a city; if it has too few people it cannot serve its own needs as a city should; if it has too many it can certainly meet all its essential requirements, but as an ethnic conglomerate not as a city Such size makes it difficult for any constitution to subsist. For who will be military commander of the excessive population?

Who will be their crier unless he has the voice of a Stentor? Therefore, when first the population becomes large enough to be able to provide for itself all that is needed for living the good life after the manner of the city-state community, then we can begin to speak of a city. It is possible to go on from there; a city greater in population than that will be a larger city, but as we have said this process is not unlimited. What the limit of size should be can easily be determined by an examination of the facts. The activities of a city are those of the rulers and those of the ruled, and the functions of the ruler are decision and direction. In order to give decisions on matters of justice and for the purpose of distributing offices in accordance with the work of the applicants, it is necessary that the citizens should know each other and know what kind of people they are. Where this condition does not exist, both elections and decisions at law are bound to suffer; it is not right in either of these matters to vote at haphazard, which is clearly what takes place where the population is excessive. Another drawback is that it becomes easy for non-citizens, foreigners resident in the country, to become possessed of citizenship; the great size of the population makes detection difficult. Here then we have ready to hand the best definition of a city: it must have a population large enough to cater for all the needs of a self-sufficient existence, but not so large that it cannot be easily supervised. Let that be our way of defining the size of a city.

5

The case is similar when we turn our attention to territory. As regards quality of land, everyone would choose the most self-sufficient, that is to say the most universally productive; to have everything to hand and nothing lacking is the height of self-sufficiency. As to size and extent, these should be such that the citizens can live a life that involves no manual labour, a life of a free man but one without extravagance.*

* Whether this definition is good or bad is a question into which we must later go in greater detail, when we come to discuss property in

The general configuration of the land is not difficult to state, though there are some points on which we must take the opinion of those who have experience of conducting operations of war; it ought to be hard for a hostile force to invade, easy for an expeditionary force to depart from. Apart from that, just as we remarked that the population ought to be easily supervised, so we say the same of the territory; in a country that can easily be seen it is easy to bring military assistance at any point. Next, the position of the city: if we are to put it exactly where we would like best, it should be conveniently situated for both sea and land. This will give three advantages: first the point mentioned above, it will be equally well-placed for operations in all directions; also it will form an entrepôt for the receipt of incoming foodstuffs; and it will have access to timber and whatever other raw materials the land may be able to produce.

The intention to discuss ownership and property is not fulfilled in the Politics *as we have it, unless the reference be to Book I.*

The advantages of a maritime situation are now argued in greater detail, perhaps partly in answer to Plato, who constantly expressed disapproval of sea-ports and navies, foreign trade and foreign travel. Aristotle in this chapter gives first some positive advantages, then some ways in which drawbacks can be met: for he agreed with Plato in holding it to have been a disastrous policy for Athens to extend citizenship to the lower classes, who provided rowers for the navy.

6

There is a good deal of argument about communication with the sea and whether it is a help or a hindrance in good government of states. Some say that to open one's city to foreigners, brought up in a different code of behaviour, is

general and abundance of resources in private hands; what are the right relations between ownership and use of property. It is a complicated question with many points of dispute, because men tend to go to extremes, some tending to extravagance, others to niggardliness.

detrimental to good order and makes for overcrowding. They say that the use of the sea leads to much coming and going of large numbers of traders and that this is inimical to the good life of the citizens. If these evil consequences can be avoided, it is obviously better both for economic and for defensive reasons that the city and its territory should have access to the sea. To facilitate resistance to an enemy a successful defender needs to be in a position to use both sea and land, and even if he cannot strike a blow against invaders on both elements, it will be easier to strike on one, if he has access to both. So too in the economic sphere; people must import the things which they do not themselves produce and export those of which they have a surplus. For when a city becomes a trading city it must do so in its own interest and not in others'. Some throw their city open as a market for all comers for the sake of the money they bring in; but a city which regards this kind of profit-making as illegitimate ought not to possess that kind of open market at all.

Again, we see in modern times many cities and territories in possession of docks and harbours conveniently situated, not too far away but not so near as to encroach upon the town itself, and dominated by walls and other such defence-works. It is therefore clear that if this intercommunication is productive of good, the city will derive advantage from it; if of evil, it is easy to guard against that by laying down regulations and stating who are and who are not to be allowed to enter the area. Then there is this matter of naval forces; clearly it is desirable that there should be a certain amount of these; for it is important that by sea as well as by land a state should be able to make its power felt or to render aid, not only internally but in relation to certain neighbours. The number of ships and the size of the naval force will have to be decided in the light of the circumstances and way of living of the state concerned. If it is to play a big part as a leading state, it will need naval as well as land forces large enough for such activities. The addition to population, which the enlistment of large numbers of seamen/will make necessary, need not swell the membership of the cities;

there is no reason why they should have a share in the state as if they were soldiers. The troops that are carried on board are free men belonging to the infantry; they are in authority and take precedence over the crews. But the rowers need not be members of the state; and a potential source of man-power for them is sure to exist wherever the outlying dwellers and agricultural labourers are plentiful. We can see examples of this today: at Heraclea, though their city is of modest size, they find crews for many triremes. So much then for territory, harbours, cities, sea, naval forces; we pass now to the citizens and population.

In the seventh chapter Aristotle is indebted to the 'Airs, Waters, and Places' of Hippocrates, a work dealing with the effect of climate on the health and character of inhabitants. It is unfortunate that Aris-totle does not develop the theme, casually suggested, of a possible unification of Hellas as a world-ruling power. The rest of the chapter refers to the second book of Plato's Republic.

7

We have already spoken about limiting the number of citi-zens; we must now ask what kind of natural qualities they should have. We could form a fair notion of the answer if we glanced first at the most famous Greek states and then at the racial divisions of the whole world. The races that live in cold regions and those of Europe are full of courage and passion but somewhat lacking in skill and brain-power; for this reason, while remaining generally independent, they lack political cohesion and the ability to rule over others. On the other hand the Asiatic races have both brains and skill but are lacking in courage and will-power; so they have remained enslaved and subject. The Hellenic race, occupy-ing a mid-position geographically, has a measure of both. Hence it continues to be free, to have the best political in-stitutions, and to be capable of ruling all others, given a single constitution. But we do observe the same differences among the Greeks themselves when we compare one set with another; some are by nature one-sided, in others the qualities of head and of heart are combined. Both are clearly needed if men are to be as we want them – the kind of person who can easily be moulded by a lawgiver and brought to a high degree of excellence. Some say that to feel friendly at the sight of familiar faces and hostile at the approach of strangers is a requirement for guardians of the state. Now friendliness springs from the heart, from that power in our souls whereby we love. We see this from the fact that our feelings are more likely to be aroused if those whom we love neglect us than by the conduct of those whom we do not know. Hence the lines of Archilochus, reproaching his friends but addressed to his own heart, are aptly spoken: 'About your friends you torture yourself.' The power to command and the spirit of freedom have their source in this faculty, which is masterful and unsubdued. But what he says about harshness to strangers is, I think, quite wrong; there is no need to behave thus to anyone and fierceness is not a mark of greatness of mind except towards wrongdoers. Rather, as we have said, is indignation aroused by the sight of friends when we believe ourselves to have been wrongly used by them. And this is understandable; where men expect to receive kindness as their due, they are indignant at being deprived of it and at losing the benefit. Hence the proverbial sayings, 'Grievous is fraternal strife' and 'Excessive love turns to excessive hate.'

So much for the members of the state, their number, and their kind, so much for the size and kind of territory; we need say no more because one cannot expect the same attention to detail in theoretical discussions as one would if the case were presented before our eyes.

Accordingly, since this is a theoretical discussion and not an observation of data, Aristotle leaves that part of the subject and turns to consider the ideal city itself. He opens with one of his now familiar abstract generalizations, incidentally reminding us that a polis *is something in accordance with nature. He draws a distinction between a part of an organism and, as he puts it, a 'without which not', a 'sine qua non', which is indispensable but need not be a part in the literal sense. Aristotle appears to disregard the effect which economic conditions exercise on the character and way of life of inhabitants.*

8

Just as, in considering any other object that exists in nature, we do not call 'parts' all those indispensable things without which the whole would not be itself, so too we must not list as parts of a city the indispensable conditions of its existence, nor would we in relation to any other form of community that made up a single definite kind; to all its members, irrespective of their degree of participation, the community is the community, one single identical whole. Food-supply, an amount of territory, and the like, these are indispensable but they are not the things that give a specific character to any form of human society. Whenever one thing is a means and another an end, there can be no other relation between them than this – that the one acts, the other is acted upon. Take any set of tools and consider it along with its users in relation to the work which they produce; for example a house and its builders. There is no other relation between house and builders, nothing that can be called cooperation, but the builder's skill with his tools is a means towards building a house. So too a state needs to own property, but property is no part of the state, though many parts of the property are living creatures. When we speak of city or state, we mean a community of like persons whose end or aim is the best life possible. The best is happiness and this consists in the exercise of all good qualities and their fullest possible use. Life is such that some can get a share of happiness, while others get little or none. Here then we clearly have a reason for the existence of different kinds of cities and the variety of constitutions. Different sets of people seek their happiness in different ways and by different means; little wonder that their lives are different or that they have different political constitutions.

We must also ask how many are those things without which there can be no city. (We include what we call *parts* of the state, because their presence too is essential.) Let us therefore make a count of all the things and actions needed, for that will show the answer. They are (1) food, (2) handicrafts and their tools, (3) arms. Arms are included because members of the constitution must carry them even among themselves, both for internal government in the event of civil disobedience and to repel external aggression. (4) Wealth too is required both for war and for all the internal needs. Then (5) the needs of religion (this might have been put first) and (6) (most essential of all) a method of arriving at decisions, both about policy and about matters of right and wrong as between one person and another. These then are the essentials; every state, we may say, has need of these. For a state is not a chance agglomeration but, we repeat, a body of men aiming at a self-sufficient life; and if any of these six is lacking, it will be impossible for that community to be thoroughly self-sufficing. It is therefore essential in setting up a city to make provision for all these activities. Quite a number of agricultural workers will be needed to supply food; skilled craftsmen will be required, and fighting men, and wealthy men, and priests, and judges of what is right and expedient.

The chapter which follows contains some of Aristotle's most characteristic observations on society. The governing class must be one; it must be identical with the citizen-body, all of whom have by definition sufficient 'virtue' to enable them to make decisions, legal and political, to bear arms, to live a gentleman's life. The exposition would have been less complicated if Greek had a word for 'age-group', but Aristotle is anxious not to divide the upper class into two; therefore the same persons will successively be soldiers, judges, politicians, and priests.

On the 'absolutely just' and the just relatively to the state or some

*other standard compare Book IV, Chapter 7 and Book V, Chapter 9
beginning.*

9

This enumeration of classes being finished, it remains to
consider whether they shall all take part in all these activities, everybody being, as occasion requires, farmer and
craftsman and councillor and judge (for this is not impossible) or shall we postulate a different set of persons for
each task? Or again, are not some of the jobs necessarily
confined to one set of people, while others may be thrown
open to all? The situation is not the same in every form
of constitution; for as we have said it is equally possible for all to share in everything and for some to share in
some. These are what make differences in constitutions;
in democracies all share in all, in oligarchies the reverse is
true.

But since our present inquiry is directed towards the best
constitution, that is to say, that by which a city would be
most happy, and we have already said that happiness cannot exist apart from virtue, it becomes clear that in the best
state with the best constitution, one that possesses just men
who are just absolutely and not simply relatively to some
postulated standard, the citizens must not live a banausic or
commercial life. Such a life is not noble and not conducive
to virtue. Nor will those who are to be citizens live an agricultural life; for they must have leisure to cultivate their
virtue and talents, time for the activities of a citizen. Now
both defence and deliberation, whether about policy or
about questions of justice, are at the heart and centre of the
state. And when we ask whether these are to be assigned to
different persons or to be kept together in the hands of the
same body, our answer is partly one and partly the other. In
so far as the tasks themselves differ in the best time of life for
their performance, one requiring wisdom, the other strength,
they should be assigned to different people. But as it is impossible to secure that those who are strong enough to

enforce their will shall always tolerate being ruled by others, to that extent they must be assigned to the same people. For those who possess and can wield arms are in a position to decide whether the constitution is to continue or not. So we are left with this conclusion: that this constitution, both in its military and its civil functions, should be put into the hands of the same class of persons, but not both simultaneously. Rather we should follow nature, the young have strength, the older have understanding, so it is both right and expedient that the distribution of tasks should be made on this basis; it takes into account fitness for the work. Property too must belong to this class; it is essential that citizens should have ample subsistence, and these are citizens. The lower-class element has no part in the state nor any other class that is not productive of virtue. This is evident from our postulates; being happy must occur in conjunction with virtue, and in pronouncing a city happy we must have regard not to part of it but to all its citizens. It is also clear that property must belong to these; the agricultural workers will be slaves or non-Greeks dwelling in the country roundabout.

Of the list which we made earlier there remains the class of priests. Their position is clear: no agricultural or commercial worker could be made a priest, since it is only right and proper that the gods should be worshipped by citizens. As we have divided citizens and their duties into military and civil, it is also right and proper that citizens who have thus spent themselves in long service should both enjoy their retirement and serve the gods. These then should be appointed to priestly offices.

We have now stated what are the essential requirements of a state and what are its parts. There must be agricultural workers and craftsmen and paid labourers; but as to parts of the state, these are the military and deliberative elements, which may be separated either permanently or successively.

The first half of Chapter 10 is a digression or rather an editor's insertion. As its conclusion shows, it is part of a demonstration of the value of studying antiquity and of a cyclic view of human history. It is not concerned with the ideal state at all, but because it refers to classes in society and to the system of communal messing, it has been inserted here just after a reference to classes and before a discussion on the financing of common meals. But there is no reason to suppose that Aristotle is not the author.

It appears from this passage that the name Italy was originally given only to the extreme toe of the peninsula.

10

That division into classes is necessary, in particular the separation of the fighting from the agricultural class, is not a recent discovery; it has been well-known to students of politics for a long time. In Egypt something very similar still exists today and in Crete too. Sesostris is said to have introduced laws in this sense for Egypt, Minos for Crete. The practice of communal feeding also appears to be ancient, introduced in Crete in the reign of Minos, but in Italy very much earlier. For the chroniclers tell us of a certain Italus in that land who was king of Oenotria, and after him the people of Oenotria changed their name to Italians, and the name Italy was given to that part of Europe's coast line which lies south of a line drawn between the Scylletic and Lampetic gulfs, where the distance across is half a day's journey. This Italus, they tell us, transformed the Oenotrians from a pastoral people into farmers and instituted many new customs and laws, including the common meals. So even to this day some of his successors continue this practice as well as some of his other customs. On the Etrurian side were the Opici, called Ausones both in ancient and modern times; on the other side, that of Iapygia and the Ionian Sea, there was the land called Siritis; and the Chones also were by race Oenotrians. Common messing, then, originated thence, and class-distinctions in Egypt; the kingdom of Sesostris goes back very much farther than that of Minos.

We must, I think, regard it as fairly certain that the rest

of the customs have been in the course of the ages discovered, lost, and rediscovered many times over. In the first place there are things we cannot do without, and this very necessity naturally teaches us them. Secondly, when once these are established, the process naturally goes on tending towards more comfort and greater abundance. So we should accept it as a fact that the same process takes place in social and political institutions. That these are all ancient is shown by Egyptian history; the Egyptians are reputed to be the most ancient people and they have always had laws and a social and political organization. Thus we ought to make full use of what has already been discovered, while endeavouring to find what has not.

Land-tenure and the cost of maintaining common feeding centres. The promises to discuss the value of syssitia *and the use of slaves in agriculture are not, so far as we know, fulfilled. But on the common meals see also Book II, Chapter 10.*

We stated above that the land ought to be possessed by those who have arms and enjoy full participation in the constitution, and why the cultivators should be different from the owners, also the nature and extent of the territory required. We must speak first about the division of the land for the purposes of cultivation and about those who will cultivate it, who and of what type they will be. We do not agree with those who have said that all land should be communally owned, but we do believe that there should be a friendly arrangement for sharing the usufruct and that none of the citizens should be without means of support. Next as to communal feeding, it is generally agreed that this is a very useful institution in a well-ordered society; why we too are of this opinion we will say later. In any case, where communal meals exist, all citizens should partake of them, though it is not easy for those who are badly off to pay the contribution fixed and keep a household going at the same time. Another thing that should be a charge on the whole community is the public worship of the gods. Thus it becomes necessary to divide the land into two parts, one publicly owned, the other privately. Each of these has to be further divided into two. One part of the public land will support the service of the gods, the other the communal feeding. Of the privately owned land one part will be near the frontier, the other near the city, so that every citizen will have two portions, one in each locality. This is not only in accordance with justice and equality but makes also for greater unity in the face of wars with bordering states. Without this dual arrangement some make too little of hostilities on the border, others too much, some underestimate the dangers of frontier quarrels, others take them too seriously, even sacrificing honour in order to avoid them. Hence in some countries it is the custom that when war against a neighbour is under consideration, those who live near to the border should be excluded from the discussion as being too closely involved to be able to give honest advice. It is therefore important that the territory should for the reasons given be divided in the manner stated. As for those who are to till the land, they should, if possible, be slaves (and we are building as we would wish). They should not be all of one stock nor men of spirit; this will ensure that they will be good workers and not prone to revolt. An alternative to slaves is foreigners settled on the countryside, men of the same type as the slaves just mentioned. They fall into two groups according to whether they work privately on the land of individual owners of property, or publicly on the common land. I hope later on to say how slaves ought to be used in agriculture and why it is a good thing that all slaves should have before them the prospect of receiving their freedom as a reward.

The chapter which follows is a good example of the way in which Aristotle expanded his notes by subsequent additions. As a result the four things to be looked for in siting a city – good air, good water, administrative convenience, defensive possibilities – are unevenly and unsystematically handled. Once again we note Aristotle's debt to the 'Airs, Waters, and Places' of Hippocrates.

I I

We have already noted that a city should have easy access both to the sea and to the interior, and, so far as conditions allow, be equally accessible to the whole of its territory. The land upon which the city itself is to be sited should be sloping. That is something that we must just hope to find, but we should keep four considerations in mind. First and most essential the situation must be a healthy one. A slope facing east, with winds blowing from the direction of sunrise, gives a healthy site, rather better than one on the lee side of north though this gives good weather. Next, it should be well situated for carrying out all its civil and military activities. For the purposes of defence the site should be one from which defenders can easily make a sally but which attackers will find difficult to approach and difficult to surround. Water, and especially spring water, should be abundant and if possible under immediate control in time of war; alternatively a way has been discovered of catching rain water in large quantities in vessels numerous enough to ensure a supply when fighting prevents the defenders from going far afield.

Since consideration must be given to the health of the inhabitants, which is partly a matter of siting in the best place and facing the right way, partly also dependent on a supply of pure water, this too must receive careful attention. I mention situation and water supply in particular because air and water, being just those things that we make most frequent and constant use of, have the greatest effect on our bodily condition. Hence, in a state which has welfare at heart, water for human consumption should be separated from water for all other purposes, unless of course all the water is alike and there are plenty of springs that are drinkable.

In the matter of defensive positions it should be remembered that what is best for one type of government is not so good for another. A lofty central citadel suits both oligarchy and monarchy, a level plain democracy; neither suits an aristocracy, which prefers a series of strongly held points. In laying out areas for private dwelling houses, the modern or Hippodamean method has the advantage of regularity; it is also more attractive and for all purposes save one, more practical. For ease of defence, the old-fashioned irregular siting of houses was better, hard for foreign mercenaries to get out of and for attackers to penetrate. It follows that both methods should be used and this is quite possible: arrange the buildings in the same pattern as is used for planting vines, not in rows but in *quincunx*, and do not lay out the whole city with geometric regularity but only certain parts. This will meet the needs both of safety and good appearance.

As for walls, it is quite out of date to say, as some do, that cities that lay claim to valour have no need of walls; we have only to look at what in fact has happened to cities that made that boast. Doubtless there is something not quite honourable in seeking safety behind solid walls, at any rate against an enemy equal in numbers or only very slightly superior. But it may happen, and does happen, that the numerical superiority of the attackers is too much for the courage of the defenders, both of the average man and of a chosen few. If then we are to save our city and avoid the miseries of cruelty and oppression, we must concede that the greatest degree of protection that walls can afford is also the best military measure. The truth of this is emphasized by all the modern improvements in missiles and artillery for attacking a besieged town. Deliberately to give cities no walls at all is like choosing an easily attacked position and clearing away the surrounding high ground. It is as if we were to refrain from putting walls round private property for fear of rendering the inhabitants unmanly. Another thing that should not be lost sight of is that those who have provided their city with a wall are in a position to regard that city in both ways, to treat it either as a fortified or an unfortified city. Those who have no walls have no such choice. And if this is so, then it is a duty not only to build walls but also to maintain them in a manner suitable both for the city's appearance and for its defensive needs, which in these days are very numerous. Just as the attacking side is always on the lookout for methods which will give them an advantage, so too the defenders must seek additional means of defence by the aid of scientific inquiry. An enemy will not even attempt an attack on those who are really well prepared to meet it.

Further details of the lay-out. The agora (*any open-air meeting-place*) *reserved for free-born gentlemen is found also in Xenophon* (Cyrop. *1, 2, 3*) *where its main purpose is said to be to keep them from acquiring a taste for the degrading practice of trade. On the duties of officials in charge of markets, streets, countryside, see Book VI, Chapter 8.*

12

We have seen that the greater number of the citizens should be distributed over a number of feeding-centres and also that the walls should be furnished at suitable intervals with forts each manned by a garrison. Hence it would seem reasonable that some of the feeding-centres should be located in the same places as the garrisons. For the rest, institutions devoted to the service of the gods and the chief feeding-places of government offices should have a central position on the same site, unless the sacral law or some pronouncement of Apollo at Delphi requires the sacred building in the case to be erected somewhere apart. Our purpose would be well served by a site which gives a frontage commensurate with our ideas of good siting and is at the same time easily defended in relation to the neighbouring parts of the city. Just below this is a good place to build a square of the kind which in Thessaly is given the name Free Market. Here nothing may be bought or sold and no member of the lower orders or countryman may be admitted unless summoned by the authorities. The amenities of this area would be enhanced if the gymnasia of the older folk were situated there; for in the taking of exercise also there should be separation of age-groups, the younger in one place, the older in another; government personnel should go in with the latter but should also mingle with the younger men, since the presence of authority's watchful eye is the best way to instil a real feeling of deference and of respect for the upper classes. The market proper, where buying and selling are done, must be in quite a separate place, conveniently situated both for goods sent up from the harbour and for people coming in from the country.

The authorities of the state being divided into secular and religious, it is right that the priests too should have their eating-places near the sacred buildings. As for the minor offices of government – those concerned with contracts, with suits-at-law, summonses, and the ordering of such matters generally (also surveillance of markets and what is called 'astynomy') – these should all be located near a market and general meeting-place. This will, of course, be the area of the dealers' market, which is intended for the exchange of necessary commodities: the upper area that we mentioned is intended for recreation. A similar arrangement should be followed in country districts; for there too the officials, forest-wardens, or field-wardens, or whatever they may be called, must have eating-places and garrison-posts to enable them to carry out their work of protection; likewise shrines of gods and heroes situated all over the countryside.

But it is really not necessary now to go on mentioning all these things in detail. It is not at all difficult to think what things are needed; it is quite another matter to provide them. Our talk is the mirror of our desires, but the outcome is in fortune's hands. Therefore we will say no more about these matters now and turn to the *politeia* itself.

Aristotle accordingly deals next with what for him is clearly the most important part of the business – the politeia *and all that that untranslatable word stands for. At this point we should remember that a* politeia *is essentially a collection of people. Whether they be many or few, they are a solid body of 'good' men, united in their acceptance of all the standards, moral and spiritual, intellectual and artistic, which belong to and are prescribed by the constitution by which they live. It follows that these standards will have to be learned by all the citizens; a man must know the* nomoi *of his* polis *and he must start learning them when he is quite young. Hence the most important part of any constitution is, as Plato saw, the education of those who are going to be its members. This for Plato and Aristotle was true at all times and is especially so when we are looking for the ideal state; for then we must also look for the ideal education. So all the rest of Aristotle's* Politics *as we have it, from here to the end of Book VIII, deals with education, its aims (down to the middle of Chapter 14), and its methods.*

But first back to happiness, since the aim of education is the good and happy life; and this is a point which Plato according to Aristotle had deliberately neglected (see above Book II, Chapter 5 at the end). The references to his own previous discussions of happiness are to the first book of the Nicomachean Ethics, *especially Chapters 9 and 10.*

13

We must now discuss the constitution itself and ask ourselves what people and what kind of people ought to form the material out of which is to be made a happy and well-governed city. All men's well-being depends on two things; one is the right choice of target, of the end to which actions should tend, the other lies in finding the actions that lead to that end. These two may just as easily conflict with each other as coincide. Sometimes for example the aim is well-chosen, but in action men fail to attain it. At other times they successfully perform everything that conduces to the end, but the end itself was badly chosen. Or they may fail in and be wrong about both, as sometimes happens in the practice of medicine, when doctors neither rightly discern what kind of condition is a healthy one for the body nor discover the means which will enable their self-set goal to be attained.

Wherever professional skill and knowledge come into play, these two must both be mastered – the end and the means to the end.

It is clear then that all men desire to have happiness and the good life, but some men are in a position to get it, others are not. This may be due to fortune or to their natural disposition; both play a part; the good life needs *some* material goods at any time, but when the natural disposition is good, fortune will need to provide a lesser amount of these, a greater amount when it is bad. Some indeed, who start with excellent opportunities, fail from the very beginning in the pursuit of happiness. But as our object is to find the *best* constitution, and that means the one whereby a city will be best ordered, and we call that city best ordered in which the possibilities of happiness are greatest; it is clear that we must keep our conception of happiness constantly in mind. We defined this in our *Ethics* and we may be permitted to make use of the definition here: happiness is activity and the complete utilization of all our powers, our goodness, not conditionally but absolutely. By 'conditionally' in this connexion I refer to actions necessary in the conditions and by 'absolutely' I mean moral or noble. For example actions relating to justice, the just recovery of damages, and the infliction of just punishment spring from the virtue justice, but they are necessary or conditional and whatever good is in them is there by necessity.* But actions directed towards honours and high standards of living are noble actions absolutely. For the former actions are but the removal of evil, the latter are not; they are on the contrary the creation and the begetting of positive good.

A good man will nobly bear ill-health, poverty, and other misfortunes, but happiness requires the opposite of these.†

---

* I would prefer to see a state of affairs in which such action would be unnecessary either for state or individual.

† This definition too was given in our ethical writings – that a good man is the sort of man for whom things good absolutely are good in his eyes on account of his own virtue, and clearly his attitudes to what befalls must be good and noble absolutely.

Hence men imagine that the causes of happiness lie in external goods and not within our minds. This is as if we were to ascribe brilliant lyre-playing to the quality of the instrument rather than to the skill of the player.

From what has been said it is clear that some things must be there from the start, others must be provided by a lawgiver. We wish for our city good fortune in all that Fortune has it in her power to bestow, that is all we can expect of her. It is not in Fortune's power to make a city good; that is a matter of scientific planning and deliberate policy. On the other hand, a city's being good rests on the citizens who share in the constitution being good; and for us all the citizens share in the constitution. The question then is, How does a man become good? Of course if it is possible for all to be good (and not just the citizens taken individually), then that is better, since all includes each. But in fact men are good and virtuous because of three things. These are nature, habit or training, reason. First, nature: a man must be born, and he must be born a man and not something else; he must have the body and the mind of a man. It may be of no advantage to be born with certain qualities, because habit and training cause changes. There are some qualities which have a dual possibility; subsequent habits may make them either good or bad. The majority of creatures live by nature only; some live by habit also to some extent. Man lives by reason as well, he alone has the faculty of reason. To make a good man requires all three working concertedly. Reason causes men to do many things contrary to habit and to nature, whenever they are convinced that this is the better course. In an earlier chapter we described what nature can do to make men such that they will easily respond to the handling of the legislator. After that it becomes a matter of education. Men learn partly by training, partly by listening.

If the principle of continuous personal rule were to be accepted, and the conditions necessary for it were forthcoming, the education of the citizens would be quite different from that required in a constitution under which the citizens would be expected to take their turn at holding office. Aristotle in his consideration of the Ideal State does not altogether reject the former type, any more than he did in Book III, where absolute monarchical rule received attention, but he lays it aside as not practicable. So the question here is how is a man to be educated for citizenship, to be made morally and intellectually fit to hold office in his turn and to behave himself when it is not his turn. This will satisfy the demand for equality, which it is dangerous to leave unsatisfied, and will at the same time do justice to merit and ability. Within the citizen or governing class only a distinction of age-group will operate, as in Chapter 9 above.

14

Since every association of persons forming a state consists of rulers and ruled, we must ask whether those who rule and those who are ruled ought to be different persons or the same for life; for the education which will be needed will depend upon which way we answer that question. If one group of persons were as far superior to all the rest as we deem gods and heroes to be superior to men, having to begin with great physical and bodily excellence and equally great mental and spiritual superiority, so much so that the superiority of the rulers is indisputable and quite evident to those ruled by them, then, I say, it is better that the same set of persons should always rule and the others always be ruled. But since this is not a condition that can easily be obtained, and since kings are not so greatly superior to their subjects as the writer Scylax says they were in India, it follows that, for a variety of causes, all alike must share in the business of ruling and being ruled by turns. For equality means the same not for all indiscriminately but for those who are like; this is fair and the established constitution can hardly be long maintained if it is contrary to justice. Otherwise there will be a large revolutionary element among the ruled all over the country, and it becomes quite impossible for even a strong governing class to withstand such a combination.

Again it cannot be disputed t at rulers have to be superior to those who are ruled. It therefore becomes the duty of the lawgiver to consider how this distinction is to be made and how they shall share in government. We noted earlier that nature herself has provided one distinction: that class which in respect of birth is all the same she has divided into older and younger, the former being more fit for ruling, the latter for being ruled. No one really objects to this method of command by seniority or thinks himself too good for it; after all he knows that once he reaches the required age, he will get what he has earned by waiting. There is then a sense in which we must say 'the same persons rule and are ruled' and a sense in which we must say that they are different persons. So too their education must be in one sense the same, in another different; for, as is often said, one who is to become a good ruler must first himself be ruled.* But since we hold that the same qualities are needed for citizen and for ruler and for the best man, and that the same man should be first ruled and later ruler, it immediately becomes an essential task of the planner of a constitution to ensure that men shall be good men, to consider what practices will make them so, and what is the end or aim of the best life.

The education of the citizens is therefore directed towards producing a ruling class, or rather a class whose members are capable of ruling when required to do so. Aristotle begins his description of the educational process with an account of the psychology on which it is based. In education only the rational part of the soul will show the end, *though others may assist in providing the* means. *We should here*

---

* Rule, as was said earlier, is of two kinds, according as it is exercised for the good of the ruler, which is despotic rule, or for the good of the ruled, which is rule over free men. The same actions may be ordered to be taken under either kind of rule, but the objects are different. Hence many activities generally considered servile may be honourably performed even by free men, by the younger among them. For the question whether an act is noble or not is to be decided not in reference to the actions themselves but in the light of their end and for whose benefit they are undertaken.

remind ourselves that the word which we translate 'leisure' does not denote either rest or recreation, but working at something worthwhile and valuable for its own sake.

Two parts of the soul are distinguished, one possessing reason in itself, the other not so possessing reason but capable of listening to reason. To these belong, we think, the virtues because of which a good man is called good. To those who accept our division of the soul there is no difficulty in answering the question 'To which of the parts does the concept of *end* belong?' For the inferior is always but a means to the superior; and this is no less clear in matters that have to be planned by human skill than it is in those which belong to the sphere of nature; and the superior in this case is that which is possessed of reason. It is our custom to make a distinction between practical reason and theoretical reason, and so we must similarly divide the rational part of the soul. Actions too will follow suit; there will be three kinds in all and those springing from that which is by nature better, that is, from the two rational parts, must be regarded as preferable by all who are in a position to make a choice from among three kinds or even from among two. For each man, that is to be chosen which is the very best that he can attain.

Again, all life can be divided into work and leisure, war and peace, and of things done some belong to the class of actions that have moral worth, while others are necessary but have no such value. In the choice of these the same principle, the lesser for the sake of the greater, must be followed in actions as in parts of the soul; that is to say, we choose war for the sake of peace, work for the sake of leisure, menial and useful acts for the sake of the noble. The statesman therefore in making laws must have an eye to all these things, with reference both to the parts of the soul and to the actions to which these give rise, and an eye even more to better things and to ends in view. In the same way too he must regard men's lives and their choice of what they shall do. For one must be able to work and to fight, but even more to be at peace and lead a life of cultivated leisure, to do the necessary and useful things, but still more those of intrinsic worth. These then are the targets at which education should be aimed, whether children's education or that of those requiring it at a later age.

These aims are not always recognized; Spartan education is greatly at fault in rating war higher than peace. Spartan militarism has been criticized before (above in Book II and in Plato's Laws). It is renewed here with more emphasis on the man who planned the system. He is not here called Lycurgus or given any name at all. Spartan military supremacy had come to an end before Aristotle's time.

It appears however that those Greeks who have the best reputation for good government and the lawgivers who drew up their several constitutions did not in fact construct societies with the best possible aim, and did not direct their laws and education towards producing all the virtues; but instead, following the vulgar way of thinking, turned aside to pursue qualities that appeared to be more lucrative and useful. And in a like manner to these some more recent writers have voiced the same opinion: they express their approval of the Lacedaemonians' régime and admire the aim of their lawgiver, because he ordered all things with a view to war and national strength. This is a view which can easily be refuted by reasoning and already in our own day has been refuted by the facts. As most men desire to dominate others, because success in this brings abundance of worldly goods, so the writer Thibran is clearly an admirer of the Laconian lawgiver, and all the others too who, writing about the Spartan constitution, have stated that thanks to their being trained to face dangers they came to rule over many others. But since today the Spartan domination is no more, it is clear that they are not a happy and prosperous nation, and their lawgiver was wrong. There is something laughable in the fact that, for all their care to keep within their own constitution and with no one to stop them from using their own laws and customs, they have lost their particular way of a good life.

They are also wrong in supposing that a lawgiver ought openly to approve the acquisition of mastery; for rule over free men is nobler than despotic rule and more in keeping with virtue. To say that a state has trained itself in the acquisition of power with a view to ruling its neighbours – that is no ground for calling a state happy or applauding its lawgivers. Such an argument may have dangerous consequences; its acceptance requires any citizen who can to make it his ambition to be ruler in his own city – the very thing that the Lacedaemonians accused Pausanias of seeking and that too though he was their king. So none of these theories or principles are of any value for a statesman; they are neither good nor true. The same guiding principles that are best for nations are best also for individuals, and it is these that a lawgiver must instil into the minds of men. And as for military training, the object in practising it regularly is not to bring into subjection men not deserving of such treatment. It has three purposes: (1) to save ourselves from becoming subject to others, (2) to win for our own city a position of leadership, exercised for the benefit of others not with a view to dominating all, (3) to exercise the rule of a master over those who deserve to be treated as slaves. The lawgiver should rather make it the aim both of his military preparations and of his legislation in general to establish peace and a cultured life. And facts support this; for the military states generally, while they fight wars, survive, but when once they establish an empire begin to decline. Like steel they lose their fine temper if they are always at peace; and the lawgiver who has not educated them in the right use of leisure is to blame.

Virtues are desirable in themselves and not for any advantage that they may bring. Education should aim at fostering all the virtues, and not as in Sparta courage only. The argument is not clear owing to deficiencies in the text in the middle of the chapter. There is a reference

*back to the end of Chapter 13, to three elements in education –
what is there at birth, what is acquired by training, what is learned
by reasoning.*

15

Since it is clear that men have the same purpose whether
they are acting as individuals or as a state, and that the best
man and the best constitution must have the same distinguishing features, it becomes evident that there must be present in the state the virtues that lead to the cultivation of
leisure; for, as has often been said, the end of war is peace
and the end of work is leisure. Of the virtues useful for the
employment of leisure some are exercised in a period of
leisure, others in a period of work, because a lot of things
need to be provided before leisured activity can become possible. Hence a city must be self-restrained, courageous,
steadfast.* We need courage and steadfastness for the work,
intellectual ability for cultivated leisure, restraint and
honesty at all times, but particularly at times of peace and
leisure. For war forces men to be obedient and honest, but
the enjoyment of prosperity, peace, and leisure is apt rather
to make men violent and self-assertive. Therefore much
sound morality and much self-restraint are demanded of
those who are conspicuously successful and enjoy the bless-
ings of prosperity, men such as might be living, in the poets'
phrase, in the isles of the blest. For these especially will need
philosophy, moderation, righteousness; and the more abundant their advantages, the greater their need. Clearly then
the state too, if it is to be good and happy, must have a good
measure of these virtues. For if it is a mark of inferiority not
to be able to behave well, it is especially so in a period of
leisure – to appear good when working or on military
service, but in leisure and peace to be no better than slaves.

Training in virtue therefore should not follow the Lacedaemonian model. The difference between them and other

* Without these men are as slaves, since those who cannot bravely
face danger are slaves to an invader and, as the proverb says, slaves have
no leisure.

nations lies not in any disagreement about what are the greatest goods but in their view that there is a virtue which will produce them. They value good things and their enjoyment more than the production of virtues, but it is clear from our argument that virtue must be practised for its own sake, and we have to consider how and by what means.

We have already distinguished three essentials – nature, training, and reason. Of these we have already dealt with the first, determining the natural conditions which it is desirable to be born into; next we must ask whether education should proceed by means of reasoning or by the formation of habits. Certainly these must work together in perfect unison; for it is equally possible to make an intellectual error about the best principle and to find oneself led astray by one's own habits and training.

One thing is clear from the start: as in everything else so here, coming into being proceeds from some beginning, and its end proceeds from a beginning which was the end of something else. So for us as human beings reason and the mind are the end to which our growth tends. Thus it is to these that the training of our habits, as well as our coming into being, must be directed. Next, as soul and body are two, so also we note two parts of the soul, the reasoning and the unreasoning; and each of these has its own natural propensity, the former intellectual, the latter appetitive. And just as the body comes into being earlier than the soul, so also the unreasoning is prior to that which possesses reason. This is shown by the fact that, while passion and will as well as appetite are to be found in children from birth, reasoning and intelligence come into being as they grow older. Therefore the care of the body must begin before the care of the mind, then the training of the appetitive element, but always for the sake of the intelligence, as the body's training is for the sake of the soul.

The general conditions of life, climate, race, etc., in which it is desirable to be born were stated earlier in this book. Now, dealing with the upbringing of children from the very start, he gives advice on birth itself, marriage, parenthood, and procreation. In ancient Greece when a child was born, it was a matter for the father's decision whether it was to be reared or left to die in an exposed place. This practice must have come under criticism by the fourth century B.C. for, although there are some textual difficulties in this part of the chapter, it is clear that there was a body of opinion opposed to using exposure of healthy infants merely for the purpose of keeping down the population.

16

Now as it is a lawgiver's duty to start from the very beginning in looking for ways to secure the best possible physical development of the young, he must consider first the marriage of their parents, what kind of people should get married to each other and when marital intercourse ought to take place. In making regulations about these matters he should have regard both to the couples themselves and to their time of life, in order that they may attain the right ages in each case at the same time. The period of the father's ability to beget and that of the mother's to bear children should coincide. A period when one of the two is capable and the other not leads to mutual recriminations and separations. Next, as regards the timing of successive births of children, there should not be too great a gap in age between father and children; there is little that the young can do for elderly parents and their fathers are of little help to them. Nor should they be too close in age, for this causes relations to be strained; proper respect is not given to fathers who are almost contemporaries, and the nearness in age leads to bickering in household affairs. And further, to go back to the point we started from, one should ensure that the physical development of the young will be in accordance with the wishes of the founder of the state.

All these purposes can be fulfilled, or nearly so, if we pay sufficient attention to one thing – the relative ages of man and wife. Since, generally speaking, the upper limit of age for the begetting of children is for men seventy years and for women fifty, the beginning of their union should be such that they will arrive at these two points of life at the proper ages. The intercourse of a very young couple is not good for child-bearing. In animals generally the products of very early unions are defective, usually female and diminutive; so the same kind of results are bound to follow in human beings.* A further objection to very early marriages is that very young women have greater difficulty and there are more deaths.† It is also more conducive to faithfulness in marriage that daughters should be rather older when their fathers bestow them in marriage; it seems that women who have sexual intercourse at an early age are more likely to be dissolute. On the male side too it is held that if they have intercourse while the seed is just growing, it interferes with future growth; for in that too there is a fixed limit of time, after which it ceases to be replenished. Accordingly we conclude that the appropriate age for marriage is about the eighteenth year for girls and for men the thirty-seventh plus or minus. Intercourse will then take place when they are both physically in their prime and they will reach the cessation of childbearing at the proper times in each case. And the succession of births, if pregnancy takes place at the expected time, will begin with the first-born at the parents' prime and end as they decline, the father now approaching his seventieth year.

We have spoken now about the time of life when marriage should take place, but not about the periods of the year best suited for sexual intercourse. However, the common practice of choosing the winter season is satisfactory. In addition those contemplating child-bearing should seek the advice of doctors and scientists; the former can give the requisite in-

* There is some evidence that this is so: in countries where very early marriages are the rule, the offspring are small and defective.
† Some say that here we have also the origin of the oracle given to the people of Troezen ('plough not the new land'), that there is no reference to the production of crops, but to the fact that frequent marriages of young girls were causing many deaths.

formation about periods in the life of the body, the latter about weather conditions; they recommend a time of northerly winds rather than southerly. On the question of what kind of physical condition is most advantageous for parents, those who want detailed information must seek it in manuals on the rearing of children; for our present purpose the following outline will suffice. Athletic fitness does not provide the best condition either for a citizen or for health in the production of offspring. A condition of much coddling and of unfitness for hard work is equally undesirable. Something between the two is needed; a condition of one inured to hard but not excessively hard toil, directed not all in one direction as an athlete's, but towards the various activities of the free-born. These provisions are applicable to men and women alike. Further, it is important that women should look after their bodily condition during pregnancy. They must not be lazy or go on a meagre diet. It is easy for a legislator to ensure this by making it a rule that they shall each day take a walk, the object of which is to worship the gods who are especially concerned with childbirth. But while the body should be exercised, the mind should not. Mental exertion is better avoided; the unborn infant appears to take good from her who is carrying it, as plants do from the earth.

With regard to the choice between abandoning an infant or rearing it let it be lawful that no cripple child be reared. But since the ordinance of custom forbids the exposure of infants merely in order to reduce numbers, there must be a limit to the production of children. If contrary to these arrangements a copulation takes place and a child is conceived, abortion should be procured before the embryo has acquired life and sensation; the presence of life and sensation will be the mark of division between right and wrong here. Since we have already decided what are the ages of male and female at which co-habitation should begin, we must also decide upon the length of time during which it may properly continue. The offspring of elderly people, like the offspring of the young, are imperfect in mind and body, those of the aged are feeble. We should therefore be guided by the highest point of mental development, and this in most cases is the age mentioned by certain poets who speak of seven periods of seven years, that is to say about the fiftieth year of a man's life. Thus anyone who has passed this limit by four or five years ought no longer to beget and openly acknowledge children. But for the sake of health or other such good reason intercourse may continue without secrecy. Extra-marital intercourse with persons of either sex is not good, and should, if possible, never be resorted to or admitted, so long as one is a husband and so addressed by a wife. If anyone is found to be acting thus during the period of his begetting of children, let him be punished by such measure of disgrace as is appropriate to his misdemeanour.

'Aristotle in this chapter,' says Newman (III, p. 478) 'says little which has not already been said by Plato.' This chiefly in the seventh book of the Laws *to which there is a reference. Education up to five years of age needs no formal teaching; from five to seven visual methods may be used. The main periods are the next two, seven to fourteen and fourteen to twenty-one. The digression interrupts the sequence by referring to the young in general, especially adolescents.*

17

The period following birth must be regarded as the time when the nourishment given to a child has the greatest effect on the development of the body. It is clear from an examination, both of other animals and of those nations that make a point of rearing their young to be fighting fit, that an abundant milk diet is very suitable for their young bodies, but a diet that includes wine is likely to upset them. Next, it is good for them to make all the bodily movements that they are capable of at that age. To prevent the still soft limbs from becoming bent some peoples still make use of mechanical devices for keeping them straight. From infancy too they ought to be used to cold; to be thus habituated is most useful for future health and for the activities of warfare. Hence among certain non-Greek peoples it is the custom to dip newly-born infants in cold river-water; others, for example the Kelts, put on them very little clothing. It is a good thing to start very young in accustoming children to such things as it is possible to accustom them to, but the process must be gradual; the warmth of the young body gives it a condition well-suited for training to resist cold. In these and similar ways the training of children in infancy should proceed.

The next stage is up to five years of age. During this period it is not a good plan to try and teach them anything or make them do tasks that would interfere with their development. At the same time they must have exercise, not a state of passivity. They will get exercise in many ways but most of all in play. Their games, like everything else, should be worthy of free men and neither laborious nor unsystematic. The officials known as inspectors of children's welfare ought also to pay attention to deciding what kind of literature and stories children of this age are to hear; for all that they hear now is to be regarded as preparation for the schooling that is to follow. Hence their games ought largely to consist in playing at or rehearsing what they will later be doing in earnest. It is wrong to try and prohibit small children from crying and dilating the lungs, as is suggested in the *Laws*; it is in fact an exercise of the lungs which is beneficial for the growth of the body. In addition to regulating the time spent on play and on exercise and the rest, those in charge should particularly see that very little time is spent in the company of slaves. Children of this age and up to seven must inevitably live at home, and even as young as that they are liable to pick up by eye or by ear 'ungentle-manliness'.

Aristotle here turns aside to urge, very much in the manner of Plato, keeping unseemly words and spectacles away from the young. First impressions count for much; this is the point of the anecdote about the actor Theodorus.

In general the legislator ought to banish from the state, as he would any other evil, all unseemly talk; the indecent remark lightly dropped results in conduct of a like kind. Especially therefore it must be kept away from youth; let them not hear or see anything of that kind. If any is found doing or saying any of the forbidden things, he shall, if he is of gentle birth but not yet old enough to be allowed to eat at the common tables, be punished by whipping, while a youth who is rather older shall be punished by loss of privileges of the free-born, just because his conduct has been that of a slave. And since we exclude all unseemly talk, we must also forbid looking at pictures or literature of the same kind. Let it therefore be a duty of the rulers to see that there shall be nothing at all, statue or painting, that is a representation of unseemly actions, except those that are in the shrines of those gods to whom the law concedes the privilege of indecency. The law further allows men who have reached a certain age to pay honour to these gods on behalf of their wives, their children, and themselves. But it should be laid down that younger persons shall not be spectators at comedies or recitals of scurrilous iambics, not, that is to say, until they have reached the age at which they become entitled to recline at banquets, and share in the drinking; by this time their upbringing will have rendered them immune to any harm that might come from such spectacles. What we have just been saying has been said only incidentally; we must later go into the question in greater detail and decide whether or not they ought to attend, and, if so, under what conditions. We have only said as much as would serve the present occasion. Theodorus the tragic actor made, I think, a very apt remark in this connexion when he refused to allow any other actor, even quite an inferior one, to appear on the stage before him, because, he said, an audience always takes kindly to the first voice that meets their ears. I think something of the same kind is true in men's relations with each other and the things they see and hear. We tend to love at first sight. Therefore we must keep all that is of inferior quality far away from the young, particularly these things that contain repulsive evil.

Aristotle returns to the succession of age-periods and looks forward to the next book.

When they have passed their fifth birthday they should for the next two years learn, simply by observation, whatever they may be required to learn. Education after that may be divided into two stages – from the seventh year to puberty and from puberty to the completion of twenty-one years. Thus those who divide life into periods of seven years are not far wrong, and we ought to keep to the divisions that nature makes. For all training and education aim at filling the gaps that nature leaves. It therefore becomes our business to inquire whether we ought to lay down a system for the education of boys, then whether it is advisable to have a public authority in charge of it, or leave it in private hands, as is the usual practice in cities at the present time, and thirdly to discuss what the system of education should be.

BOOK VIII

*Of the three questions asked at the end of Book VII the first hardly
needs answering. The second too, which we should regard as giving
the greatest scope for discussion and disagreement, is soon disposed of.
The rearing and education of the children of citizens is a matter of
public concern, since they are the future citizens, the future ruling
class. One needs to learn to be a citizen as much as a craftsman needs
to be trained. But what and how to teach the potential citizen – this
will depend largely on the type of state and on the kind of life which
it is desired to make, especially the intellectual, artistic, cultivated life
which the Greeks called scholē, usually translated 'leisure'. Hence a
great deal of the eighth book is concerned with music and singing.
But we do not know how much of the book is lost; it certainly now
appears to be unfinished, as the thirteenth-century translator William
of Moerbeke saw.*

I

No one would dispute the fact that it is a lawgiver's prime
duty to arrange for the education of the young. There is no
doubt that where this is not done the quality of the constitution suffers every time. Education must be related to the
particular constitution in each case, for the character of the
constitution is just that which makes it specifically what it is.
Its own character made it at the start and continues to maintain it, the democratic character preserves a democracy, the
oligarchic an oligarchy. And in all circumstances the best
character produces the best constitution. There must also be
the preparatory training for all the various crafts and professions and a process of habitation to the various jobs; so
it is obvious that there must also be training for the activities
of virtue. But since there is but one aim for the entire city, it
follows that education must be one and the same for all and
that the oversight of education must be a public concern,
not the private affair which it now is, each man separately

bringing up his own children and teaching them just what he thinks they ought to learn. In all matters that belong to the whole community the learning to do them must also be the concern of the community as a whole. And it is not right either that any of the citizens should think that he belongs just to himself; all citizens belong to the state, for each is a part of the state; and the care bestowed on each part naturally looks also towards the care of the whole. In this respect the Lacedaemonians earn our approval; the greatest possible attention is given to youth in Sparta and all on a national basis.

2

It is clear then that there should be laws laid down about education and that education itself must be made a national concern. But we must not forget the question what that education is to be, and how it is to be brought into operation. For in modern times there are opposing views about the practice of education. There is no general agreement about what the young should learn either in relation to virtue or in relation to the best life; nor is it clear whether their education ought to be directed more towards the intellect than towards the character of the soul. The problem has been complicated by what we see happening before our eyes, and it is not certain whether training should be directed at things useful in life, or at those conducive to virtue, or at non-essentials. (All these answers have been given.) And there is no agreement as to what in fact does tend towards virtue. Men do not all prize most highly the same virtue, so naturally they differ also about the proper training for it.

Then as to useful things – there are obviously certain essentials which the young must learn, but they do not have to learn all useful things, since we distinguish those that are proper for a free man and those that are not. The citizen must take part in only those useful occupations which do not degrade the doer. Among degrading activities and vulgar pursuits we must reckon all those which render the body or soul or intellect of free men unserviceable for the demands and activities of virtue. We therefore call degrading those occupations which have a deleterious effect on the body's condition and all work that is paid for. For these make the mind preoccupied and unable to rise above menial things. Even in the liberal subjects there is a limit beyond which their study becomes illiberal. Too great concentration on them, too much mastering of detail – these are liable to cause the same degradation of spirit that we have been speaking of. In this connexion a most important criterion is the purpose for which the action or the study is undertaken. It is proper for a free man to do something for himself or for his friends or on account of its value in itself, but he that does the same action on others' account may on occasion be regarded as doing something paid for or servile.

The chief aim of a gentleman's, that is, a citizen's, education is to enable him to employ his intellectual and artistic faculties to the full, to live a life of 'virtue' and of 'leisure'. The following chapter is one of the best sources for understanding what Aristotle meant by scholē. *If the promise made below of further discussion 'on a later occasion' was fulfilled, what he said has been lost. The end of the chapter is confused. The omission of arithmetic is surprising.*

3

The subjects nowadays regularly studied serve both virtue and utility, as we have already noted. About four are generally taught to children, (1) Reading and Writing, (2) Physical Training, (3) Music, and (4), not always included, Drawing. Reading and writing and drawing are useful in daily life in a variety of ways, gymnastic because it aims to make men strong and brave. But about music there is a real question. Most men nowadays take part in music for the sake of the pleasure it gives; but some lay it down that music is fundamental in education on the ground that nature herself, as has often been said, aims at producing men not

merely able to work properly but fit also for the life of cultivated leisure. And this latter, we repeat, is the basis of the
whole business. It is true that we need both; but if not-
working is preferable to, and is the end sought by, working,
we must ask ourselves what are the proper activities of leisure.

*There are many things that we may legitimately do when not work-
ing, but the question is which of them can be classed as* 'scholē'.
Music is clearly one of them.

Obviously not play; for that would be to make play the
object of living, our end in life, which is unthinkable. Play
has its uses, but they belong rather to the sphere of work;
for he who works hard needs rest, and play is a way of resting, while work is inseparable from stress and strain. We
must therefore for therapeutic reasons admit the necessity of
games, while keeping them to their proper times and proper
uses; taking exercise in this way is both a relaxation of the
mind and, just because we enjoy it, a recreation. But the way
of leisure that we are speaking of here is something positive,
in itself a pleasant happy existence which the life of work
and business cannot be. For he that is working is working
for some hitherto unattained end, and happiness is an end,
happiness which is universally regarded as concomitant not
with toil but with enjoyment. Admittedly men do not agree
as to what that enjoyment is; each man decides for himself
following his own character and disposition, the finest character choosing the highest kind of enjoyment on the loftiest
plane. Thus it becomes clear that preparation for spending
time at leisure requires a great deal of learning and education. The educational processes and the subjects studied
must have their own intrinsic merit, as distinct from those
necessary professional subjects which are studied for reasons
outside themselves. Hence, in the past, men laid down
music as part of the curriculum of education, not as being
necessary, for it is not in that category, nor yet as being useful in the way that a knowledge of reading and writing is
useful for business or administration, for study, and for

many citizen activities, or as a knowledge of drawing is useful for the better judging of artists' works, nor again as gymnastic is useful for health and strength; for we do not see either of these accruing as a result of playing music. There remains one purpose – to provide an occupation for leisure; and that is clearly the reason why they did introduce music into education, regarding it as an occupation of free men. Thus Homer wrote 'to summon him alone to the rich banquet' and after these words he introduces certain others 'who summon the bard whose singing shall delight them all'. And elsewhere he speaks of Odysseus saying that the best recreation is when men get together and 'sit in rows up and down the hall feasting and listening to the singer'.

Clearly then there is a form of education which we must provide for our sons, not as being useful or essential but elevated and gentlemanly. We must on a later occasion discuss whether this education is one or many, what subjects it includes and how they are to be taught. But as it turns out, we have made some progress in that direction; music at least must be included. We have the evidence of the ancients derived from the subjects laid down by them.

The case of music makes that clear, but it does not stand alone; there are other subjects which the young must learn, for example their letters, not only because they are useful but because these are often the means to learning yet further subjects. Similarly drawing and a knowledge of design are useful not merely for the avoidance of mistakes in one's private purchases but that one may not be taken in when buying and selling furniture, or rather more especially because it teaches us to be observant of beauty in any physical object. But to be constantly asking 'What is the use of?' is unbecoming to those of superior mentality and free birth.

Since it is obvious that education by habit-forming must precede education by reasoned instruction (as that of the body precedes that of the mind), it is clear that we must subject our children to gymnastic and to training in wrestling and fighting; the former produces the condition of the body, the latter its actions.

And so to physical training, the right and the wrong.

4

In our own day those cities which have the greatest reputation for looking after their youth either aim at producing an athlete's condition, to the detriment of both the appearance and the development of the child's body, or else like the Spartans who have avoided that particular error, by severity of treatment they render them like animals, under the impression that this is conducive to courage. But, as has often been pointed out, the care of the young must be directed not to producing one quality only and not that more than the rest. And if courage is their aim, they do not even manage to secure it. For neither among animals nor among less civilized peoples do we find courage to be a characteristic of the most fierce, but rather (among animals) of the gentler and feline species; and among human beings there are many tribes that enjoy slaughter and the consumption of human flesh, in Pontus Achaeans and Heniochi and some of the mainland tribes, some better, some worse; raiders they may be, but they are not endowed with courage. And of the Lacedaemonians themselves too we know that so long as they applied themselves to strenuous training, they were superior to the rest, but nowadays they fall short of others both in war and athletics. For their former superiority was not due to their particular way of training the young but merely to the fact that they trained, and their opponents did not. The prime object therefore must be not any animal quality but nobility of character. One cannot imagine a wolf or any other animal engaging in a dangerous struggle because it is the right thing to do; but that is what a brave man will do. Those who put their young to excessive military training, neglecting their education in essentials, are in sober fact rendering them vulgar and uneducated, making them useful for one part only of citizen life and even for that, as our argument shows, less useful than others. We should judge the Spartans by their present-day performance, not by what they used to be like. They now have rivals in the field of education, which formerly they did not have.

There is to be sure a place for gymnastic in education and there is general agreement as to what that place should be: up to puberty the exercises should be light and easy; nothing should be done that would interfere with the body's growth, no heavy dieting or strenuous forced hardships; for these are liable to have just that ill-effect, as is shown by the fact that it is rare for the same men to be successful in the Olympic games both as boys and as men; their severe gymnastic training as boys has caused them to lose their strength. But when for the three years after puberty they have been engaged in learning other things, then the subsequent period may very properly be devoted to strenuous exercise and compulsory heavy dieting. Vigorous exercise of mind and body must not be combined; each naturally works in the opposite direction from the other, bodily toil interfering with the mind, mental with the body.

Thus, while the needs of the body are straightforward, the needs of the mind are not; and so Aristotle returns again to music. It was shown in the third chapter that learning music was not an essential in the same way as learning to read and write, but that it was traditionally a subject of a liberal education. But to learn the rudiments of music in childhood is one thing; it is quite another in manhood to cultivate, understand, and perform. Music is something more than an amusement; yet one of its great merits is that it gives pleasure. But the pleasure needs some degree of previous training, unlike the pleasures of eating. It is worth noting that for a Greek a man's taste in music or dress or anything is part of his character.

5

We have already discussed some of the questions that arose about music, but it would be well to resume the subject and carry it further, because I think that what I have to say will provide a key to any future discussions about music. To begin with, it is not easy to define either what the effect of music is or what our object is in learning it. Is it for our amusement and refreshment, like taking a nap or having a drink? I hardly think so, because these things are not in themselves of prime importance, though they are pleasant and help us to forget our worries, as Euripides says.* Must we not rather regard music as a stimulus to goodness, capable of having an effect on the character, in just the same way as gymnastic training produces a body of a certain type, and so capable of forming men who have the habit of right critical appreciation? Thirdly, it surely has a contribution to make to the intelligent and cultivated pastimes.

It is clear then that we are not to educate the young with a view to amusement. Learning is hard work; while children are learning they are not playing. They are as yet too young for the cultivation of the intellect by means of music as an occupation; the complete life does not belong to the incomplete body. Still one might perhaps say that serious study in childhood may have for its aim the amusement of the complete and adult man. But if this is so, what need is there for themselves to learn music? Why not do as kings of Persians and Medes do, have others to make music for them, so that they may listen and enjoy? For surely those who have perfected their skill in the making and production of music will give better performances than those who have devoted to learning music only such times as will enable them to listen intelligently. If we reject that and say that we must ourselves work hard at producing music, does it follow that we must also learn to produce good meals? Certainly not.

The same question arises when we ask whether music has the power to improve the character. Why learn music oneself and not rather do as the Lacedaemonians do – acquire the art of right judgement and good taste by listening to others? They claim that without learning music they are capable of correctly distinguishing good music from bad.

* This is what causes some people to put all three on the same level, sleep, drink, and music, and to use them all in the same way. Dancing is also sometimes added.

The same argument applies also when we ask whether music ought to be used as a means to making pleasant and cultivated pastimes for gentlefolk. Why must they learn to perform themselves instead of simply enjoying the fruits of others' study? We may in this connexion refer to our conception of the gods; the poets do not depict Zeus as playing and singing in person. In fact we regard professional performers as belonging to the lower classes, though a man may play and sing for his own amusement or at a party when he has had a good deal to drink.

Perhaps this question should be postponed till later; our chief inquiry now is whether or not music is to be put into education and what music can do. Is it an education or an amusement or a pastime? It is reasonable to reply that it is directed towards and participates in all three. Amusement is for the purpose of relaxation and relaxation must necessarily be pleasant, since it is a kind of cure for the ills we suffer in working hard. As to the pastimes of a cultivated life, there must, as is universally agreed, be present an element of pleasure as well as of nobility, for the happiness which belongs to that life consists of both these. We all agree that music is among the most delightful and pleasant things, whether instrumental or accompanied by singing,* so that one might from that fact alone infer that the young should be taught it. For things that are pleasant and harmless belong rightly not only to the end in view but also to relaxation by the way. But since it rarely happens that men attain and keep their goal, and they frequently rest and amuse themselves with no other thought than the pleasure of it, there is surely a useful purpose in the pleasure derived from music.

On the other hand, men have been known to make amusement an end in itself. No doubt there is something pleasant about one's own chosen end but it is a very special kind of pleasure, and men in seeking pleasure mistake the one kind for the other. For there is indeed a resemblance;

* The poet Musaeus says 'singing is man's greatest joy'. Hence because it makes men feel happy, it is very properly included in entertainments and in the pastimes of social intercourse.

the end is not pursued for the sake of anything that may accrue thereafter but always for its own sake; similarly these recreation-pleasures are not for future but for present benefits; their pleasure arises from what is past – labour and pain finished. This would seem to be a reasonable explanation of why men try to get happiness through these pleasures. But it is certainly not for this reason alone that men take up music; the main reason, it seems, is that it provides relaxation.

This may be the operative reason why music is taken up but it is not its chief value.

Nevertheless we must ask whether, though this is commonly the case, the true nature of music be not something of greater value than filling the need for relaxation. Music certainly has a pleasure of its own; all ages and all types like and enjoy it. But we must do more than merely share in the general pleasure which all men find in it; we must consider whether music has any effect on the character and the mind. We could answer this question if we could say that we become of such and such a disposition through music. And surely it is obvious from many examples that music does indeed have such an effect, not least from the tunes composed by Olympus. These are well known to affect the personality, making men wildly excited – a frenzied excitement which is both a mental and a moral condition. Again, when listening to theatrical performances all men are affected in a manner in keeping with the performance, even apart from the tunes and rhythms employed. Since music belongs to the class of things pleasant, and since it is virtue therein to enjoy rightly, to like and dislike the right things, clearly there is no more important lessons to be learned or habit to be formed than that of right judgement and of taking pleasure in good morals and noble actions.

Now in rhythms and in tunes there is a close resemblance to reality – the realities of anger and gentleness, also of courage and moderation, and of the opposites of these, indeed of all moral qualities; and the fact that music heard does indeed cause an emotional change in us is an indication of this. To have the habit of feeling pleasure (or pain) in things that are like to reality is very near to having the same disposition towards reality. I mean if a man enjoys looking at a statue of someone for no other reason than that he likes the look of it, then inevitably he will enjoy looking at the original, whose likeness he is at the moment contemplating. Now it is true that objects perceived by the senses, touched or tasted, do not present any similarity to moral qualities,* but in music moral qualities are present, represented in the very tunes we hear. This is obvious, for to begin with there is the natural distinction between the modes or harmonies, which cause different reactions in the hearers, who are not all moved in the same way. For example, men are inclined to be mournful or tense when they listen to that which is called Mixo-Lydian, they are more relaxed when they listen to the looser harmonies. An equable feeling, mid-way between these, is produced, I think, only by the Dorian mode, while the Phrygian makes men greatly excited. These are the results of some excellent work which has been done on this aspect of education; the investigators have made practical tests and based their conclusions on them. The same is true also of the different types of rhythm; some have a steadying effect, others an unsettling, and of these latter some give rise to vulgar movements, some to more gentlemanly.

It follows from all this that music has indeed the power to induce certain conditions of mind, and if it can do that, clearly it must be applied to education and the young must

* Perhaps objects seen do, since appearances may have such an effect, but only to a small extent; and not all people share this reaction to such perception. Moreover the shapes and colours that we see are not strictly representations of character but indications rather, and these indications are visible on our bodies when strong emotion is felt. It does, however, make a great deal of difference what it is we look at; the young ought not to contemplate the paintings of Pauson but rather those of Polygnotus and of other painters and sculptors who are truly ethical.

be educated in and by it. And the teaching of music is particularly apt for the young; for they because of their youth do not willingly tolerate anything that is not made pleasant for them, and music is one of those things that are by nature made to give pleasure. Moreover there is a certain affinity between us and music's harmonies and rhythms; so that many experts say that the soul is a harmony, others that it has harmony.

Once again the subject is dropped, to be taken up again in Chapter 7. The question now discussed is how far the education of a gentleman can be permitted to include playing a musical instrument, which is a form of manual labour. This is followed by a digression on the aulos, the chief Greek wind-instrument.

6

We must now return to a question raised earlier – must they learn to sing themselves and play instruments with their own hands? Clearly actual participation in performing is going to make a big difference to the quality of the person that will be produced; it is impossible, or at any rate very difficult, to produce good judges of musical performance from among those who have never themselves performed.* And all that we have been saying makes it clear that musical education must include actual performing; and it is not difficult to decide what is appropriate and what is not for different ages, or to find an answer to those who assert that learning to perform is vulgar and degrading. First, since as we have seen, actual performance is needed to make a good critic, they should while young do much playing and singing, and then, when they are older, give up performing; they will then, thanks to what they have learned in their

*At the same time learning an instrument will provide children with a needed occupation. Archytas's rattle was an excellent invention for keeping children occupied; they cannot be expected to remain still, and playing with this toy keeps them from smashing things about the house. Of course it is only suitable for the very young; for older children education is their rattle.

youth, be able to enjoy music aright and give good judge-ments. As for the objection, brought by some, that musical performance is degrading to a gentleman, this can easily be answered if we consider to what extent boys, who are being educated to discharge the highest functions in the state, ought to take part in music, what tunes and what rhythms they are to perform, and on what instruments they are to learn to play, for that too will make a difference. In the answers to these questions will be found the answer to the objection; and an answer must be found, for it is very likely that certain kinds of music do have the effect mentioned.

It is clear therefore that learning music must not be allowed to have any adverse effect on later activities, or make the body banausic and ill-fitted for the training of citizen or soldier, the practice in youth, the theory in later years. What is needed is that the pupil shall not struggle to acquire the degree of skill that is needed for professional competitions, or to master those peculiar and sensational pieces of music which have begun to penetrate the com-petitions and have even affected education. Musical exer-cises, even if not of this kind, should be pursued only up to the point at which the pupil becomes capable of appreciat-ing good melodies and rhythms, and not just the popular music such as appeals to slaves, children, and even some animals. From these considerations we can see the answer also to the question what kinds of musical instruments are to be employed. We must not permit the introduction of wind-instruments into education or any that requires the skill of a professional, the cithara and such-like, but only such as will make good listeners to musical education and education in general. Furthermore the pipes are not an instrument of ethical but rather of orgiastic effect, so their use should be confined to those occasions on which the effect desired is not intellectual but a way of working off the emotions. We may add to its educational objections the fact that playing on the pipes prevents one from using the faculty of speech. For these reasons our predecessors were right in prohibiting the use of wind-instruments by the young of the upper classes, though at an earlier period it was permitted. This is what took place: as abundance increased, men had more leisure and acquired higher standards both culturally and socially. Just before, and still more after, the Persian wars, in which their success had increased their self-confidence, they fastened eagerly upon learning of all kinds, pursuing all without distinction. Playing on the pipes was introduced into education and at Sparta the chorus-leader himself piped for his chorus to dance to, and round about Athens the pipes took such firm root that many, perhaps the majority, of the gentry learned them. Thrasippus, who, when he acted as chorus-trainer for Ecphantides, dedicated a picture, is an indication of this. But at a later date as a result of actual experience the pipes went out of favour; men became better able to discern what tends to promote high standards of goodness and what does not. Many other older instruments were found to have similar drawbacks as a means of musical education, for example the plucker, the barbitos, and those which merely titillate the ear, the heptagon, triangle, sambuca, and all those that require manual dexterity. There is sound sense too in the story told by the ancients about the use of the pipes – that Athena invented them and then threw them away. It may well be, as the story says, that she did this because she disliked the facial distortion which their playing caused. But a far more likely reason is that learning to play upon the pipes contributes nothing to the education of the mind; after all, Athena, as we believe, was intelligent, as well as nimble with her fingers.

We reject then as education a training in material performance which is professional and competitive. He that takes part in such performances does not do so in order to improve his own character, but to give pleasure to listeners, and vulgar pleasure at that. We do not therefore regard it as a proper occupation for a gentleman; it is rather that of a paid employee. Inevitably the consequences are degrading, since the end towards which it is directed – popular amusement – is a low one. The listener is a common person and influences music accordingly; he has an effect on the professionals who perform for him; the music which he expects of them, and the motions which they have to make to produce it, affect detrimentally their bodies and their minds.

The effects caused by listening to the various kinds of music were briefly touched upon in Chapter 5, but not specifically in relation to education. This is now done, with remarks also about listening to music in the theatre. The reference to the Poetics *cannot be to the well-known sixth chapter of that work as we have it, for there too an understanding of 'the purging of the emotions' is taken for granted and there is no discussion. So the reference is to some writing unfortunately lost.*

7

We must investigate a little this matter of harmonies and rhythms and its relation to education. Are we to make use of all the harmonies and rhythms or should we not make distinctions? And will the same basis of classification serve also those who are concerned with education, or must we lay down a third? Certainly music is, as we know, divided into melody-making and rhythm, and we must not omit to consider what bearing each of these has on education, and whether we are to rate higher music with a good tune or music with a good rhythm. I believe that these topics are very well dealt with both by some modern musicians and by others whose approach is philosophical but who have actual experience of music in relation to education. I would advise those who want detailed treatment of the several questions to seek advice in that quarter. Here let me give a conventional account and simply refer to the usual typology.

We accept the classification of melodies as given by some educationalists – ethical, active, and emotional, and regard the harmonies as being appropriate one here and another there in that scheme. But we say that music ought to be used not as conferring one benefit only but many; for example, for education and cathartic purposes,* as an intellectual pastime, as relaxation and for relief after tension. While then we must make use of all the harmonies, we are not to use them all in the same manner, but for education use those which improve the character, for listening to others performing use both the activating and the emotion-stirring or enthusiastic. Any feeling which comes strongly to some exists in all others to a greater or less degree, pity and fear, for example, but also this 'enthusiasm'. This is a kind of excitement which affects some people very strongly. It may arise out of religious music, and it is noticeable that when they have been listening to melodies that have an orgiastic effect they are, as it were, set on their feet, as if they had undergone a curative and purifying treatment. And those who feel pity or fear or other emotions must be affected in just the same way to the extent that the emotion comes upon each. To them all comes a pleasant feeling of purgation and relief. In the same way cathartic music brings men an elation which is not at all harmful. Hence these are the harmonies and melodies that ought to receive particular attention from those who are concerned with contests in theatrical music.

In the theatre there are two types of audience, the one consisting of well-educated gentlemen, the other of common persons, drawn from the menial occupations, paid workers and such-like. For the relaxation of this latter class also competitions and spectacles must be provided. But as their minds have become distorted, removed from the condition of nature, so also there are deviations from the norm in their harmonies, in the unnatural pitch and tone of their melodies. Each group finds pleasure in that which is akin to its nature. Therefore allowances must be made for theatrical producers when they use the type of music that appeals to this class of audience.

But as to education, as we have said, for its purposes we must use tunes in accordance with their ethical value and

* Here I use the term *catharsis* without further qualifications; I will treat of it more fully in my work on *Poetics*.

the same with harmonies. The Dorian mode, as we mentioned earlier, is in that category, but we must also admit other modes if they have passed the scrutiny of those authorities who combine the teaching of philosophy and musical education. It is to be regretted that Socrates in the *Republic* singled out the Phrygian mode to be added to the Dorian, while rejecting altogether the use of the pipes. Yet among the harmonies the Phrygian has exactly the same effect as the pipes among instruments; both are orgiastic and emotional. Poetical composition illustrates this; the feeling aroused by Dionysiac and other such poetry is that which belongs to the pipes among musical instruments, and such poetry finds its appropriate expression in tunes composed in the Phrygian mode. The dithyramb, for example, is universally regarded as Phrygiamb. Experts in this field point to numerous examples, notably that of Philoxenus, who tried to compose his myths for dithyramb in the Dorian mode, but could not do so; the very nature of his material forced him back into the Phrygian, the proper mode. But about the Dorian mode all are agreed that it is the steadiest and that its ethical quality is that of manliness. Further, since we approve of that which is mid-way between extremes and assert that that is something to be aimed at, and since the Dorian as compared with the other harmonies does possess this merit, it is clear that Dorian tunes are more suitable than the others for the education of the young.

Two things we keep constantly in view – what can be done and what should be done; every set of men must set out to grasp both things possible and things proper. But these two are different for different ages; those who through age have grown weary do not find it easy to sing the high-pitched harmonies, but for such men nature offers a whole range of lower-pitched. Hence once again some of the musical experts rightly take Socrates to task because he rejected as useless in education all the more relaxed harmonies; he regarded them as having the same effect as drink, not the intoxicating but the soporific effect. (Intoxication produces rather a Bacchic frenzy.) So, looking to our later years, a time of life which will come, we must keep hold of harmonies and melodies of this kind. Furthermore, if there is a harmony of this type, which because of its power to combine orderliness with educative influence is suitable for the age of childhood (the Lydian would seem to be a case in point), it is clear that we have three distinct features to look for in education – the happy mean, the possible, and the appropriate.

INDEX

319